FOOD AND

INTEGRATING FOOD, TRAVEL AND TERRITORY

T
st:

—

—

2

—

CABI TOURISM TEXTS are an essential resource for students of academic tourism, leisure studies, hospitality, entertainment and events management. The series reflects the growth of tourism-related studies at an academic level and responds to the changes and developments in these rapidly evolving industries, providing up-to-date practical guidance, discussion of the latest theories and concepts, and analysis by world experts. The series is intended to guide students through their academic programmes and remain an essential reference throughout their careers in the tourism sector.

Readers will find the books within the CABI TOURISM TEXTS series to have a uniquely wide scope, covering important elements in leisure and tourism, including management-led topics, practical subject matter and development of conceptual themes and debates. Useful textbook features such as case studies, bullet point summaries and helpful diagrams are employed throughout the series to aid study and encourage understanding of the subject.

Students at all levels of study, workers within tourism and leisure industries, researchers, academics, policy makers and others interested in the field of academic and practical tourism will find these books an invaluable and authoritative resource, useful for academic reference and real-world tourism applications.

Titles available

Ecotourism: Principles and Practices
Ralf Buckley

Contemporary Tourist Behaviour: Yourself and Others as Tourists
David Bowen and Jackie Clarke

The Entertainment Industry: an Introduction
Edited by Stuart Moss

Practical Tourism Research
Stephen L.J. Smith

Leisure, Sport and Tourism, Politics, Policy and Planning, 3rd Edition
A.J. Veal

Events Management
Edited by Peter Robinson, Debra Wale and Geoff Dickson

Food and Wine Tourism: Integrating Food, Travel and Territory
Erica Croce and Giovanni Perri

FOOD AND WINE TOURISM

Integrating Food, Travel and Territory

Erica Croce and Giovanni Perri

Meridies – itinerari di cultura e turismo®
Chieti
Italy

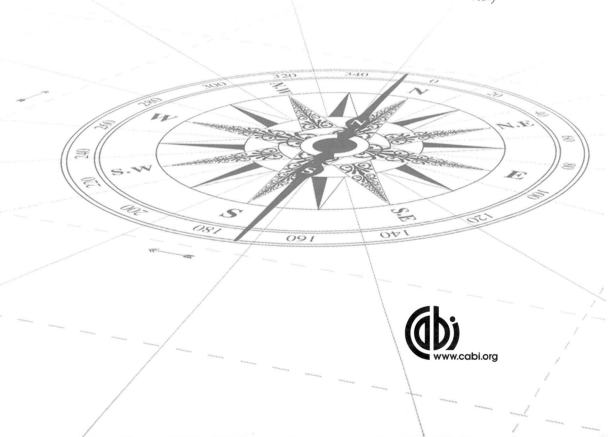

www.cabi.org

CABI is a trading name of CAB International

CABI Head Office
Nosworthy Way
Wallingford
Oxfordshire OX10 8DE
UK

Tel: +44 (0)1491 832111
Fax: +44 (0)1491 833508
E-mail: cabi@cabi.org
Website: www.cabi.org

CABI North American Office
875 Massachusetts Avenue
7th Floor
Cambridge, MA 02139
USA

Tel: +1 617 395 4056
Fax: +1 617 354 6875
E-mail: cabi-nao@cabi.org

A catalogue record for this book is available from the British Library, London, UK.

Library of Congress Cataloging-in-Publication Data

Croce, Erica.
  [Turismo enogastronomico. English]
  Food and wine tourism : integrating food, travel, and territory / Erica Croce and Giovanni Perri.
     p. cm. -- (CABI tourism texts)
  Includes bibliographical references and index.
  ISBN 978-1-84593-661-7 (alk. paper)
  1. Tourism and gastronomy. 2. Wine tourism. I. Perri, Giovanni. II. Title. III. Series.

  G155.A1C74516 2011
  641--dc22

                                                        2010016389

Translated and adapted from Croce, E. and Perri, G. (2008) 'Il turismo enogastronomico. Progettare, gestire, vivere l'integrazione tra cibo, viaggio, territorio', FrancoAngeli s.r.l., Milan, Italy (ISBN: 978-88-464-9536-5).

Figures and photos by Erica Croce and Giovanni Perri with the exception of Figure 5.1 (© Photoservice Electa/Photoshot) and Figures 5.7 to 5.9 (credit Elisabetta Cane).

Translated into English by Suzanna Miles.

ISBN-13: 978 1 84593 661 7

Commissioning Editor: Sarah Hulbert
Production Editor: Tracy Head

Typeset by SPi, Pondicherry, India.
Printed and bound in the UK by Cambridge University Press, Cambridge.

Contents

About the Authors   vi

Preface   vii

Acknowledgements   ix

01   The Spirit of a Place on a Plate   1

02   The Environment: Tools of the Trade   18

03   Tourists on the Food and Wine Trail: Who Are They?   45

04   Transforming a *Terroir* into a Tourist Destination   60

05   The Supply Side: the Actors Involved in Food and Wine Production   87

06   Food and Wine Tourism Best Practice: Case Studies from Around the World   116

07   Supply Operators in the Food and Wine Tourism Industry   137

08   Designing a Life Experience: Itinerary Planning and Organization   157

Bibliography   187

Index   193

About the Authors

Erica Croce and Giovanni Perri currently teach Food and Wine Tourism at the University of Gastronomic Sciences, Pollenzo, Italy. For many years they have been actively involved with the International Research Centre of Tourism Economics (CISET) at the University of Venice, both as teachers on the masters programme (Master in Tourism Management) and as research consultants.

As the founders of Meridies – itinerari di cultura e turismo®, specializing in tourism and culture, they provide consultancy services and training for the hospitality industry in both the public and private sectors, carry out research projects and specialize in the development of effective communication and marketing strategies for food and wine tourism.

They are the authors of several guide books and cultural and regional publications, and are regular contributors to specialist magazines and tourism journals. They are regularly invited to give training seminars and share their experiences to tourism operators and students at masters level.

Meridies – itinerari di cultura e turismo®
Piazza G.B. Vico, 15
66100 Chieti
Italy

www.meridies.net
info@meridies.net

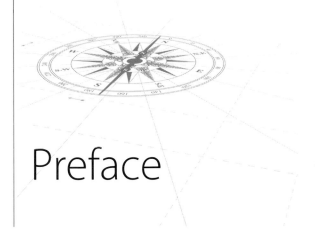

Preface

Tourism is a key driver of economic growth worldwide. There is widespread awareness that not only is tourism a strategic factor for growth, but in some countries it is one of the most important industries. This is true when geographic areas have resources that can be enhanced and the know-how to design, plan, manage, safeguard and, with great ability and clearness of vision, regularly update and requalify their tourism offer. The need to have clear development policies in place and be aware of the importance of rebranding and relaunching a tourist product is particularly pertinent for those destinations that are going through the maturity stage (at least in certain traditional types of tourism), if they wish to stay in the market. As demand evolves, these destinations are forced to adopt new tactics and strategies in order to respond to new demand needs and expectations.

The current situation in which there is global competition between countries, regions and localities offering a myriad of different environmental features and tourist products (even though the market cannot always make a distinction between them), requires operators in the sector to be knowledgeable about the products they construct, as the role they play is fundamental to the ongoing success of a destination. They must know how to communicate a place by describing its unique characteristics and identity. Their mission should be to build quality tourist products in line with sustainable principles and to foster partnerships based on reciprocal respect between all supply-side actors, with the objective of constructing meaningful and memorable experiences for visitors.

Food and wine tourism can present ideal opportunities for operators to create extraordinary holiday experiences: if carefully planned and managed, it can give visitors the opportunity to savour the unmistakable flavour of a destination through all five senses.

Furthermore, food and wine tourism mitigates the effects of an economic monoculture that results when tourism-related activities drive out any other economic activities, as has happened in many destinations. In fact, gastronomic tourism, by its specific nature, complements and interacts with other economic sectors, such as agriculture, breeding and rearing livestock, and the food industry.

In order to study the relationship and interaction between the two components of oenogastronomic tourism, *tourism* and *food and wine production*, a methodological and analytical approach together with field research *in situ* is essential. Identifying a destination's distinctive characteristics, processing the information and then enhancing resources and destination identity requires going beyond the application of models and theories, particularly when models are based on non-tourism subjects. Sensitivity and a certain amount of courage are needed to begin thinking about food and wine tourism from a 'tourism' perspective. So this means bringing into play other disciplines that should be seen as complementing the science of gastronomic tourism and not as alternatives to it.

The textbook therefore examines gastronomic tourism in all its potential. It offers theoretical considerations and practical advice. It is the result of direct observation and the authors' own personal experiences in visiting literally hundreds of food and wine producers and destinations. The reader is invited to leaf through its pages and explore.

Acknowledgements

Our thanks go to all those who believed in our ideas and the spirit in which this book was written, and who have supported us in our project to publish this book in English:

ASSOCIAZIONE STRADA DEL SAGRANTINO
Piazza del Comune, 17
06036 Montefalco (PG), Italy
www.stradadelsagrantino.it

CISET (International Research Centre of Tourism Economics) – University of Venice
Villa Mocenigo
Riviera San Pietro, 83
30034 Oriago di Mira (VE), Italy
venus.unive.it/ciset/

COMUNE DI CISTERNINO (Cisternino City Council)
Via Principe Amedeo, 72
72014 Cisternino (BR), Italy
www.comune.cisternino.brindisi.it

FRANTOIO GALANTINO snc
Via Corato Vecchia, 2
70052 Bisceglie (BA), Italy
www.galantino.it

ONAOO (National Organization of Olive Oil Tasters)
c/o Camera di Commercio I.A.A.
Via Tommaso Schiva, 29
18100 Imperia (IM), Italy
www.oliveoil.org

To Giulio and Flora

chapter 1

The Spirit of a Place on a Plate

FROM ANCIENT ORIGINS TO MODERN TRENDS

Food and wine have enhanced people's lives ever since our ancestors developed a taste for good food and good living. The ancient Romans, who were without doubt masters of the art of *bien vivre*, still have something to teach us today about the importance of eating, drinking and living well. Take the rich and influential Mecenate, for example, living in Rome in the 1st century AD, accustomed to drinking top-quality prestigious wine. His friend, the poet Horace, knew all about Mecenate's educated tastes and wrote, almost excusing himself, that he was not in a position to be able to drink the same nectar: 'At home you will drink Caecuban wine and the grape which is squeezed in the Calenian press; my cups are not graced with vines from Falerno nor from the hills of Formia' (Odes, I, 20). Horace also mentions oil and vinegar in his writings, referring to 'the olive oil of Venafro obtained from the first pressing' and to the vinegar made from Metimna grape juice (Satires, II, 8). Classical literature can in fact take us on a virtual tour of convivial banquets and food-laden tables, divulging ancient pleasures and tastes.

Over time, intellectuals, writers, poets and chefs gradually created a geography of taste and, although the appreciation of fine food and wine products was initially confined to a small group of wealthy connoisseurs, a growing awareness began to emerge of the strong and direct links that a geographical region has with its products and its cuisine.

It would be interesting to know if Mecenate and personalities of the same calibre, other than enjoying Falerno wine and similar culinary delights, would have been prepared (or would maybe even have entreated) to leave their place of residence with the idea of arriving in a destination noted for its prestigious agro-alimentary production, understanding its cultural heritage, making direct contact with the producer, visiting the area to see the process of transformation of the primary material into the final product, tasting the product in its place of origin, eventually buying supplies of the delicacy and returning home enriched by the experience. In synthesis, this is a description of what gastronomic tourism entails. As an academic subject it is relatively new and it is difficult to give a precise date to its origins. In the French regions of Alsace and Burgundy, where gastronomy has been embedded in the regional culture for centuries, the custom of going directly to the producer to purchase wine seems to be rooted in the local population's DNA. And Robiola cheese from Piemonte is an inherent part of the cultural landscape, cited and praised by the great Italian writers of the neorealist movement in the 20th century.

In some areas today, food and wine tourism is well-developed and in demand, in others it is still a niche market attracting a small number of curious visitors, and in some cases it remains an untapped source. For a food or wine production area to transform itself into a tourism destination, exciting interest on the part of visitors who are moved by a desire to get to know a product and its region better (and enjoy themselves at the same time), it must create the right type of 'cultural atmosphere'. It is possible to identify some key points that are essential for the creation and development of a successful gastronomic tourism destination. As each place is unique, however, each individual locality gradually becomes more aware of its role as a tourist destination over time, and develops and matures in different ways and at a different pace.

To get some idea of how a small group of pioneers can gradually over the years leave space for an ever-increasing body of gastronome travellers, we will stop here and take a look at how food and wine tourism has evolved in Italy. From a didactic point of view, Italy is in fact an ideal case to study as not only is it famous worldwide for its extraordinarily rich gastronomy, it also ranks as one of the world's top tourist destinations.

To begin with, there is an enormous amount of documented evidence – from manuals about regional specialities to tourist guides and other publications – that has stimulated readers with an interest in food and wine to set off on journeys of gastronomic discovery.

As long ago as 1841, *L'Italie confortable, manuel du touriste* by Valery (pseudonym for A.C. Pasquin) was a French guide expressly written for tourists giving practical information to assist them during their travels in Italy. The guide includes information about the climate, gives the names of doctors, provides advice on food and customs in different destinations, hotels, means of transport and connections, tariffs and prices, book shops and libraries, jewellers, dressmakers and tailors, and a multitude of other useful details. There are also suggestions about which dishes to try and which gastronomic products to sample and purchase, with the names and addresses of the best shops to visit to find local delicacies.

It was not until 1931, however, that the Italian Touring Club published its *Gastronomic Guide to Italy* (*Guida gastronomica d'Italia*). Described as being 'above all a tourist guide, and therefore packed with practical information', it was written and compiled with the explicit aim of presenting Italy's rich patrimony of '*specialità*' to 'those Italians who travel to become better acquainted with our country' and to 'those foreign tourists who come to Italy to admire its beauty, its art treasures and its history'. In the preface, we read, 'as here stands one of the most useful aspects of the Guide, in other words, it will accompany tourists on their own quest to discover a local speciality, that they may have heard mention of or even tasted, but without ever really knowing precisely where it is from'. Another distinct aim was to endorse the practice of sampling product *in loco*. However, the Guide does not make mention of product transformation or invite tourists to seek out places where it might be possible to view raw material being processed and transformed into an end product. There are no suggestions either as to where tourists could possibly buy food or wine products. Today's gastronomy guides, on the other hand, are full of suggestions about where visitors can go and see the full cycle of food/wine production and where they can buy gourmet products and local specialities. Animated by a lively and patriotic spirit, the Touring Club Guide is, however, an invaluable record of different places and destinations of great culinary interest, in that they all offer a product of high gastronomic worth. The Guide also served as a precious resource for later guides and publications. What is more, the role it played in educating the public about the links between culture and gastronomy in Italy was no less important than the one played by Pelligrino Artusi's enlightening book, *La scienza in cucina e l'arte di mangiar bene* (*Science in the Kitchen and the Art of Eating Well*), published in 1891.

More or less around the same time, the Italian Tourist Board (Ente Nazionale Italiano per il Turismo) commissioned the publication of a map detailing the principal gastronomic specialities in the different regions of Italy (*Carta delle principali specialità gastronomiche delle regioni italiane*). The map is 'artistic' rather than being a useful geographical reference. The Italian peninsula is literally invaded by all kinds of pictures of local dishes and products printed on each region. Each region is identified by a scroll, leaving the tourist with just the embarrassment of choosing where to start their journey in a country entirely painted with dishes of steaming pasta, flasks and bottles, cured meats and all other kinds of culinary delights.

An important step towards defining gastronomic tourism, as we know it today, was journalist Mario Soldati's book *Vino al vino* (*Wine to Wine*) published in 1971. The book is actually a collection of articles written by Soldati referring to three exploratory journeys around the Italian peninsula to search out the best locally produced wine, as opposed to big-name industrially produced wines. His comments and observations are still useful in that they highlight the cultural significance of the gastronomic experience:

> Because, knowing more about a particular wine entails much more than having two or three sips or even a large glass. Above all, it means having a few basic notions about the area where the wine is produced; we should therefore have some knowledge about its geology and geography, its history and its socio-economic conditions. It means going to the place in person and managing to be taken to *that precise vineyard* where *that specific wine* comes from. It also means walking and walking, attentively observing the surroundings, following the quality and direction of the wind, noting, with the passing of the hours, the evolving shadows on the hills, contemplating the shapes of the clouds and scrutinizing the distinctive architecture of the farmhouses and buildings; and perhaps even more important, it means talking to the winemaker, to the workers in the vineyards and in the cellars, to the oenologist and so on... It means exploring at length the wine vaults, the underground cellars, the warehouses and the vinification rooms amid the concrete vats: inspecting the ways the barrels are made up, smelling the wine while it is still fermenting, seeking out concealed appliances used for cooling or, even worse, pasteurization; and finally patiently tasting, alternating slowly from one to another, at regular intervals, the different vintages.   (Soldati, 1971)

As we can see from Fig. 1.1, from the 1920s onwards in Italy (and other Mediterranean countries famous for their gastronomy), evolving social and economic conditions tied to food production and the land eventually provided the right conditions for the growth in gastronomic tourism. It was only after people had experienced what it was like to live in a society where eating well was the norm, but paying the price due to the standardization of taste by mass food production, were the conditions right for a younger generation of consumers, cut off from rural life, to go back to their roots and reclaim the authentic tastes of another era, while welcoming new trends and innovative products.

In recent years there has been an upsurge of interest in eating organic or biodynamic foods, or foods that are commonly deemed to be 'safe' or certified. This has partly been influenced by a growing awareness of the need for environmental sustainability, the pleasure of eating good food and the search for holistic well-being. It is also due to a number of food scares in recent history that have driven people to seek out higher-quality food products. Increasingly passionate about food and moved by a desire to discover more about the *terroir* of particular products, changing consumer behaviour has had a decisive impact on food and wine tourism. The desire for a healthier lifestyle has also led to people wanting to find out more about the production cycles of food products. Food producers have gradually begun to respond to consumer interest and engage directly with habitual clients as well as potential customers by opening up and

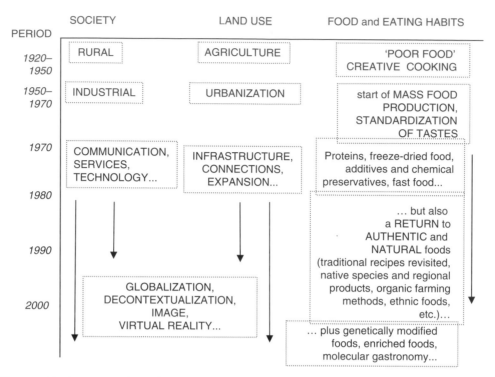

Fig. 1.1. Evolving social conditions and changes in attitude towards land use and food in Italy between 1920 and 2000.

inviting visitors to step inside and experience the production process first-hand (in this respect it is worth noting the amount of public interest aroused in 2004 by Jonathan Nossiter's award-winning documentary *Mondovino*).

Changing attitudes to mass food production also provided the impetus for different movements in the 1980s both in Italy and abroad and gave new dignity to the pleasures of the palate. A plethora of food and wine guides and gastronomy reviews came on to the market, satisfying a growing number of connoisseurs, while tasting seminars and exciting new events added a cultural dimension to food/wine production, appealing to the non-professional public.

Slow Food was set up in 1986, the very same year in which an enormous scandal broke over Italian wine being contaminated with methanol. It was the first association to champion the joys of slow eating, rejecting 'fast life' (Slow Food, 1989), and made it its mission to raise public awareness about the pleasures of good food, respect for nature, natural lifecycles, the dignity of farmers, biodiversity and eco-gastronomy. The Slow Food movement was immediately acclaimed in Italy and is still growing, having thousands of international members. In 1987, the association, in collaboration with Gambero Rosso, published the first edition of a guide to Italian wines (*Vini d'Italia*). This was followed three years later by *Osterie d'Italia*, a guide to Italy's traditional small restaurants. Apart from organizing taste workshops, seminars and other initiatives aimed at educating the public's palate, it also continues to organize a number of high-profile media events such as the 'Salone del Gusto' (since 1996), 'Cheese' (since 1997) and 'Slow Fish' (since 2004). Since 2000 it has set up 'Presidia' in order to protect endangered products, and since 2004 it has been the driving force behind 'Terra Madre', a huge international event organized every 2 years that brings together all those directly involved in food production and supply, providing a platform to share and exchange experiences, hopes and aspirations. Also in 2004, Slow Food founded the University of Gastronomic Sciences, the first of its kind.

Working alongside Slow Food is Gambero Rosso, a leading multimedia organization promoting the culture of taste. Apart from publishing magazines, books and guides, it also has its own satellite television channel dedicated to gastronomy with guest appearances by food and wine celebrities. Gambero Rosso's purpose-built 'City of Taste' in Rome also organizes cooking classes.

No less important in shaping public opinion and transforming the way people view and consume food are food writers and critics as well as award-winning chefs. Through the media, they have passed on their passion and concern to both real and potential clients about the importance of supporting locally produced products and taking a regional approach to creating recipes. Then there are all those who work in taste education, from sommeliers to oil, cheese, coffee and chocolate tasters, who organize national and local events and courses for professionals in the field, connoisseurs and curious amateurs. Whatever the level, these courses provide participants with a precise framework and lexis to describe a specific product and to carry out a sensory analysis of its organoleptic qualities while reinforcing the crucial concept of *terroir*.

In the last few years, aware consumers have gradually learnt to recognize the various acronyms printed on product labels, certifying them as being recognized by the European Union as regional quality food products, such as PDO (Protected Designation of Origin) and PGI (Protected Geographical Indication), as well as those used to indicate wine denomination of origin (AOC, DO, DOC, etc.).

It was not until 1993, however, that food and wine tourism in Italy officially moved into the mainstream, with perhaps the most ambrosial and evocative product of all, wine. This was thanks to the Wine Tourism Movement that managed to persuade a number of Tuscan wineries to adhere to an open doors initiative called 'Cantine Aperte' ('Open Cellars'). From just a few dozen wineries in 1993, the number has now grown to hundreds scattered over the length and breadth of Italy, each welcoming visitors on a guided tour every year on the last Sunday in May. This initiative has met with such success that some wine producers have decided to remain open to the public all year round.

In 1999, legislation was introduced to regulate the Italian 'Wine Routes' (France already had its own system of wine itineraries from the 1950s onwards). Contemporarily, other product routes and discovery trails began to open up at an international level, in search of quality extra-virgin olive oil, or artisan bread products, or beer (e.g. in the Czech Republic), or spirits (e.g. the 'Malt Whisky Trail' in Scotland), etc.

On a local level, in Italy a number of associations were created to promote regional products. One of the first was Wine Cities, which was specifically established to counter the terrible damage done to the reputation of Italian wine following on from the methanol scandal. It was a combined effort by 39 municipalities to help and support winegrowers and producers in their areas. Subsequently, other associations came to be established: Bread Cities, Olive Oil Cities, Cherry Cities and so on.

Food and wine tourism continues to attract an ever-increasing number of aficionados, and is instrumental in identifying products with their areas of production. At the heart of food and wine tourism are the producers and their businesses; radiating out from the heart are the places and events that enhance and optimize the core resource, e.g. restaurants, wine bars and shops, museums, local food or wine festivals, tasting sessions and cookery courses. Finally, it spreads out to include points of sale, accommodation facilities and tourist services; indeed all the actors that are part of the tourist supply (and those who are not) of a destination.

Apart from having the experience of tasting a product where it is actually produced, visitors learn to appreciate the link between a product and its area of origin, even more if they can try the product at restaurants, cafés or bars in the immediate vicinity. When a product is an essential ingredient of an exquisite, local dish, tourists not only enjoy a gastronomic experience, they also enter into contact with the host community's culture. Not all specialities are 'easily visited' however. Hygiene regulations may not allow tourists into a production area or extremely rare delicacies have to be treated with particular care, away from curious groups of visitors. Truffles, for instance, have to be picked during the night and, more often than not, the places where they grow are a well-kept secret. If visitors do not have the opportunity to come into direct contact with a product, they must have the chance to interact with the producer. This is a fundamental characteristic of gastronomic tourism.

The current boom in gastronomic tourism is also a demonstration that the significant attributes that are given to food in the Western world have grown in correspondence with changing lifestyles and living standards. From initially being a form of sustenance to satisfy a primary need (as well as being a trading commodity), the role food plays in today's society is essentially about social pleasure, about gathering around a table or pleasing the taste buds. Food has become an object to analyse critically at tasting courses; it has become an object of art. In food and wine tourism it is a transmitter of culture, an important economic factor and the embodiment of regional identity.

Today, everyone seems to be talking about gastronomic tourism (indeed there seems to be more talk than action). It has become a trend. Films are made about it; articles and books are dedicated to it; television programmes proclaim it. But like all fashions and trends, it could easily just fade and die away. We believe, however, that it is still an untapped resource in many parts of the world and, if managed and planned properly, has the power to bring recognition, wealth and prestige to many areas that have a real vocation for food or wine production.

A TYPE OF INTEGRATED CULTURAL TOURISM

Food and wine tourism shares many of the same features as cultural tourism. Once upon a time, cultural tourism meant visiting historic centres, admiring art treasures and sightseeing famous monuments. Over the last few years however, it has come to mean more than just an interest in art and history and now includes an enthusiasm for folk heritage, for gastronomic production, for learning more about different communities, traditions and ways of life. It is plain to see that there is a very strong link between the two types of tourism: a holiday that is based around offering a gastronomic experience will necessarily include one or more components of cultural tourism.

One of the most positive aspects of food and wine tourism is that it integrates so easily with other types of tourism, as can be seen in Fig. 1.2.

When elementary or middle schools go away for a school trip, it is perfectly easy to insert a visit to a model farm into their programme of activities. High-school students could easily be taken on a tour of a food production centre to learn about the technical side of food processing. Monasteries clearly appeal to religious tourists, but the artisan jams, wine and beer produced by the monks also attract people with a passion for natural foods and products. A hike in the mountains could easily include a stop at a dairy hut to see how alpine cheese is made and to taste it, ideally while sitting at a table overlooking herb-rich meadows and savouring the aromas of those precise herbs in the cheese. A cultural visit to the medieval town of Montepulciano (Tuscany) could easily be extended to visit some of the wine cellars in its

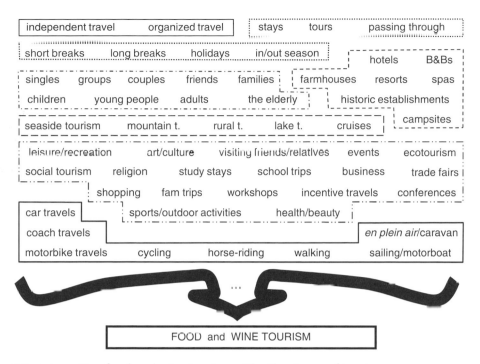

Fig. 1.2. Integrating food and wine tourism with other types of tourism.

historic palaces. Tourists enjoying a health and leisure break at an elegant spa can sometimes be pampered with treatments made from locally produced products, such as wine, grapes, extra-virgin olive oil, milk and yoghurt.

There are obvious links between gastronomy and rural tourism, making it particularly easy to integrate food and wine tourism, especially if we think of the type of settings where people usually enjoy a gastronomic holiday experience (Fig. 1.3). But we can also combine gastronomy with other types of tourism that are quite removed from food and wine production. Take cruise holidays, for example. Numerous gastronomic experiences can easily be organized on board ship: tasting courses and workshops, food and wine pairing seminars, cooking classes with a celebrity chef, lessons on using herbs in cooking and organic food with well-known names leading the classes, and so on. It is even possible to organize an excursion to a winery or farm or olive mill while the ship is in port. For passengers, activities like these give added value to the cruise experience, while the companies themselves gain a competitive edge over market rivals. In New Zealand, visitors to Marlborough can enjoy a day-long gastronomic experience, by first visiting a winery and then taking part in a wine-tasting session comparing different wines from the surrounding areas. The difference with this experience is that the tasting session takes place on board a boat with a skipper, and passengers can relax and enjoy the scenery, or even do some fishing.

Non-motorized travel exists in several countries where special routes known as 'greenways' have been created. Greenways follow tracks and trails, old trade routes and disused railway lines. When a greenway crosses an area known for its food or wine production, it offers obvious opportunities to integrate gastronomic tourism. The existence of these traffic-free routes is a key factor of strength for the territories they cross, and can also be an incentive to safeguard and protect the rural environment and landscape.

Fig. 1.3. Hiking in the vineyards.

Some examples of European greenways are:

- Vías Verdes. Spain has converted over 1500 km of disused railway lines into cycling and walking paths. The greenways are an invitation to everyone, residents as well as tourists, to get to know Spain, its culture and landscapes, in an environmentally friendly way. No one is excluded. The greenways are accessible to people of all ages, including people with mobility problems where certain tracts have been adapted for wheelchairs. Walking and cycling along viaducts and tunnels once built for rail travel, greenway users get the chance to discover previously little-known areas and communities. The 55 km-long 'Vía verde del Aceite' that runs between Jaén and the Guadajoz river, crosses the very heart of the olive-growing region of Andalusia. The landscape dotted with *pueblos blancos* surrounded by olive groves is an intrinsic part of the Via verde cycling or sports experience. Indeed, as one of Spain's foremost oil-producing regions, with large cooperatives for olive grinding and pressing and sales of olive oil, the area has given this particular greenway its distinctive name: 'The Olive Oil Greenway'.
- The Vienna–Prague Greenway. The two cities are joined together by a network covering hundreds of kilometres of paths, tracks and country roads. The greenway users can choose from a series of different themed itineraries and discover castles, lakes, forests, Renaissance towns and country villages along the way. Traces of the Iron Curtain are still apparent and serve as a warning for future generations. The greenway also includes a wine route in the area between Znojmo and Mikulov (South Moravia in the Czech Republic). Touring maps explicitly invite visitors to discover the wine production area by cycling 'towards wine and history'.
- Visitors can take a slow and rhythmic pace to discover the sceneries and production areas of Burgundy through 'Le tour de Bourgogne à vélo', which offers five different itineraries along greenways and cycling paths.

- The region of Alsace is criss-crossed by numerous *winefootpaths*, giving visitors the chance to stop every now and then at a local *wistub*, and discover its villages and churches as well as its magnificent white wines. Visitors to the area can pick up brochures with information about the *winefootpaths* from the local tourist information offices.

Canal holidays are another way of combining the pleasures of gastronomy with a slower pace of life. There are many fine production areas such as Armagnac or parts of the Camino De Santiago de Compostela pilgrimage route, that can be visited by navigating the areas' waterways in a houseboat. Along the way there are plenty of opportunities to stop off and enjoy a gourmet meal or visit a local winery or distillery.

TOURISM AND THE ENVIRONMENT: FINDING THE RIGHT BALANCE

The impact of tourism on a destination is necessarily felt in a number of ways. It leaves its mark on the geographic, visual and relational space, with consequences on the environment in its natural, social, economic and cultural components (Fig. 1.4).

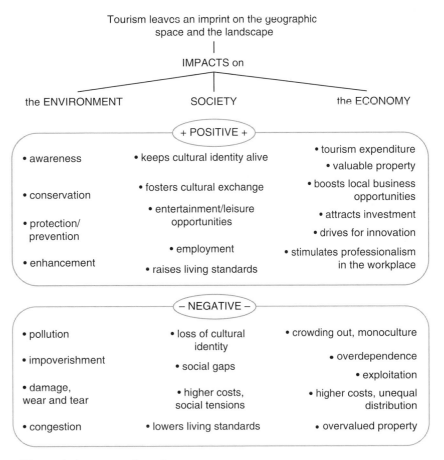

Fig. 1.4. The main impacts of tourism.

Studies undertaken to determine tourism impact have all pointed to the fact that, all too often, the negative impacts outweigh the positive. Many geographic, ecological, economic, social and anthropological studies clearly illustrate that far too often tourism organization is banal and that mass tourism generates negative effects (as it is based on the short-sighted premise that it will bring immediate economic benefits to the destination).

Tourism is widely held to be responsible for the abuse and overuse of resources and for creating social tensions and loss of cultural identity as a result of unequal distribution of economic gains. The local economy is often crowded out and is replaced by a monoculture. The destabilization or loss of destination identity and authorized forms of economic colonization is however due to inadequate tourism planning, not to tourism itself or to spontaneous tourism development – a factor not helped by the widely held but erroneous belief that tourism is the only possible solution to reignite economic wealth in regions that have seen other production sectors shrink and stagnate.

The tourism industry needs to respond to a social need for pleasure and relaxation, but at the same time it needs to acknowledge that different types of clients are looking for a cultural experience as well, or have high self-affirmation needs. Only by creating different and varied products can the industry respond to and satisfy demand.

Tailor-made or customized tours, however, are often as guilty as all-inclusive packages in giving tourists just a fleeting acquaintance with a destination. No matter how brief the relationship, it is still invasive for the environment and the host community. This usually happens when the tourist product is based on familiar images and preconceived notions about the destination. Even before departure, the tourist feels secure in the knowledge that they already know all they need to know about the destination (e.g. through the media or tourist guides). All that remains to do when they actually arrive there is to quickly verify their preconceptions.

Other tourist products respond to demand from independent travellers for exclusive discovery tours by offering adventure or exploration holidays (often not nearly as adventurous as they would like to make out). These types of holiday are usually to faraway destinations that are considered to be exotic and full of cultural meaning, much more so than destinations favoured by mass tourism. In reality, the tourist who embarks on this type of holiday is hoping to come into contact with something outside their own experience, to discover a completely new culture and way of life that they can live intensely just for a brief moment, before they return to the safety of their home comforts and reassuring daily routine.

Clients often buy into promises that have no connection with reality, but instead are nostalgic versions of a way of life that has long since disappeared. Images such as a man and donkey on a narrow mountain path, or a woman balancing a basket of food on her head, or a lone fisherman hauling in his meagre catch come to mind. They may well reflect real situations but more often than not are merely romanticized views of other people's lives. And yet, the tourist is searching for an authentic experience which is strangely contradictory, in search of isolation and a complete experience, in the hope of finding places that do not remind them of the socio-cultural conditions to which they belong.

The tourist industry anticipates and launches new trends, satisfies needs that often the industry itself creates, and projects stereotyped images of places and destinations specifically created to attract demand. It is often the case that where geographically marginalized countries or destinations (not always because they are distanced from the principal tourism markets) have been able to maintain more traditional and authentic ways of life, they seem to be more exposed to the dangers of tourism. This happens because they do not have the ability or the necessary measures in place to be able to resist the enormous wave of social, psychological, economic and environmental impacts that tourism brings with it. With tourism policies based purely on satisfying visitor needs and desires, they succumb to the illusion that tourism will bring quick, easy and painless growth. The risk then is that these places become merely surreal cultural representations of themselves.

The tourism industry and visitor behaviour therefore do not always bring the positive effects that in theory tourism should generate. Technically, tourism should raise awareness about the cultural identity of a destination and be responsible for enhancing the lives of the host community. It should foster cultural exchange and provide greater opportunities for leisure and entertainment. It should generate new job opportunities, attract investment, and stimulate new business approaches and a desire for growth and innovation.

Seen in this light, food and wine tourism should be seen as an ideal opportunity and occasion to revisit the past and appreciate its values and traditions in the present day. In essence, the past is a rich resource of cultural, economic and managerial elements from which the entire tourism system can draw on.

Once upon a time, the classic or romantic meaning of a journey ideally signified open and curious travellers (who left behind any preconceptions or prejudices) actively seeking to establish a rapport with the people and places they visited during their travels. In today's media-savvy world, with everything at our fingertips, with so many choices and an overwhelming input of images and information about other people's experiences, travel in the original sense of the word no longer exists; it has been supplanted by tourism.

From a logistical, psychological and experiential point of view, the meaning of travel today is totally different from travel in the past. However, something of the original spirit lives on in the minds of those tourists who set out to enjoy themselves but are ready to embrace the unfamiliar and learn something new, so that they return home enriched by the holiday experience. This is as true for the single, lone traveller as it is for a group of senior citizens out together on a day trip. Actors in the tourism industry can help keep the original character of travel alive in the products they construct for their clients, receiving visitors with warmth and hospitality, guiding and sharing the pleasure of the travel experience with them. The host community also plays an important role here, as it needs to welcome visitors with an open mind but also be capable of managing tourism in the long term. This entails a delicate balancing act between defending and protecting the destination's natural resources and cultural identity and opening up to new and exciting possibilities. On the other hand, the tourist should be open to an awareness of the needs of the destination, and have a desire to experience emotion, savour new tastes and play.

What then are the ingredients for a positive approach to tourism in a destination? How can negative impacts be minimized? How can we link food and wine tourism to sustainable development?

SUSTAINABLE PRACTICES

A premium food or wine product transmits flavour and taste, it reflects traditional or innovative production methods, it is capable of exciting emotions, it is an expression of regional culture and history, and generates wealth for that region. Food and wine tourism generates many opportunities and gives added value for destination development, but it must be managed and organized in a responsible and sustainable way.

What is sustainable development?

- 'Sustainable development is development that meets the needs of the present without compromising the ability of future generations to meet their own needs. It contains within it two key concepts: the concept of "needs", in particular the essential needs of the world's poor, to which overriding priority should be given; and the idea of limitations imposed by the state of technology and social organization on the environment's ability to meet present and future needs' (World Commission on Environment and Development, 1987).

- Sustainable development is about 'improving the quality of human life while living within the carrying capacity of supporting ecosystems' (International Union for Conservation of Nature and Natural Resources, United Nations Environment Programme and World Wide Fund for Nature, 1991).

- 'Sustainable development is development that delivers basic environmental, social and economic services to all residents of a community without threatening the viability of the natural, built and social systems upon which the delivery of these services depends' (International Council for Local Environmental Initiatives, 1994).

The definitions given above are just three of many that have been put forward to explain what is meant by sustainable development from the 1980s onwards. They help us to understand how a sustainable approach can be applied to tourism.

No matter at what level sustainable practices are implemented, from individual citizens to large companies, from micro areas to macro areas, from a single product to an entire range, there are three fundamental elements that have to be carefully balanced to underpin sustainable development. These are the protection of the ecosystem, and the principles of social justice and economic efficiency:

- Protecting the balance of ecosystems means guaranteeing biodiversity and production, in terms of energy flows, food chains and interactions between biotic and abiotic components, etc. It also signifies understanding at what point damage becomes irreversible and respecting the limits of resilience; in other words, the capacity of an ecosystem to renew itself.

- The principle behind social justice is that everyone has a natural right and should have equal access to environmental patrimony (intragenerational equity), and that the environment should be protected and preserved for the enjoyment of future generations (intergenerational equity).

- Economic efficiency goes beyond the principle of striving for economic growth; it means maintaining a correct balance between the economic system and the environment, with the idea that environmental capital and social capital together constitute a rich resource for collective well-being. In practical terms, this means activating production methods that use renewable resources, improving wealth distribution, raising living standards, investing in technological innovation, aiming for more product diversification, defending cultural identity, developing economic potential at a local level and preventing all forms of economic colonialism, meritocracy, etc.

In tourism, respecting and maintaining the ecosystem balance implies taking account of the carrying capacity of a destination. This means that tourism policy makers need to analyse the maximum number of visitors a place and its resources can support, in that a tourist consumes space even though it is not always that evident. Once visitor numbers go beyond this point the impact of their presence will be economically, physically and socially damaging to the destination. This holds true for all visitor destinations, whether they are historic city centres, museums, churches, beaches or even wineries or dairy farms. 'Damage' is in the sense that the systems in place, e.g. transport and infrastructure, begin to cease functioning properly and the costs of tourism begin to outweigh the benefits.

The concept of carrying capacity can be applied to the environment (e.g. analysing visitor presence and any resulting damage to the ecosystem or to a monument, a farm or a winery); in a social sense (e.g. assessing effects on the social relationships and quality of life of the host population, or on workers in an olive mill open to visitors, or even on the internal harmony of tour groups themselves); and in an economic sense (e.g. measuring decline in demand – and consequent decline of tourism revenues – as a result of overcrowding and dissatisfaction with the quality of life in the destination and with the holiday itself).

Analysing and measuring carrying capacity is therefore an essential first step to successfully managing tourism impacts on a destination and its host community. Studies need to be conducted over fairly protracted periods of time, supported by statistics and analyses in social, economic and geographic indices (income, quality of life, impact on resources, etc.).

Sustainable policies to protect the environment are based on the cardinal principles of restoration, conservation, prevention and enhancement. If policies are to be effective in minimizing negative impacts on a destination, they need to be carefully planned and based on detailed research. Prevention in particular needs to be carried out by constantly monitoring and analysing repercussions on the environment due to tourism presence. As an investment, prevention does not seem to give any apparent or immediate returns; however, in the long term, careful analysis of environmental impacts enables policy makers to develop environmental education and awareness-raising campaigns for both visitors and residents. These policies can naturally be applied to gastronomic tourism, with the aim of incrementing knowledge about environmental systems within food and wine regions, disseminating information with regard to resource management and increasing awareness about opportunities for development. Specific geographic regions, small, precious areas and food and wine production enterprises all have the opportunity to develop new production methodologies to underpin sustainable development and maintain the correct balance between environmental and social issues and economic development.

It must be admitted however that developing and implementing sustainable development policies is not always straightforward:

- It is not always easy to outline precise objectives for policy management.
- It can be difficult to identify the exact parameters for evaluating and measuring the effectiveness of sustainable policies.
- Reaching a common consensus about what policies to adopt can be problematic because multiple interests often prevail.
- Sustainable activities often entail higher costs because initial investments into reducing consumption and waste can be quite considerable, particularly as effects are not felt immediately and require medium- to long-term planning.

Tourism planning must have a systematic and global vision of a destination and its geographical area. Tourism must avoid consuming those resources on which it depends, it must not alter cultural identity and it must not be responsible for creating social tensions. Tourism should bring added value without driving out other socio-economic activities in the destination. The success of tourism planning is based on whether it is able to achieve a dynamic relationship between: residents and the quality of life in the destination; tourists and the quality of their holiday experience in the destination; and the way both categories, residents and tourists, interact with the environment. The way the environment is used reflects the value given to it by its users. If this balance is to be achieved, all actors in the destination need to be involved, including the local community and local businesses, public and private bodies, education and research institutes and the media.

Fig. 1.5. At the farmers' market: good practices.

Individual actors and operators all have a contribution to make. A sustainable approach adds value even to a single tourist product or service and can easily be achieved if business strategies are well-organized, flexible and professional. For example, sustainability can be integrated into a food and wine tour or visit by adopting the measures below:

- carrying out market research to identify and select the most appropriate target;
- making sure that visitor numbers can comfortably be accommodated in the spaces available for the visit;
- channelling and disseminating information;
- giving a coherent and recognizable theme to a food and wine tour;
- informing clients about the environmental strategies adopted by the single enterprises involved in the tour (Fig. 1.5);
- devising a tour or visit that is both entertaining and informative;
- constructing a tour that ensures economic success and/or continued visibility in the market;
- monitoring the effects that a tour or visit has on the destination and on production; and
- ensuring that tour participants come away from the experience with an increased awareness.

QUALITY

According to ISO standards (ISO 8042:1986, 3.1), quality can be defined as 'The totality of features and characteristics of a product or service that bear on its ability to satisfy stated and implied needs'. In traditional marketing, this notion of quality is interpreted as an opportunity to overlap in a strategic way the specific characteristics of the supply with those of the demand, and to render a product more appealing than its competitors. Quality is therefore seen to lie within the specific characteristics of a product or service that are useful for satisfying a need.

However, when we speak about quality, we must consider the way a product responds to sustainable needs (environmental, social and economic) as well as its ability to perform satisfactorily, to be safe, pleasing and reliable.

There is no doubt that in today's world awareness about environmental issues, whether it is generated by grass-roots activists or filters down from governmental organizations, plays an important role in the qualitative satisfaction when purchasing/using a product or service. In the case of tourism, this is even more true thanks to the strong relationship that exists between a journey/holiday and the environment in which the journey or holiday takes place. Among all the characteristics that distinguish tourist services from other types of products (e.g. immateriality, transversality, heterogeneity, perishability, strong subjective component), the one that stands out more than any other is the omnipresence of the environment. And this is not simply linked to the fact that one of the principal motives for travelling is to enjoy the beauty, culture and resources of the destinations visited through the consumption of public and private goods.

In fact, in marketing terms, the strong presence of the environment in tourism is also due to an inversion in the production and distribution processes that are common to most material goods. In the case of tourism it is the market that moves towards the product (environmental resource–tourist destination) and not the other way round: the product is used and consumed in the holiday destination. To optimize tourism planning and management therefore, it is necessary to develop a strong sensitivity to the geographical and cultural aspects of a destination as well as developing good hospitality practice.

A quality product does not necessarily have to be expensive. The concept of quality is often linked to loyalty towards a particular producer or to brand preference, and even in some cases to the name given to a type of product or service offered. A good example is the appeal that a prestigious wine estate or DOC region has for a wine connoisseur, or the effect that the name of the cultivar or species of the primary food materials (particularly if it is a rare speciality) has on a gourmet food lover. In both cases, the name of the product is synonymous with quality. Quality is always linked to the *terroir*, to the region of production. It can be traced back to the ancestry of the noble grape varieties or to the artisan production methods used to create a distinguished cheese. Quality can even be found in the personality of a producer who epitomizes the very nature of his products or the fascination of the productive landscape.

The preference or loyalty given to a product or service by the consumer-tourist even before it has been tried is connected with the instrumental quality of the product/service in question. This is because the quality is 'fabricated'; we can see this in food and wine tourism where quality is demonstrated by the characteristics of the product or services, but also by the nutritional and organoleptic attributes of the product.

In conclusion, if we are to apply the concept of quality to tourism, and in particular to food and wine tourism, giving value to the holiday experience, we must consider the ongoing interaction between product quality and environmental quality as a set and act accordingly, by integrating all the qualitative features that make up the subsets.

As Fig. 1.6 demonstrates, a lot of attention is given to assessing the correspondence between expected and experienced quality, or in other words how the supplied quality matches up to perceived quality. These concepts are very much linked to the relationships that exist between the character and identity of the host destination, those of the visitors in the destination (with their needs and wants) and of the producers (with their sensitivity and their ability). Perceptions, experiences, ways of demonstrating hospitality and developing product potential are absorbed and emanated through the critical spirit of the tourist and the host destination or the tourist operator.

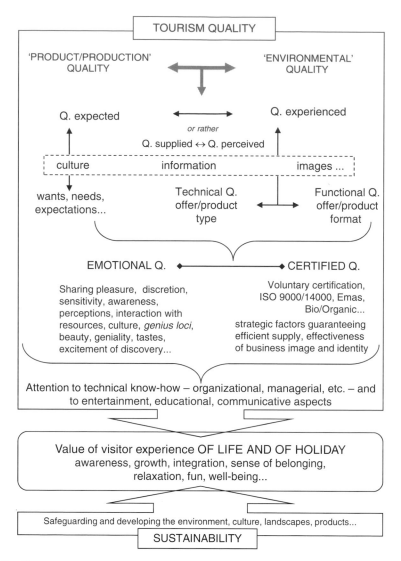

Fig. 1.6. Quality.

A tourist region, a food or wine production business, a restaurant, etc. can all demonstrate quality if they possess the correct characteristics and can show that they are in a position to provide all that is necessary for tourism from the point of view of infrastructure, the environment, production, social conditions and sustainability. The price:quality ratio must also be correct; otherwise there is a risk of asymmetrical information. But this is not all.

Seen from this point of view, it is easier for us to consider the dual definition that is often given to quality: technical quality (how the offer translates itself) and functional quality (how the offer is given). The traditional marketing approach saw quality (expected–perceived, technical–functional) as being almost exclusively related to processes and products. Nowadays, it is necessary to integrate the 'technical' aspects (processes, production methods, management manuals, guides) with the value/role that people/their environment play and the emotional aspects linked to hospitality.

Quality can also be subdivided into two macro areas: certified and emotional. International quality certification for production procedures and environmental performance (e.g. Ecolabel, Emas, ISO 9000/14000) is useful for standardizing quality levels and confirming to stakeholders that the production methods used have minimal environmental impacts. As market demand becomes increasingly aware of the need for environmentally friendly business practices, certification is a bona fide guarantee of product quality for aware consumers. In fact, environmental certification is an extremely important marketing tool as client-tourists who would describe themselves as being 'responsible travellers' perceive it as adding value to a product. Certification on its own however is not sufficient. Contact with the destination and its environment and the impact that this has on the tourist have strong emotional connotations due to the pleasure involved in getting to know a new place and the sensory experiences enjoyed during the visit. A tourist needs to relate to and interact with a destination and be moved by its beauty, its cultural and natural resources, its authentic flavour and unique spirit.

The human factor is equally important in contributing to the atmosphere and quality of a client's experience in a destination. As operators in the 'human contact industry', all sector workers need to be able to interact with their clients and communicate an enthusiasm for their work. As well as having excellent communication skills, tourism operators also need technical know-how and must be naturally open to making contact with the general public. Attending professional training courses to consolidate and develop business skills while keeping abreast with industry trends is essential.

In food and wine tourism, tourism quality and sustainability join forces to enhance the visitor experience by improving overall planning and management and by safeguarding the natural beauty of the destination and its surroundings.

The carrying capacity of a destination (wineries, olive mills, churches, museums, vineyards, protected areas, a wine-tasting session, an art workshop, even a trek on horseback), as we have already mentioned above, is a determining factor in safeguarding a destination's resources, but it also has a significant impact on how successful operators are in being able to satisfy their clients. Measuring success, however, should not just be considered in economic terms. Supply-side actors must also take into account socio-environmental results. The technical and administrative aspects of their work need to be fully integrated with what goes into creating a satisfying and memorable psychological and physical experience of a destination. In order to guarantee a fulfilling and satisfying experience, operators need to be aware of certain essential key elements that combined together ensure a sense of visitor well-being. It goes without saying that fun and relaxation are important components of the tourist product, as are moments of emotion and pleasure, and opportunities to learn something new; but one of the principal elements by which the success of a product can be judged is whether it has given the client-tourist a sense of belonging to the destination and, as a result, an increased sense of responsibility towards it and a more complete sense of well-being.

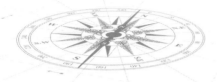

chapter 2

The Environment: Tools of the Trade

Whatever tourism sector we are dealing with, the region and its environment, for obvious reasons, are always the chief attraction and main resource. Before going ahead with plans and management strategies therefore, tourism policy makers must begin by defining the features of the environment, its aptitude and potential for tourism development within the host destination.

As we have already seen in Chapter 1, in other economic sectors, marketing strategies focus on bringing products to a point of sale where the consumer can appraise the product before making a purchasing decision. For example, if we are thinking of buying a car, we can go to a local dealer to see what they have to offer; or in the case of financial services, we can go to a bank and check interest rates before opening a bank account. In tourism, the tourist-consumer (demand) can only verify what they have purchased by experiencing it in the destination (product). This is the only way a tourist product becomes tangible. It makes no difference whether a holiday has been booked and paid for over the Internet or whether it has been organized by a retail travel agent: the tourist invests in a set of variables that cannot be evaluated before consumption. Furthermore, tourism experience in a destination involves the consumption of goods and services and public and private resources (or a mixture of both) that cannot be distinguished from those used and consumed by non-tourists and residents.

In food and wine tourism, a visitor's relationship with the physical environment, in all its manifold connotations, can be stronger than in other tourism sectors: the parameters by which individual tourists judge the success of their holidays, in terms of sensory and emotional experiences, tend to be much greater in gastronomic tourism, as they render the holiday experience unique and memorable. For this reason, tourism planners need to have cultural and environmental sensitivity as well as keeping in mind that marketing strategies cannot just focus on satisfying demand at all costs.

As has already been mentioned, the only way forward for supply-side actors to realize economic goals and offer satisfactory holiday experiences is by cultivating an awareness of the environment and its resources, and making use of them in a sustainable way, offering a quality experience. This means being familiar with certain aspects of geographic theory and having a precise geographic knowledge of the destination in which they work or which they wish to promote. To enable them to apply this knowledge, there are certain key instruments that can help in interpreting geographic features, ranging from the general to the specific, from cross-sectional to specialized, by taking an interdisciplinary approach to all the environmental resources inside an area.

TERROIR, MILIEU, TERRITORY/REGION, LANDSCAPE

Food and wine tourists travel in environments marked by two theoretical–practical extremes: the *cru*, a high-quality product that is intrinsically linked to a particular region (usually a small, well-defined area), and the physical, geographical space within which it is confined. The gastronomic tourism experience is essentially a metaphorical journey between these two poles; an experience which becomes richer and more enhanced if the journey touches upon the fundamental concepts of *terroir*–milieu–territory/region–landscape. These concepts, in fact, bring together the geographic, economic, sociological and anthropological aspects of food and wine tourism.

    The endless possibilities of connecting one concept to another and the ample space for manoeuvre presented by each of the individual 'themed' stops, listed below, make it easy to construct diverse mental geographical itineraries. Tourists are not obliged to discover the different geographical components of a tourist product in any particular sequence, nor is there any need to analyse the concepts in order. The all-important factor is that operators in the sector take into account the *terroir*–milieu–territory/region–landscape relationship, and adopt an interdisciplinary and interactive approach to finding the best possible ways to enhance the gastronomic tourism experience.

    If we take a closer look at the meaning and significance of these four words, we will see that there are a number of strategic features that can be applied and used whatever the context or situation (Fig. 2.1):

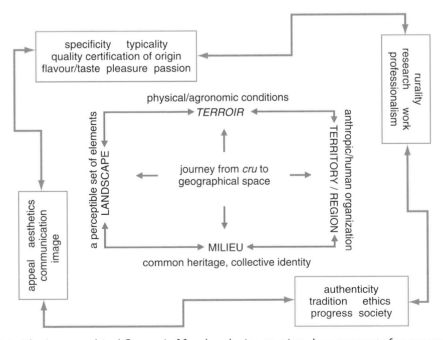

Fig. 2.1. The 'geographical flavour' of food and wine tourism: key concepts for successful planning.

- The French term *terroir* is a key point of reference for food and wine tourism. It is defined as 'an expanse of land with certain characteristics identifying it from an agronomic perspective. These characteristics originate from the *terroir*'s physical qualities (e.g. elevation, climate, exposure, soil, etc.), and are also a consequence of human intervention such as irrigation, drainage, terracing...' (Vaudour, 2003). It is the *terroir* that is the *genius loci* or spirit of a place, giving it its distinctive atmosphere. It is the *terroir* that produces quality food and wine products, and this is perhaps the most important aspect of any activity linked to gastronomic tourism. The agronomic and scientific meaning given to the term *terroir* is linked to the three physical markers of agricultural production, earth/rock–soil–atmosphere, and as a consequence, geology, geomorphology, topography, pedology, climate and so on. However, it also encapsulates the impact of human intervention (cultural, technological, etc.) on the land.

    The interaction between a *terroir*'s physical features and those caused by human activity create in specific places a set of singular conditions for producing high-quality agro-alimentary products with unique characteristics that reflect their region of origin. It is this unmatched geographic specificity, so closely linked to the *terroir*, which gives some gastronomic products their outstanding reputation. This also explains why recognition and certification of quality (e.g. in wine products) are associated with the geographical areas from which the products originate (AOC, DO, DOC, PDO, PGI, etc.). A *cru* therefore (and indeed any native species of the *terroir*) possesses organoleptic, socio-economic, symbolic and communicative resources that combined together give it its special quality. To sum up then, when defining the term *terroir* in its widest possible sense, we should also include the special features and qualities of the milieu, the environment and the landscape. We will look at this in more detail below. *Terroir* can also be translated as meaning 'land or birthplace'. Given this definition, a *terroir*'s connection with its cultural milieu, resources, traditions and characteristics is evident, as is its relationship with the environment and the way that the landscape has been shaped. Let us now turn to the other components of the gastronomic journey.

- Milieu represents common heritage and collective identity, both of intrinsic importance in shaping the entity of a place or region. Together, they combine all those tangible and intangible elements, natural resources and socio-cultural conditions that, over time, go into creating a precise geographic reality and are responsible for making that place or region what it is today and shaping its potential for development in the future.

- A geographic analysis of any physical space must be conducted by examining the characteristics of its territory/region. The quality of life that can be supported by the territory/region is obviously an important factor in all sectors of tourism, food and wine tourism in particular. The territory/region is an expression of human intervention and organization. It is an extremely complex, dynamic and symbolic entity with multiple elements constantly interacting with one another, e.g. its orographic features interconnecting with administrative and functional aspects. Territories/regions are the result of social actions and the way individuals perceive their environment: the stronger is the impulse to seek out and understand how all the different threads tie together, the more complete and accurate that perception turns out to be (Fig. 2.2).

- The landscape is the most immediately perceptible aspect and is the most susceptible to territorial/regional systems; for this reason it is probably the most important aspect of the tourism experience. The landscape is a cultural reality, the result of human endeavour. It reflects all the different ways that humans interact with the environment and use its resources; it is a subject for observation, consumption and speculation.

Fig. 2.2. Tangible and intangible elements in the environment (source: the authors' own adaptation of Caroli, 2006).

We could even say that, without an observer, the concept of landscape would not exist. The impact that a landscape has on an observer depends very much on their cultural background and their powers of perception and interpretation. 'When we find ourselves before a landscape whose majesty strikes us to the heart, the pure pleasure that we feel comes from a desire to belong, to be part of it. In that particular instant, we have a longing to be in total unison and harmony with what we see before us' (from the art exhibition 'Sitting and Admiring Landscapes, 1966–2009', Ascoli Piceno, 2009).

These words by painter Tullio Pericoli explain perfectly what we mean by 'affective inhabitancy': linked to the beauty of the landscape, it is one of the main factors determining the quality of visitor experience in a destination. Very often, the tourist considers the landscape as simply a scenic backdrop or something that, although unfamiliar, adds atmosphere to their holiday. However, they need to be totally immersed in their surroundings if they are to give a positive appraisal of their holiday experience. In cultural and food and wine tourism, immersion is not enough: the landscape and the environment must be visited, interpreted and inhabited. A landscape is full of symbols and signs that have objective meanings as well as existential subjective values; they need to be sought out and examined by all those residing in a destination, whether long-term residents or short-stay visitors, to enable them to gain a better understanding of what life is like in that particular place at that particular moment in time. It is almost impossible to have a complete picture or understanding of a landscape however, as it depends very much on the individual's standpoint or frame of reference. The objective should always be to gain as much knowledge as possible about life as it is lived in the place, to appreciate its unique personality and identity, and to live the experience to the full. This is true for tourists as well as residents, who can enhance their experience of a destination even further by involving all their senses in discovering the flavours of the food and/or wine produce/products that are connected with that particular place. This approach can be applied to all geographic scales of observation, whether it a valley view or a city view, a mountain range or a rocky coastline. As we go up the scale, it could be a church façade or the fascinating interior of a cheese maturing room, until we arrive at the 'micro landscape' of an artisan baker's shop window. It can even be applied to the landscape offered by a particular dish in a restaurant whose colours, aromas and flavours are a tribute to the local area and its products. It is the landscape that, through the sense of sight, is the first to take a visitor on a multi-sensory journey of a region or area. The multi-sensory experiences that are potentially offered by a landscape are something that tourism marketing should focus on more. If this were the case, it would erase the conflict between the value of use (linked to the identity and culture of a place) and the value of exchange (linked to market needs) in a tourist destination. What is more, the qualities, inherent values and products of a *terroir*–milieu–environment–landscape that belong to the host community would become the very same elements sought after by visitors.

> The true journey, as introjection of an 'outside' different from our normal one, implies a complete change of nutrition, a digesting of the visited country – its fauna and flora and its culture (not only the different culinary practices and condiments but the different implements used to grind the flour or stir the pot) – making it pass between the lips and down the oesophagus. This is the only kind of travel that has a meaning nowadays, when everything visible you can see on TV without rising from your easy chair. (Calvino, 1988)

GEOGRAPHIC THEORIES

In order to analyse the implications of tourism development on the environment, we need to turn to specialized documentation: numerous geographic models exist dealing with the configuration and organization of space for tourism purposes and are useful instruments for tourism planners and operators (as well as tourists). The specialist knowledge gained by analysing the models helps the supply side to decide what type of tourism activity is currently most suitable in a destination and can also indicate what future is likely for the destination as a whole and for individual tourist products.

Geographic theories originally dealt with tourism as a whole, which was seen as an abstract concept and did not refer to specific sectors. However, we have seen that it can easily be adapted and applied to food and wine destinations.

Spatial models put forward abstract theories that are the result of observation and examination. They give us instruments by which it is possible to interpret, classify, illustrate and represent the state and evolution of extremely complex realities that are not always easy to pin down or define, as they do not seem to fit into any predetermined structure. It is up to the researcher-operator to keep up to date with socio-economic and environmental developments and the theories that gradually evolve as a result of these developments, e.g. in technology, human and land settlement, transport, markets, communication, culture and lifestyles.

Spatial models are therefore excellent learning instruments and provide useful frameworks with which to undertake research and make comparisons. It is possible that they may give only partial or incomplete readings if they are used with the aim of identifying and interpreting every single feature of an area. This kind of detailed research must be conducted with caution and further studies and analyses, such as fieldwork, need to be carried out to verify the individual qualities or characteristics of a given destination. Successful analysis therefore requires a theoretical approach combined with on-the-spot research experience.

Configuring tourist flows and space

Geographic space is criss-crossed by ever-increasing national and international tourism flows. With countless destination choices, different forms of organization and means of transport, and motivated by a myriad of reasons, more and more people are travelling worldwide.

The Lundgren model (Lundgren, 1984) is a hierarchy of four different geographic systems relating to the country of origin and the chosen destination (see Fig. 2.3); in other words, four different types of place of origin and destinations analysed on the basis of their function and geographical position. As these configurations frequently correspond to traveller behaviour, the model is extremely useful because:

- it gives a starting point for considering tourist flows and their distribution in various areas – the number of arrivals and typologies of tourists, the relationship between different places of origin, reasons for travelling to and typology of chosen destination, etc.; and
- it offers a potential framework (although partial) for devising business and tourism development strategies and for designing promotional strategies to appeal to specific targets according to their country of origin.

The original model did not take into account different typologies of tourism, but we can apply the theory behind it to the food and wine tourism sector if we consider the quantitative and qualitative aspects of tourist movements:

- Metropolitan or urban areas. These are at the top of the Lundgren scale: located within a network of interconnected infrastructures, they are easily accessible. There is an exchange of large numbers of visitors between one area and another (domestic and international inbound/outbound tourists). These large city centres offer visitors a vast choice of entertainment and leisure opportunities, including gastronomic experiences. Certain cities in the world have a reputation for culinary excellence and, very often, companies renowned for prestigious food production can be found inside the city limits. For example, within the flows of tourists between Paris and Tokyo, there are undoubtedly tourists whose main motive for travel is to enjoy French or Japanese cuisine. Urban areas can also act as hubs through which residents and incoming tourists travel to get to other areas or localities (perhaps divided into concentric zones) in the immediate vicinity or to reach more distant destinations. This brings us to the next stage in the spatial system.
- Suburban areas. These are areas linked to nearby cities by outgoing and incoming (by far the greater number) tourist flows. They tend to be areas that offer possibilities for recreation or that have a particular attraction that draws city residents, as well as temporary visitors who are passing through the city or those who have specifically chosen the city as a holiday destination, out of the city for a day trip or short break (mainly at weekends or holiday times).

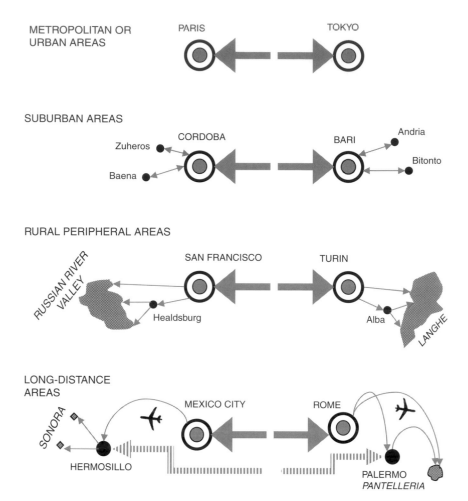

Fig. 2.3. Hierarchy of spatial systems in origin–destination of tourist flows (source: the authors' own adaptation of Lundgren, 1984).

An emblematic example for food and wine tourism is the potential system in the area of Andria–Bitonto in the province of Bari (Italy), dotted with small towns famous for their Romanesque art, surrounded by olive groves and mills. Or similarly, in the area south of Cordoba in Spain, there are the famous whitewashed towns of the *pueblos blancos de l'aceite* set among olive trees and olive farms.

• Rural peripheral areas. Tourists either pass through an urban centre to reach these areas directly, or they may choose to stay in a small country town or village and use it as a base to venture further afield and to explore the rural surroundings. For example, there are possible parallels between the configurations of two wine tourism systems: Russian River Valley←Healdsburg←San Francisco (USA) and Langhe←Alba←Turin (Italy). It is also possible that tourism presence (mainly domestic) in rural locations is due to the number of city dwellers who own second homes, especially in areas that lie within a short/medium distance from the city. In the same way, a similar situation is represented by multi-property or time-sharing (an exception to the theory put forward by the model) that is responsible for tourism presence in more distant destinations.

- Long-distance areas. These are reached after lengthy journeys or long-haul flights. Inbound foreign visitors arrive through airports/ports, etc. collocated near a metropolis (useful as points of reference for foreign tourists) before continuing their journey into the hinterland. Lundgren identifies them as 'green areas, natural environments', nature parks, protected areas, exotic destinations, etc. As examples of gastronomic destinations, we could cite *haciendas* in Bacanora on the Sonora coast that can be reached through Hermosillo–Mexico City, or the gastronomic seaside area of Pantelleria in the south of Italy, accessed by travelling through Palermo–Rome.

An analysis of the Lundgren model could give us a scenario in which tourist space is organized in concentric zones, possibly crossed by preferential corridors of movement connecting major destinations to each other. The way these circular spaces are organized depends on the volume and intensity of tourist flows and the particular characteristics displayed by destinations and radial centres inside the transport networks. We can even hypothesize exchange and collaborative partnerships and projects between different areas inside the zones. These theories certainly offer a framework for describing and analysing the mechanisms and development potential of tourism systems, but they do need to be contextualized and take into account the specific features of the destination/region under examination. Further factors needing to be taken into consideration are:

- the typology of tourism in question (seaside, cultural, food and wine, sports, etc.), typology of travel organization (independent/organized, individual/group), seasonality, length of stay, length of holiday/tour (research evidence suggests that there is a correlation between the length of time a tourist is prepared to stay away, the use of transport and the distance to the destination: the further away the destination, the longer the period of time spent on holiday);
- transport means and network connections (e.g. low-cost airlines have had a substantial impact on the relationship between length of holiday and travel time);
- costs, which vary according to distances covered, level of service, reputation of the destination, transport used, length of holiday, seasonality according to theme of visit or destination; and
- information available to the market and tourist perception of the destination (the media exercise an enormous influence over consumer perception and market choice, creating destination images to appeal to different targets – familiar, innovative and original, pioneer, exclusive and trendy, etc.).

Other aspects to be considered when analysing a particular area should include the activities of the supply side, the level of hospitality, the socio-political-economic situation and the actual stage of tourism development. We will look at this aspect in more detail when we come to the section dedicated to evolutionary theories.

The work of Lozato-Giotart (2008), a French geographer, on classifying tourist space also gives us some instruments and a methodology which we can apply to analysing spatial forms and relationships in tourism destinations.

Lozato-Giotart's theory is based on the principles of:

- the environmental value of tourism, which makes a distinction between specialized destinations that are exclusively for tourism use (e.g. purpose-built holiday resorts) and multipurpose destinations where tourism is integrated with other socio-economic activities (e.g. cities, seaside towns);
- the spatial distribution of tourist settlements, particularly in the way they connect with other occupied spaces such as industrial areas, shopping areas, transport hubs and residential areas,

which makes a distinction between mononuclear localities (in which tourist areas and tourism infrastructure are concentrated in one place) and polynuclear localities (where tourist areas and infrastructure are distributed in more than one place); and

- the spatial distribution of tourist sites and resources, which makes a distinction between localities with one major tourist resource (one pole of tourist attraction) and multi-attraction destinations.

If we want to apply Lozato-Giotart's theory with regard to multi-attraction destinations, we need to take an in-depth look at the nature of the attractors. In this way, we can create a scale of possibilities between monothematic destinations, where tourist appeal depends on one specific kind of resource/attraction, and polythematic destinations where tourists are drawn to the locality by two or more integrated elements, such as nature, art, culture, shopping, conferences and events, fairs and exhibitions, health and leisure, food and wine. With gastronomic destinations, it would be useful to understand if they are monoproductive (in which case their appeal depends on one specific quality product) or polyproductive, where the locality or region's attraction is connected to two or more locally produced quality products.

We should also consider other possible situations, such as:

- Absence of any pole attractions, where tourist appeal is connected to aspects of the landscape or scattered natural resources, e.g. desert dunes, glaciers at high latitudes, forests, extensive plantations.
- Absence of any nuclearity (core infrastructure), a rare possibility as wherever there is a tourist attraction or resource there is usually some type of infrastructure in place; however, situations still exist where there is a total lack of tourism infrastructure/services, e.g. in protected national parks that are difficult to access, remote monuments and isolated farmhouses. We should also take into account holiday destinations that attract free or 'nomadic' travel, where overnight accommodation is under canvas.

There is a risk that using different methodological criteria when applying these types of models could result in different geographical observations: for example, if the perception of a destination and depth of analysis are different, this could bring about a cause/effect reaction with analyses conducted on a totally different geographic scale. It is extremely interesting (and useful) to note that the same tourist destination can belong to different spatial typologies according to the objective of the study and if different geographical visions are used. It is possible that any attempt at geographical schematization is the result of partial attributions or visions that are not absolute truths if seen from a different point of view, or if different research methodologies and methods of analysis are used.

Returning to the model, if we apply the parameters listed above to the study of spatial configurations in food and wine tourism, we can identify two macro-categories of destination types, characterized by further internal subdivisions:

- Urban spaces, which are generally multi-purpose and polynuclear. Figure 2.4 indicates how food and wine tourism sites are distributed and we can see how they can be interpreted within one of the following categories.
- Multi-attraction cities such as Reims, Cognac (France), Jerez (Spain), Porto (Portugal), Marsala, Montepulciano and Canelli (Italy), famous for their wine cellars; Munich (Germany) for its beer; Brussels (Belgium) for its chocolate; Campbeltown (Scotland, UK) for its whisky; Imperia and Cartoceto (Italy) or Baena (Spain) for their olive mills; and, again in Italy, Paestum for its dairy products, in particular buffalo mozzarella cheese; Campofilone

and Gragnano for pasta; San Daniele for ham; Altamura for bread. They are all fairly large urban centres that have quite an extraordinary distribution of traditional and renowned agro-alimentary companies.

- Cities/sites with one pole of attraction, examples of destinations where visitor appeal is based on one gastronomic company are Lynchburg in Tennessee (USA) and Midleton (Ireland), both famous for their distilleries. There are also examples of cities that have two poles of attraction, in other words two strong attractors capable of drawing tourists autonomously, such as Bra (Italy). Its urban centre is a strong pull for visitors (famous for its meat and cheese products, the headquarters of the Slow Food movement and its Baroque architecture), while the University of Gastronomic Sciences is located just outside, in the ancient hamlet of Pollenzo. Temporary gastronomic events, such as food fairs, exhibitions or farmers markets, can also function as a pole attraction, bringing visitors to a locality exclusively for a particular occasion, or acting as an added attraction to a destination for the duration of the event. Although these are temporary events and time spent in a destination may be brief, if they are successful they leave an imprint on the destination and a positive impression in the attentive visitor's mind. Depending on the size and duration of the individual event, the type of image that it manages to transmit and the perceived image of the host destination, these occasions can become so popular they become part of a fixed calendar of organized events and attract an ever-increasing number of devotees.

If we look instead at how accommodation structures are distributed, it is very rare to find examples of infrastructure confined to just one or even two zones of an urban centre, although it is possible to find concentrated pockets of accommodation facilities in certain areas of a city such as in the historic quarter, around central transport hubs or in business districts where trade fairs and exhibitions are held.

Regional and rural spaces are generally polynuclear with multiple poles of attraction. It can happen that a rural area, although an attraction in itself, depends on the pull of a particular town or locality in the region. The potential for food and wine tourism in these areas is generally limited to well-defined regions characterized by multiple resources with the same appeal and a widespread range of tourist activities. Spatial configuration is based on where the attractors are localized and the different shapes of the tourist itineraries derive from where these attractors are located. The distribution of visitor stops is very often connected to the morphology of the terrain, e.g. along the coastline, on the plains, along a valley, the slopes or crest of a mountain, on a plateau. It also depends on the theme of the tour and organizational aspects such as transport networks and connections and the distribution of hospitality, catering and food and wine production facilities. It is worth noting that the polarization of tourism expresses itself in different ways and it is possible to identify a number of different configurations even within the same area:

- Regions with centralized poles of attractions. These are cities from where it is possible to organize tours or excursions to visit famous localities with food or wine production enterprises in the immediate vicinity, e.g. Verona, Ragusa, Siena, Montalcino and Montefalco (Italy); Bordeaux, Chablis and Roquefort (France); Bruges and Antwerp (Belgium); Logroño (Spain); and, outside Europe, Mendoza (Argentina) and Cape Town (South Africa). In the case of large urban centres that have rural environments immediately outside the city limits, e.g. Melbourne (Australia) surrounded by the wine-growing areas of Yarra Valley, Mornington Peninsula and Sunbury, or, still in Australia, the McLaren Vale and Adelaide Hills surrounding Adelaide, we have a typology of tourism that we could refer to as 'rururban'.

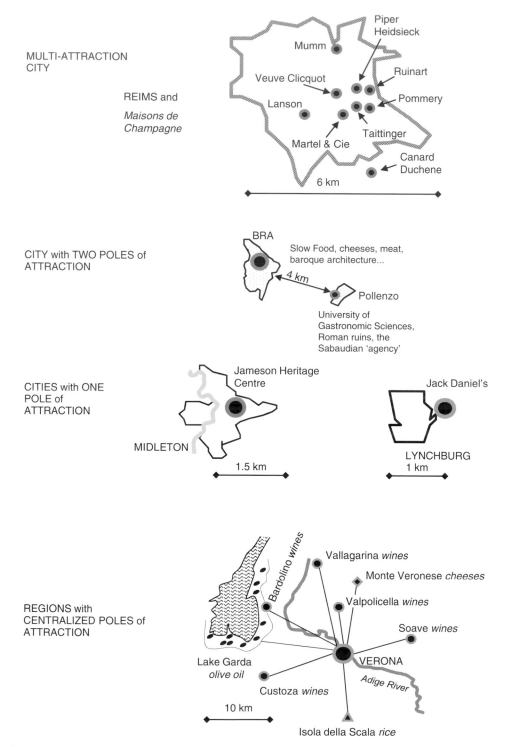

MULTI-ATTRACTION CITY

REIMS and

Maisons de Champagne

Piper Heidsieck

Mumm

Veuve Clicquot

Ruinart

Lanson

Pommery

Martel & Cie

Taittinger

Canard Duchene

6 km

CITY with TWO POLES of ATTRACTION

BRA

Slow Food, cheeses, meat, baroque architecture...

4 km

Pollenzo

University of Gastronomic Sciences, Roman ruins, the Sabaudian 'agency'

CITIES with ONE POLE of ATTRACTION

Jameson Heritage Centre

Jack Daniel's

MIDLETON

LYNCHBURG

1.5 km

1 km

REGIONS with CENTRALIZED POLES of ATTRACTION

Bardolino wines

Vallagarina *wines*

Monte Veronese *cheeses*

Valpolicella *wines*

Soave *wines*

Lake Garda *olive oil*

VERONA

Adige River

Custoza *wines*

10 km

Isola della Scala *rice*

Fig. 2.4. Spatial configurations in urban and regional gastronomic tourism (source: the authors' own adaptation from Lozato-Giotart, 1993).

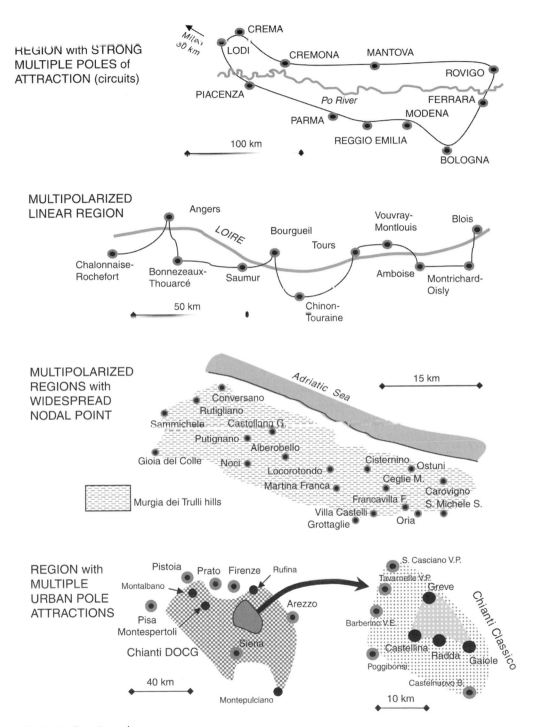

REGION with STRONG MULTIPLE POLES of ATTRACTION (circuits)

CREMA
LODI
CREMONA
MANTOVA
ROVIGO
PIACENZA
Po River
FERRARA
PARMA
MODENA
REGGIO EMILIA
BOLOGNA
100 km
Miles 30 km

MULTIPOLARIZED LINEAR REGION

Angers
Vouvray-Montlouis
Blois
LOIRE
Bourgueil
Tours
Chalonnaise-Rochefort
Bonnezeaux-Thouarcé
Saumur
Amboise
Montrichard-Oisly
Chinon-Touraine
50 km

MULTIPOLARIZED REGIONS with WIDESPREAD NODAL POINT

Adriatic Sea
15 km
Conversano
Rutigliano
Sammichele
Castellana G.
Putignano
Alberobello
Gioia del Colle
Noci
Cisternino
Ostuni
Locorotondo
Ceglie M.
Martina Franca
Carovigno
Francavilla F.
S. Michele S.
Villa Castelli
Oria
Grottaglie

Murgia dei Trulli hills

REGION with MULTIPLE URBAN POLE ATTRACTIONS

Pistoia
Prato
Firenze
Rufina
Montalbano
Arezzo
Pisa
Montespertoli
Chianti DOCG
Siena
40 km
Montepulciano

S. Casciano V.P.
Tavarnelle V.P.
Greve
Barberino V.E.
Chianti Classico
Castellina
Radda
Gaiole
Poggibonsi
Castelnuovo B.
10 km

Fig. 2.4. Continued.

- Multipolarized regions, which can be divided into:

  ○ Regions with multiple urban pole attractions. These are areas delimited by urban centres that give historic interest and character to the local food or wine production. The strong bond that exists between these cities and the areas in between is a constant reminder of the close links of culture and the environment. Examples in Italy include the area of Chianti that lies between the cities of Florence, Pistoia, Arezzo, Siena and Pisa or, on a larger scale, the heart of the Chianti region between Greve, Radda, Castellina and Gaiole; in France we have the Armagnac region between Eauze, Condom and Auch or the Champagne region between Reims, Epernay, Troyes and Verdun. In certain cases, we also have to consider tourist regions with strong but intermittent multiple poles of attraction. This refers to situations where there is a notable difference between the amount of attention given to urban poles in contrast to their immediate surroundings. In this case, the identity of the rural environment is shaped by its urban component. This can be observed when the major attractions for visitors touring a region are concentrated in the main urban centres and the areas between them are considered only from the point of view of transit, providing a scenic backdrop for travellers between the main destinations. The art and gastronomy tours in the Padana region (Italy) are a good example of this, where the area stretching from the south of the region to the north embraces three different territorial levels (Via Emilia, the Po River and the lower plain of Lombardy), offering a unique mosaic of art and history and high-quality production of cured meats and cheeses.

  ○ Multipolarized regions with widespread nodal points. These are areas dotted here and there with small urban centres, such as the Altopiano di Asiago or the Murgia dei Trulli (Italy), Provence (France), Extremadura (Spain) and Santa Barbara (USA). They can also include entire localities or districts, such as the wine-growing areas of Sonoma–Napa Valley (USA) and Somerset West–Stellenbosh–Franschhoek–Paarl (South Africa). We should underline the fact that, in many cases, these regions can also be considered as being both multipolarized and monothematic in the sense that they are famous – or are perceived as being so – above all for their specialized gastronomic production. Furthermore, we often find that localized production areas, while being in the vicinity of urban towns and settlements (from which they often take their name), are in fact famous because of the entire region to which they belong and where poles of attraction are concentrated on the various production companies scattered throughout the area. Apart from the examples already mentioned above, we could also add the 'Malt Whisky Trail' of Speyside (Scotland) or some of the other wine-growing areas in South Africa (Lutzville), Australia (Margareth River, Barossa), New Zealand (Central Otago) and South America (Bio Bio).

- Multipolarized linear regions. These are areas where gastronomic destinations can be found along the course of a river, along old trade routes, along a section of coastline, etc. Examples include: the wine route in Alsace that connects Strasbourg, Colmar and Mulhouse; the 'route des grands crus' in Burgundy, from Dijon to Montagny; the Loire Valley (France); the Moselle Valley (Germany); the Barossa Valley (Australia); but also the route between Calistoga, St Helena and Napa in the Napa Valley (USA). There are also gastronomic destinations strung along parts of the Santiago de Compostela route in the Rioja region (Spain), or along the old Roman roads; in Italy, certain tracts of the Adriatic coastline are famous for their *brodetto* (fish soups) between the Marche and Abruzzo;

both the Po Delta (Italy) and Galicia (Spain) are renowned for their series of shellfish breeding centres; *tonnare*, tuna fishing and processing plants (parts of the Sicilian and Sardinian coastlines); exotic or Mediterranean ports where fishing tourism is a strong attractor. Multipolarized seaside destinations are particularly interesting as they offer a wide catchment area and are convenient bases for exploring gastronomic destinations further inland. Good examples include the olive- and wine-growing areas of Abruzzo, Maremma, Veneto, Friuli Venezia Giulia and Puglia (Italy), or Priorat or Penedes inland from the Costa Dorada between Barcelona and Tarragona (Spain), which are continuing to attract an ever-increasing number of visitors who make the journey up from the coast.

In the last few years another category of spatial configuration has emerged, which can be defined as multipolarized mononuclear centralized: in essence this refers to an accommodation establishment that has established a reputation for the quality of its hospitality connected to the surrounding environment and whose tourist offer also includes a gastronomic component. Clients have the possibility to enjoy a range of different activities without ever having to leave the accommodation structure. The most obvious examples are self-contained holiday resorts, beauty farms, luxury hotels, farmhouse stays and rural holiday centres immersed in the countryside and connected to food or wine production enterprises, such as wineries, olive mills and dairy farms. More and more of these offer other services such as on-site restaurants, beauty treatments using natural ingredients, hands-on activities (e.g. helping with the harvest, fruit-picking), workshops and courses (e.g. painting, cooking, food or wine tasting) and sports activities (e.g. horse-riding and mountain-biking). In these particular contexts, the region and its landscape can be 'only' a pleasing scenic backdrop to the holiday rather than being considered as a production area for quality food or wine products. However, the gastronomic experience still has an important role to play: guests can be offered the possibility to tour production premises, to participate in a tasting session and to purchase products to take home with them. Fine wining and dining, where dishes are based on regional products, also enhance the gastronomic experience.

Evolutionary theories

All places are shaped by social, economic and cultural factors. Tourist destinations are no different; in fact, to understand the spirit of a place (an all-important factor in pinpointing and understanding perception and appeal), we need to study these factors and analyse the role they play in modelling spatial and temporal developments in tourism. A number of studies have led to the construction of dynamic models that can help us towards understanding these spatial and temporal patterns. Environments, places and destinations evolve over time; they are in a state of constant change as they adapt to different temporal phases. The defining or inherent character of a place that sets it apart from others would suggest that we use these theories as a starting point for analysis and verification, and if we carry out more in-depth fieldwork, we should be able to pinpoint correlations, deviations and applications.

The effects of polarization, hierarchy and saturation on tourism destinations can also be understood by looking at Miossec's theory (Miossec, 1977). The model can be applied at various scales and describes the gradual evolution of an area touched by tourism. This evolution is summarized into five temporal phases (Fig. 2.5) and each one can be looked at from four different perspectives:

- the organization of the geographic space;
- the development of infrastructure and transport;

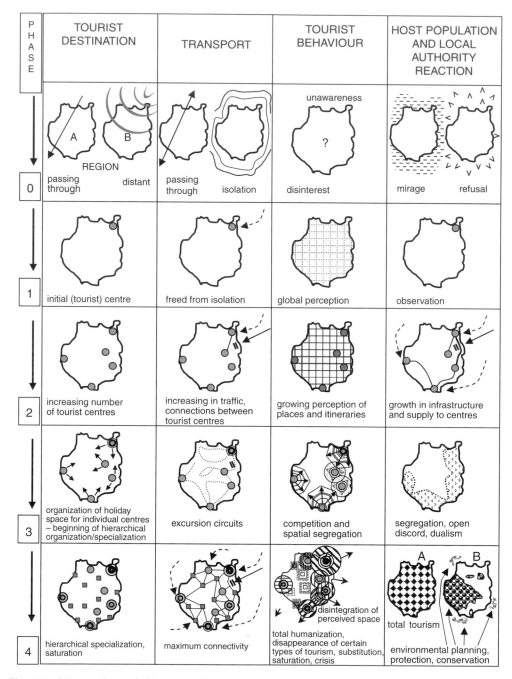

Fig. 2.5. Miossec's model (source: the authors' own adaptation from the original model).

- tourist behaviour; and
- the attitude of the host community (residents and administrators).

According to Miossec, when residents who have always lived in a place untouched by tourism come into contact with the first pioneering visitors, it is common that either they feel tourism is a mirage or they refuse the presence of tourism in their community. In a second moment, however, this is followed by curiosity and observation. This is helped if there is only point of access to the destination. From the point of view of the visitor, as the area is still unknown, the image that they have of the destination tends to be rather generic (phases 0 and 1).

Phase 2 sees tourist flows increase and visitors begin to show a desire/need to explore and get to know the destination better; at the same time as more infrastructure and facilities are being developed. At this point, the host population sees tourism as something to be capitalized on. The last phases see an ever-increasing consumption of space: tourist locations established during the earlier phases become more specialized and the area begins to develop a hierarchical organization structure, concentrated in nodes, some more significant than others. There are substantial differences between areas and interests (the presence of tourism is not the same throughout the whole region); destinations begin to compete against each other and there is growing evidence of spatial segregation: there is a clear division between luxury destinations and those attracting mass tourism (phase 3). Saturation, highly concentrated infrastructure, congestion, loss of environmental features and identity (the original perception of these is also lost), are all responsible for transforming the tourism offer into something more banal and unoriginal, focusing exclusively on attracting large numbers, and bringing down prices rather than concentrating on the validity of the offer. And so begins a downward spiral that leads to phase 4, 'total tourism'. In this last phase, the area or locality is completely consumed by tourism, the relationship between tourism and the local community is incompatible and destination image collapses. This deterioration then triggers off a fall in the number of visitors who are also perturbed about the worsening environmental conditions. In spite of falling visitor numbers, there is an overwhelming number of tourism establishments and services designed to meet peak season demand.

Nevertheless, Miossec also considers another possibility: a growing awareness of the necessity to intervene and put a stop to total paralysis. Policies can be put into place and spaces in tourism localities can be subdivided, creating protected areas to safeguard the environment (e.g. by creating nature reserves and national parks, with limited or no access), where it is possible to set up alternative itineraries and tours. This kind of evolution is common in many areas (including the Mediterranean and beyond), particularly in seaside tourism.

The model does however display a substantial weakness. This is the non-contextualized empty space that represents the situation in an area before the advent of tourism. It does not take into account any other economic sectors that may have been active before tourism development. This approach, where interaction between the tourism industry and other sectors is not taken into consideration, is also applied to subsequent phases. In reality, food and wine tourism by its very nature embodies other socio-economic aspects and merges with at least two sectors: tourism and agro-alimentary production. This would lead us to believe that it is a rare occurrence to feel a loss of regional identity in gastronomic destinations, if necessary attention is given to the ethical and aesthetic quality of rural production (on which tourism development is based), in total harmony with the agronomic, physical, social and economic characteristics of the *terroir*.

Attention must also be given to the type of image that is projected of the destination. Very often, images tend to be stereotyped and do not reflect true potential. This tends to happen more often in regions or urban centres that base their appeal almost exclusively on their fame and reputation. Unfortunately, these areas, that historically have always attracted visitors, have not been able to evolve successfully over time. They have not known how to implement innovative measures and strategies to ensure success while preventing museumification. The same situation happens in areas where social layers and traditional production activities and craftsmanship have completely altered over time and become inadequate to the situation, obsolete or extinct. The geographic space that they occupy has become 'souvenirized'; the destination is a mock-image of itself, with 'traditional' products being bought in from outside, supporting and maintaining a culture that is merely a false imitation of the original.

> The typical course of development has the following pattern: painters search out untouched and unusual places to paint. Step by step the place develops as a so-called artist's colony. Soon a cluster of poets follows, kindred to the painters: then cinema people, gourmets and the *jeunesse dorée*. The place becomes fashionable and the entrepreneur takes note. The fisherman's cottages, the shelter-huts become converted into boarding houses and hotels come on the scene. Meanwhile the painters have fled and sought out another periphery – periphery as related to space, and metaphorically, as 'forgotten' places and landscapes. Only the painters with a commercial inclination who like to do well in business remain: they capitalize on the good name of this former painter's corner and on the gullibility of tourists. More and more townsmen choose this place now en vogue and advertised in the newspaper. Subsequently the gourmets and all those who seek real recreation, stay away. At last the tourist agencies come with their package-rate travelling parties; now, the indulgent public avoids such places. At the same time, in other places, the same cycle occurs again: more and more places come into fashion, change their type and turn into everybody's tourist haunt.   (Christaller, 1964)

Aside from the irony contained in these lines, Butler (1980) does well to cite from Christaller to introduce his tourist destination life cycle model (Fig. 2.6). He also points out how the dynamics of a tourist destination are linked to changes in consumer tastes and choice, to how area resources have been maintained (or to the degree to which they have deteriorated), to changes in local development plans and policies, and to how infrastructure and attractions are used according to the socio-economic-environmental conditions of the area in question.

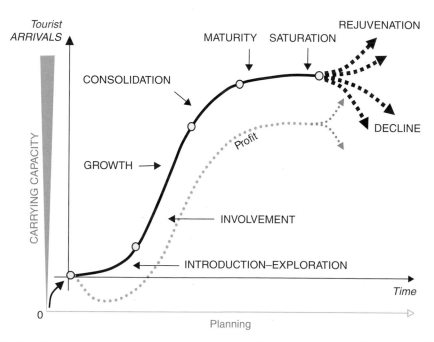

Fig. 2.6. The life cycle of a tourist product (source: the authors' own adaptation of Butler, 1980).

This model also describes the different environmental configurations that a destination goes through when tourism activities develop spontaneously. Within each of these configurations, any eventual differences in attitude and/or reaction on the part of all the actors involved in that particular phase of impact (visitors, tourism operators, residents, local policy makers, investors, etc.) come to light. In each of the evolutionary stages, it is possible to observe changes in how the destination is perceived and the way destination image is projected. These have repercussions on the potential for tourism enhancement and development in a destination:

- Introduction–exploration. The locality is unknown, the environment is unspoilt. The first pioneer tourists begin to arrive and enter into direct contact with the local population. Any organized tourist products are virtually non-existent. The only actors on the supply side tend to be residents, who either voluntarily or spontaneously offer basic services such as food and overnight accommodation. Tourism impact on the destination is practically nil.

- Involvement. As tourist flows increase, local residents begin to see potential for growth. Transport connections, hospitality services and facilities are still undeveloped; as a consequence the organization of infrastructure is speeded up to respond to improve the quality of supply. Tourism impact remains modest.

- Growth. The destination is now in the spotlight and attracts increasing attention from tourism markets. Outside investors and a growing presence of external organizations drive local businesses out. The public sector invests heavily in infrastructure and develops communication policies aimed at large-scale promotion. Visitor arrivals soar and reach levels of maximum growth. Prices rise and so do profits. It is not long before tourist arrivals outnumber residents during peak seasons. Outside labour is needed to boost the workforce. The consumption of space and resources becomes ever more evident, causing damage to the environment with many residents unprepared to pay the brunt of the ensuing costs. Earnings from tourism are not distributed evenly among the host community. Mass tourism crowds out the original tourist explorers who do not return to the destination.

- Consolidation. The tourist sector dominates the local economy, and in some cases local production is completely driven out. By this stage, the loss of cultural identity could be total. Visitor numbers are still on the rise but less intensely than before. The first measures are put in place to try to create incentives for further development. Congestion and environmental degradation are now consolidated and bring about the first signs of intolerance and strong rejection on the part of the host population.

- Maturity–saturation: flat growth, visitor numbers peak. Impact on the destination is considerable and environmental appeal is irretrievably lost. The authentic image of the destination is compromised and clientele is confined to the mass market. Prices begin to drop. The local population's hostility is tangible. Market share diminishes in spite of attempts to attract new segments. Dependence on public sector financing grows, although this does not always deliver. Investments are sought to activate artificial resources, such as theme parks, that are totally out of context and have nothing to do with the original identity of the destination. In many cases, businesses grind to a halt and are forced to sell up. Companies and enterprises frequently change hands.

At the end of the cycle the destination can move in two possible directions:

- Decline. Internal conflicts and a fall in visitor numbers are tangible signs that decline is underway. The tourist function of the destination is replaced by real estate and residential and commercial sectors.

- Rejuvenation. Investments and shared smart planning aimed at relaunching the destination's image through new products/services and recuperating previously undervalued resources can impede decline. As market interest picks up again, the destination manages to re-enter the tourist circuit but with different functions compared with its original use, e.g. by creating theme parks, casinos, golf courses or other sports facilities, exhibition and conference areas, cultural events. Positive results can also be obtained by restoring urban heritage sites and relaunching areas or resources whose potential had not been realized or taken into account the first time round.

According to Butler's model, it is often not until the final stages of the life cycle that the stakeholders begin to wake up and feel the need to properly plan tourism development without compromising the environment, by which time the environment has already been degraded or damaged. When territorial plans are adopted to develop tourism in a particular area, they can in fact modify the descriptors given in the model. A plan of action can put a halt to a process of deterioration, it can postpone it, it can bring it forward and make things worse, or, in certain cases, a whole phase in the life cycle can be omitted. For instance, the creation of a conservation area or regional nature park will obviously have ramifications on a tourist product's life cycle and slow down the process of deterioration, while planning to construct a purpose-built resort in a unique geographic space and unspoilt, natural environment (e.g. by a deserted tropical beach, in an isolated mountain valley or in some wine-producing regions) will naturally speed up tourism development in the area and lead to eventual environmental deterioration. It is absolutely essential that tourism development is planned from the outset according to sustainable principles and that the situation is constantly monitored to prevent any negative impact on the environment. In this way, it is possible to predict potential areas of conflict between the need to develop the tourist product and the need to protect environmental quality. The fact that the situation is monitored and kept under control also means that it is easier to intervene in time and correct any errors that could be potentially damaging. We should therefore be looking at other stages of the life cycle to see the effects of carrying capacity on destinations and not just concentrate on the last phases, although it is true that the signs of environmental distress are more evident towards the end of the cycle. In fact, each stage has a threshold of resilience that should be determined by first making a comparison and then making a compromise between respect for the environment and planning objectives, and should take into account the capacity and efficiency of visitor facilities and services, market research results, the approval of the host community and socio-economic opportunities.

The carrying capacity is not a precise limit: it should be considered instead as a variable concept open to the effects and influences of technological advances and innovations, to models of consumer behaviour (hopefully responsible towards the environment) and efficient management of resources.

Some useful parameters for analysing tourism impacts on the environment are:

- the ratio of tourists to the host population, or the ratio of accommodation structures (including second homes) to the surface area of the destination or to the number of inhabitants, also the quality of hospitality services and facilities, occupancy rates of hotels and other types of tourist accommodation;
- land use and usage of geographic space;
- organization of tourism supply based on type of demand, visitor motivation and environmental feasibility;
- administrative policies;

- residents' attitude towards tourists and vice versa and opportunities for tourism development;
- economic and social differences between residents and the demand side;
- the impact of tourism on commercial activities already present in the area;
- local business health;
- the quality of local employment in the tourism sector and connected industries;
- supply and costs of basic services (in and out of peak seasons);
- congestion and discomfort;
- internal destination image and perception; and
- external destination image and perception.

Rather than thinking about limiting growth in a destination, we should perhaps be thinking about intelligent growth and improved quality of life. Perhaps by focusing on these two aspects it would be possible to avoid or at least slow down the natural process of decline. It must be stressed however that not all destinations or products (even brand products) follow every single stage of the life cycle model. Although useful as points of reference, these models should never be regarded in an absolute sense or be considered perfect and complete: real interpretation of data and rational forecasts can only be made after comparing specific situations in a precise context.

We can also find some parallels between the theories elaborated by both Miossec and Butler and Plog's psychographic travel model (Plog, 1974). The model, described in Fig. 2.7, was originally constructed for a well-known American airline with the objective of identifying potential strategies for flight connections between New York and other destinations. The psychological traits of travellers out of New York were measured according to their perception and choice of their favourite destination. The results follow a Gaussian distribution pattern, with data sets classified into three large categories of tourist types:

- Allocentric travellers crave adventure and excitement. In search of far-flung destinations and new cultural experiences, they make their own travel arrangements and choose to

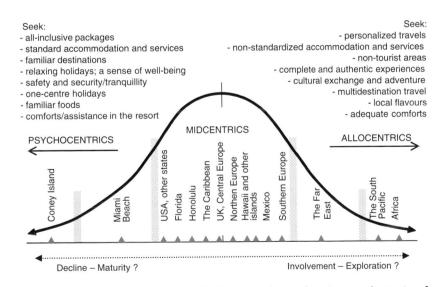

Fig. 2.7. Plog's psychographic travel model (source: the authors' own adaptation from Minca, 1996).

stay in accommodation that can offer the right degree of comfort without being banal or standardized.

- Psychocentrics, on the other hand, are self-inhibited and unadventurous. Their choice of destination falls on places that are familiar and reassuring. They buy all-inclusive holidays aiming to rejuvenate body and mind through sports and relaxation, and are happy to stay in standardized accommodation.
- Midcentrics are placed in the middle and are by far the largest group. Their destination choices range from tried-and-tested holiday resorts to more adventurous holiday experiences. They generally prefer to have an intermediary organize at least some part of their holiday, so will use the services of tour operators, travel agents or incoming assistance in the destination itself.

If we turn things around and look at the model from a different point of view, it can give us a useful framework to analyse the evolution of a tourist destination based on the characteristics of its visitors. It is more than likely that allocentrics choose destinations that are in the initial phase of development, while psychocentrics would be the only group to opt for a mature (or even declining) destination. To be able to identify the exact psychographic group to which visitors belong, many factors need to be taken into account and analysed: their place of origin, their demographic characteristics (including level of education and profession), lifestyle, willingness to pay, personal tastes and disposition towards the various opportunities offered by the market and, last but not least, the image that the destination projects in the various market segments that it attracts, in relationship to motivation for visitor choice.

In today's world however, where the travel market is so segmented, it is no longer possible to simply divide travellers into three large groups: improved means of transport, specialized tour operators able to offer customized travel all over the world, a tendency to holiday at different periods throughout the year with different aims and objectives, all point to the fact that a more in-depth analysis is needed beyond the model proposed by Plog. For instance, an English tourist exploring Taurasi, a little-known high-quality wine-growing area in Campania (Italy), by mountain bike and sleeping under canvas in the great outdoors could easily be an allocentric traveller. That same tourist, on a different gastronomic holiday later in the year, could decide to become psychocentric by going to Provence, Napa Valley or even by choosing to stay in an all-inclusive resort in the very same region of Taurasi. For this reason, in the same way that the previous analytical instruments cannot give us absolute truths about real-life situations, Plog's model cannot be used to make predictions or give a precise and authoritative description of tourist behaviour. We need, in fact, to take into account the following factors:

- The complexity of human behaviour does not allow for individuals to be classified into single 'closed' categories. Tourists travel for a variety of reasons and adopt different attitudes according to different types of holiday experiences.
- The results described in the model only refer to characteristics displayed by travellers in North America. Tourists from other parts of the world are likely to display different traits.
- The choice of destination does not always correspond to the personality trait of the visitor. In many cases, the choice of an unfamiliar holiday destination does not necessarily mean an allocentric outlook; on the contrary, if travellers arrive unprepared for a totally new or adventurous experience, it could have the effect of discouraging any further attempts at exploring new territories in the future.

- There can often be significant discordance between the ideal choice of holiday and the actual choice, between present intentions and future aspirations. A lack of time and money, circumstances, media influence, particular needs at the moment of decision making, etc., can all determine a leaning towards a less adventurous choice even among travellers who would classify themselves as being allocentric.

The negative impacts of uncontrolled tourism development also emerge from the results given in the models. The progressive loss of references to time–space due to an overload of information and a greedy post-modern attitude to cultural, aesthetic and geographic consumption has led to an inability to distinguish between the reality of a place and its projected image. This in turn has led to a change in the type of relationship that individuals have with their surroundings and the environment in general.

Very often, the bond established with a place of residence or a tourist destination is experienced in a totally instrumental way: as a means to an end, to confirm a preconceived idea, as a place of refuge, to realize personal or social ambitions, or as part and parcel of an individual's personal collection of holiday experiences. An intelligent tourist is open to new possibilities and the relationships offered by 'another' place, and is aware of the environmental implications of their visit. Even a brief stay in a destination for purely hedonistic reasons should increase the visitor's awareness of the true spirit of a place. If the host territories can maintain and reflect this spirit, the visitor experience becomes even more significant and more meaningful.

Gastronomic tourism, used as a tool for sustainable development, is an opportunity for all regions involved in quality food and wine production, as it contributes to maintaining and developing the environment, the economy, culture and society (Fig. 2.8). While other types of tourism have brought impoverishment, gastronomic tourism can reinforce the environment

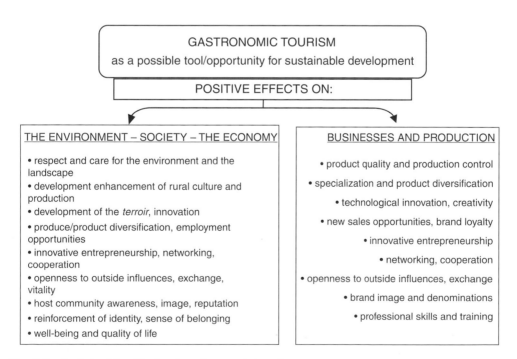

Fig. 2.8. Sustainable effects of gastronomic tourism.

and the autonomy and identity of a region, interacting with other economic sectors in a constructive way without crowding them out. This can be realized when:

- The authentic beauty and cultural vivacity of a region, together with prestigious agro-alimentary production and a stable and well-balanced social environment, gain a well-deserved reputation and image in the market. The natural resources of the pre-tourist environment remain the essential requisites for the quality of life for residents, while becoming one of the main factors for a successful tourist experience in the destination. This leads to recognizing the need to plan for tourism development. By selecting the best way to use geographic space so that the most appropriate market segment can be targeted, the trap of adopting strategies directed at solely making a profit can be avoided. The art of hospitality and welcoming visitors should be based on a desire to encounter new experiences and cultural exchange.
- The perception of a place from within (and its projected image) is seen as being of intrinsic value and not merely a factor in measuring tourist satisfaction (of tourists who may even sometimes be totally disinterested).
- The host community's contact with intelligent and interested tourists stimulates openness and innovation leading to socio-economic-cultural growth.
- The strength of the ties between traditional, local production and the *terroir* are such that they are capable of blocking any attempts by external policies or organizations to take away their autonomy or identity.
- The ability and necessity to guarantee product reputation and quality presupposes a professional approach to monitoring environmental impacts, establishing correct relationships with suppliers and clients, embracing new technologies and being open to creativity, innovation and ongoing professional training. This dedication combined with the pleasure of doing business spills over into the other socio-cultural aspects of the area, including tourism.

AN INTERDISCIPLINARY APPROACH

We have seen that a gastronomic destination needs in-depth analysis. Geographic models and theories need to be applied to fully understand the value of area resources (*terroir*–milieu–territory/region–landscape). We have also seen how these models can assist in creating sustainable policies for tourism development and quality management in a destination. However, a further step still needs to be taken if we want to be absolutely sure that the stakeholders in a destination (residents, visitors, tourism operators, policy makers, etc.) have a clear and precise picture of its true identity; an identity that is dynamic and alive with possibilities and not merely an icon or image created by tour operators.

In order to communicate a destination's true spirit and identity, tour operators must develop a 'geographic sense'. This signifies being able to present a mental image of the geographic space, identify its resources and then look at them from an interdisciplinary point of view. Beginning from one key component in the space, e.g. a gastronomic product or a work of art, the tour operator must then consider all the other visible elements that make up the set. This technique should be at the heart of strategic planning for food and wine tourism.

If the objective of tourism planning is to enhance the development of an area, a flexible and interdisciplinary approach and plurality of language must be adopted. It is the key to building an integrated product for cultural and gastronomic tourism. Depending on the type of programme

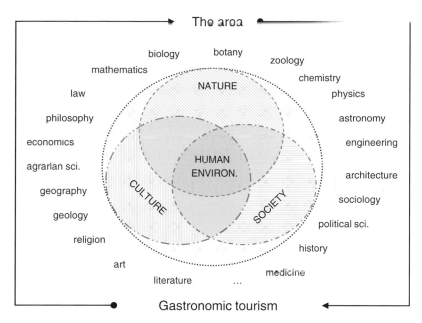

Fig. 2.9. An interdisciplinary approach to interpret the landscape and create multiple experiences in a gastronomic destination.

a tour operator wishes to construct, the area and its environment need to be looked at from every possible angle by moving from one discipline to another and exploring all the various possibilities that they present. Different methodologies and approaches (didactic, scientific and recreational) need to be adopted to realize the full interdisciplinary potential of an area in order to offer the visitor different themes and stories set within the same landscape.

As can be seen in Fig. 2.9, an area incorporates multiple disciplines that could be combined in any number of ways to create different interpretations of the environment.

A few examples are set out below to illustrate how gastronomic destinations and production regions can be considered from an interdisciplinary point of view:

- History, history of art, geography and history of landscape can all be combined in a visit to the Palazzo Pubblico Siena (Italy). Here visitors can admire the *Buon Governo* (*Good Government*) fresco cycle, painted by Ambrogio Lorenzetti between 1337 and 1339. The cycle of paintings also depicts *Cattivo Governo* (*Bad Government*) and the resulting impact on the city and countryside. Lorenzetti's masterpiece can be read as a propaganda manifesto: the city of Siena is painted with luminous vivacity, the timeless elegance of its buildings and the iconographic elements in the frescos leave little doubt with regard to the good government and power of the Nine, the city governors (as long as the population remained obedient). Indeed, as far back as 1309, the constitution of Siena underlined that whoever governed the city must hold in their hearts 'the beauty of the city for the delight and joy of visitors, to honour it and bring prosperity and growth to the city and its citizens'. In the part of the cycle dedicated to the potential effects of the good, stable government on the city's rural surroundings, we are offered an idealized vision of today's Sienese countryside, an area of high-quality gastronomic production. The well-irrigated richly cultivated landscape that we see in the fresco, and the distant but apparently easily accessible sea, are not a true depiction of what the countryside in reality looked like, but it is interesting to note

Fig. 2.10. A fragment of rural Tuscany (Italy).

a substantial similarity between the landscape as it was in medieval times and as it is today (Fig. 2.10). The strong analogy between the painting and today's landscape is also evident in the description of Val d'Orcia (south of Siena) as a World Heritage Site, by UNESCO: 'The Val d'Orcia is an exceptional reflection of the way the landscape was re-written in Renaissance times to reflect the ideals of good governance and to create an aesthetically pleasing picture' and 'The landscape of the Val d'Orcia was celebrated by painters from the Sienese School, which flourished during the Renaissance. Images of the Val d'Orcia, and particularly depictions of landscapes where people are depicted as living in harmony with nature, have come to be seen as icons of the Renaissance and have profoundly influenced the development of landscape thinking' (UNESCO, 2004). Inside the valley, in the rolling, clay Sienese hills, characterized by badlands, history and tradition resonate in the extraordinarily rich and varied agro-alimentary production that still continues today. Truffles grow in the more humid soil under the shade of oak trees; the slopes are covered in vineyards and olive trees. In the fresco a Cinta Senese pig is just about to enter the city: this pig is still bred today in the same hills around Siena.

- Thematic cartography is an extremely useful discipline for interpreting and illustrating food and wine production regions. A thematic map can be constructed in many ways, ranging from giving a very simple representation of an area by focusing on its links with one particular type of product to illustrating a much more complex situation where production in the region revolves around several gastronomic products (e.g. cheeses, cured meats and wine). According to the needs of the analysis, other disciplines can be classified and added to the map, e.g. architecture, economics, history, literature and geology. This kind of map can also be very useful for tourism planning as it clearly illustrates how the resources of a given area are distributed and how they relate to each other within the geographic space (how well

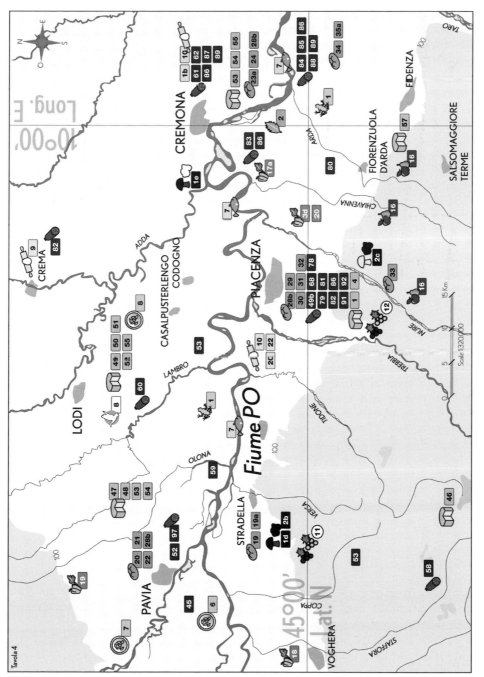

Fig. 2.11. Focus on the *Map of Gastronomic Production in the Po Valley* (Italy).

different systems function, the relationship between the poles of attractions, tourist flows, thematic connections, etc.). A good example is the *Carta dei prodotti agroalimentari del Po* (*Map of Gastronomic Production in the Po Valley*) (Perri and Croce, 2007), which illustrates the hundreds of agro-alimentary products to be found in localities along the course of the river valley and their renowned organoleptic qualities (Fig. 2.11).

- The 'typical' architectural style of an area can also be representative of its identity and its vocation for gastronomic production. In Italy, the west coast of Sicily where Marsala wine is produced is characterized by old country houses known as *bagli*; the wood and stone farms (*masi*) in the mountainous area of the South Tyrol still represent today an economy based on lumber production and dairy farming and the indivisible ownership of property; in the rice-growing area of Piedmont, the *cascine* (farmhouses built around a closed, internal courtyard) are a living testimony of the communities who lived within; the Palladian villas of the Veneto region beautifully combine their function as agricultural enterprises with their need to represent the nobility of the families that owned them (particularly the Venetian aristocracy who gradually began to invest more in agriculture, abandoning their traditional maritime business activities).

- Literature also has a very strong connection with many food and wine areas. The sensitivity of an author towards a particular area can enrich a visitor's experience, as their sentiments and points of view about the geographic space filter through their writings. There are of course many writers and books that would make ideal travel companions. We have chosen Pavese (1950), who describes the hills of his childhood in the Langhe (along with brief annotations of the pedoclimatic conditions): 'The sun shines down on these hills, there is a reverberation of crickets and *tufi* that I had completely forgotten. Here the sun comes up through the earth, not from the sky, the heat comes from the soil where tangled vine shoots have consumed every bit of green. It is a pleasurable heat, it has its own smell'.

chapter 3

Tourists on the Food and Wine Trail: Who Are They?

TOURIST BEHAVIOUR

People who expressly choose food and wine tourism are essentially cultural tourists. Generally speaking, they tend to be persons who:

- Enjoy food and wine and are interested in finding out more about production methods. They either consider themselves to be 'educated' consumers or, if not, would very much like to be more knowledgeable.
- Are open to new experiences and see food as a delightful way to discover new and different cultures and identities (food becoming as much a cultural expression as a work of art).
- Are educated and have a good cultural knowledge. They have a desire for lifelong learning and are willing to spend time, at some point during their holiday, on educational activities (through farm visits, guided tours and tastings, etc.).
- Are independent travellers used to making their own travel arrangements. As a result, they are not that keen on using the services of tour operators, even when they are specialized in organizing food and wine itineraries.
- Have high expectations with regard to the region they are visiting (in terms of discovering its distinct flavour and character, its unequivocal beauty and the quality of its services and facilities).

These descriptors give us some of the characteristics that are common in cultural tourists who are drawn to food and wine tourism. However, there are other types of visitors attracted by the oenogastronomic experience who also deserve our attention. They may be less knowledgeable, they may only be occasional visitors and they may be interested solely in indulging themselves and embarking on a gastronomic adventure just for fun. For many, the leisure aspect of their trip is their overriding concern, while others enjoy the kudos that comes from dining at a renowned restaurant or being cooked for by a celebrity chef. Armed with the latest guides, avid readers of travel reviews, always on the look out for the trendiest destinations, they are the type of people who will combine a visit to a chic restaurant and wine cellar with a shopping trip or a weekend away at a five-star casino hotel.

Whatever the case, the successful outcome of a visit depends largely on supply-side actors having a clear understanding and a thorough knowledge of consumer choice and purchasing behaviour. Operators in the sector need to take into account certain factors in order to construct a satisfactory experience for the users and enable the supply side to plan parallel strategic actions and appropriate marketing initiatives.

First, if we look carefully at tourist movement, we can see that it involves not just travel to and from a destination; there are, in fact, at least four distinct moments:

- Deciding to leave. A decision to travel generally implies seeking out relevant information beforehand according to the needs and motivations of the individual, perceiving the element of risk concerning the choice of destination and the experience to be had, and deciding on a realistic budget to cover holiday expenses and purchases.
- The act of travelling. Moving away from a familiar environment and travelling towards an unknown destination can create a sense of vulnerability, but at the same time can be extremely liberating.
- In the destination. On arrival, the tourist experiences a state of revelation (positive or negative) according to their preconceived expectations; the quality of life *in situ*, the gradual discovery of what the location can offer and the coming to terms with their inner selves in a completely different context, are all decisive factors in their satisfaction with their holiday experience.
- Going home. Returning home to everyday life, the holiday experience is consolidated by sharing accounts of it with family and friends, and consequently validating the choice of destination.

Another factor to take into account is that the traditional model for purchasing behaviour does not always reflect current practice. It is perhaps an anachronism to expect consumers to follow certain steps in a standardized chronological order, beginning with the realization of a need (e.g. a desire for relaxation or enjoyment) and then going on to make a decision on the best way to meet that need (e.g. taking a holiday rather than a short break from work); this should then be followed by information-gathering regarding the various possibilities on offer (e.g. an adventure holiday in an exotic destination or a package holiday in a seaside resort), making the decision to purchase the most suitable product and finally enjoying the holiday experience. Lastly, according to the traditional model, on return home the tourist-consumer meditates and reflects on holiday memories, shares them with others (word of mouth) and passes final judgement on the holiday experience.

The trend today is to study tourist behaviour using an experiential approach, in which the tourist-consumer is seen to be a proactive participant at each stage of the purchasing process. In fact, at each phase of tourist consumption – before, during and after the holiday, from the very moment that a need is perceived until the return home – information is being sought to make informed purchasing decisions. While on holiday, the tourist continues to find out more about the destination and what else it has to offer, and once home looks for further information to confirm their own holiday experience. The tourist-consumer can also be actively involved in the planning phase, either by organizing an independent travel itinerary or, if the services of a tour operator are used, having a customized itinerary drawn up. Sharing the holiday experience with others is no longer confined to immediate friends and family, but enters the public domain through discussions with other holidaymakers, entering into contact with residents of the host destination, giving feedback to travel agents and operators, and through online forums and blogs.

Tour operators therefore now find that, more often than not, they are dealing with very knowledgeable clients who wish to take an active role in their holiday planning and organization. In order to satisfy demand, supply-side actors must possess specific professional skills. Not only must they demonstrate that they are well-informed about a destination and can give up-to-date information about it, they must also be flexible and capable of creating innovative and original holidays and be prepared to work with clients on customized itineraries. It is important to keep in mind that each client is a person with individual needs and ideals, and that a holiday for them represents a life experience.

Once in a destination, a cultural tourist seeks to experience at least four myths:

- The myth of the Golden Age. Exploring and reliving the past.
- The myth of Minerva. Acquiring new cultural knowledge and also making discoveries through tangible objects such as traditional produce/products and handicrafts.
- The myth of the Desert. Experiencing feelings evoked when surrounded by beauty and scenic harmony; not only desert mirages and wind-sculpted sand dunes but also rolling hills covered with grape vines, groves of centuries-old olive trees, magnificent mountain meadows, all breathtaking landscapes capable of communicating strong emotions.
- The myth of Oedipus. Needing to belong, to be part of a place even for a short space of time, and to conserve something that reflects the spirit of the destination to take home and treasure. It could just be a sensation or memory or it could be something more discernible such as a bottle of wine, some cheese or local handicrafts.

A highly motivated tourist on a food and wine trail therefore seeks out a region's resources, sets out to enjoy with all five senses a region's products and aspires to buy an object or souvenir to 'savour' when the holiday is over. In order to enter the hearts and minds of tourists and leave a lasting impression, destinations (and actors working on the supply side) must be able to offer unique, complex and emotionally stimulating experiences.

DEFINING TARGET GROUPS

It is difficult to construct a precise profile of the exact target. The market is made up of many different possible consumer types, each one with its own individual personality, set of ideals, culture and approach. Furthermore, an individual will act differently and display a different set of characteristics in different circumstances. A person's mood at the moment of purchase, their inclination to be involved in a food and wine experience at a particular moment, and the behaviour of other travel companions are just some of the factors that can determine an individual purchasing decision. Having said that, destination managers, operators and producers in the food and wine industry who are already involved in tourism or who intend to become involved, may find it useful to refer to studies that have made some attempt at building a profile of what constitutes an oenogastronomic tourist.

The relatively large volume of available data and the high number of studies conducted into wine tourism, compared with the amount of research that has been carried out in other areas of gastronomic tourism, are due to the greater visibility enjoyed by the wine industry. In fact, in terms of tourist flows, appeal and demand remain consistently high, bringing obvious economic benefits to this particular sector.

Purchasing behaviour and consumption practices in food and wine tourists have been classified and analysed in a number of research projects. These are useful in helping us to have a clearer idea of the target and we could begin by looking at a study carried out by Tourism Research Australia, in which 'a winery visitor is defined as a domestic or international visitor who visits at least one winery during their trip in Australia. A food visitor is defined as a domestic or international traveller who eats at a commercial food establishment during their trip in Australia' (Tourism Australia, 2006).

According to research carried out in Italy from the early 1990s onwards, the results of which have been confirmed in later studies, the 'prototype' of a wine tourist has been defined as a consumer-connoisseur-explorer, usually male, aged between 26 and 45, of medium-high socio-economic level, who generally travels by car or uses his own means of transport, tends not to travel solo and prefers to travel in spring or autumn. However, oenogastronomy is now a cultural phenomenon and is evolving in a decidedly positive direction: today's food and wine tourists are not just interested in finding out about a particular product, they also want to discover more about the land from which the produce/product originated and come into direct contact with the region by experiencing its resources first-hand. They are willing to travel far greater distances than in the past, they may not necessarily be connoisseurs and have, in fact, diversified into different segments of demand. Travelling is no longer restricted to spring and autumn, the summer months have also become popular. Tourists may very well include an oenogastronomic visit in their holiday programme or on their journey home from a seaside or mountain resort. The range of accommodation now available also reflects diverging demand, with the proliferation of B&Bs alongside the more traditional choices of farmhouses and hotels (Antonioli Corigliano and Viganò, 2004).

Another classification divides the market into two categories: gastronauts and foodtrotters (Paolini, 2000). The first segment is an 'exclusive' target, in that it is made up of 'tourists whose motive for travelling is exclusively dedicated to the gastronomic experience'. A gastronaut is prevalently male, aged between 30 and 50, and shows a preference for travelling on Saturdays or Sundays to nearby destinations, usually on a day visit. Gastronauts organize their own travel arrangements, and travel either solo or with family or friends. Their main reason for travelling is to enjoy a gastronomic adventure and hence they give less importance to visiting other tourist attractions in the region. A foodtrotter, on the other hand, is someone who views the gastronomic experience as being 'the principal motive for travel but considers the other resources and attractions in the region important for the overall travel experience'. A foodtrotter will therefore spend more time away from home than a gastronaut, although the holiday may just be a short break for a few days. Because of the longer stays involved, the quality of services plays an important and decisive role.

Foodtrotters also tend to be mainly male, aged between 30 and 50 and generally live fairly near the gastronomic destination of their choice (usually within a radius of 200 km). If they do choose a location further away, it generally tends to be somewhere that is easily accessible. Foodtrotters are usually professionals with a medium-high level of education and cultural background. They travel on their own, with family or friends, and are responsible for making their own travel arrangements. They generally stay at least 2 or 3 days in a destination. Having a choice of 'accommodation to suit all pockets' is regarded as being just as important as having a choice of tourist attractions. People who are motivated to travel because of a particular event could also be added to these two main segments. They are also gastronauts in the sense that the reason for their trip is linked in some way to food or wine, e.g. a visit to a food festival, a farmers' market or a country fair. These kinds of occasions often attract a wide target of visitors who may be not food and wine tourists in the strictest sense.

Other studies (Cinelli Colombini, 2007) have identified different typologies of wine tourists:

- Accidental wine tourists. Aged between 35 and 45, they generally enjoy shopping (in all sorts of sectors) and are attracted to buying wine, wine accessories and related products or services. They are particularly keen on young, simple, inexpensive wines and tradition is held in higher esteem than technological innovation. They do not require or appreciate detailed explanations about products or production methods. Visits tend to be brief, usually as part of a group, and they prefer to eat in traditional, local restaurants.

- Wine tourists. Mainly male adults with relatively high disposable incomes and a passion for wine, they are well-informed and appreciate top-quality wines with established reputations and rare vintages. They are also interested in new wine blends and are curious to try newcomers to the market. While visiting a wine cellar, they would expect to be accompanied by an expert and to meet the producer in person or an oenologist. The role technology plays in wine production is regarded with interest. The tasting session is a fundamental part of the visit, which they prefer to enjoy as an individual rather than as part of a group.
- Opinion leaders. High earners and spenders, they are extremely knowledgeable in all matters to do with wine and are open to new ideas and developments in oenology and viticulture. They purchase only the most prestigious and fine rare wines on the market. Appreciative of innovation and quality, they expect to be among the first to try new wines and to meet the estate oenologist. As individual independent travellers they like to take their time and visits tend to be fairly lengthy and extensive.
- Talent scouts. Extremely knowledgeable, they are always on the look-out for excellence and originality. As frequent visitors to gastronomic destinations, they often make new discoveries even before the specialist press. They can play an important role in the destiny of a new wine cellar or region of production by bringing them to public attention and putting them on the map.

The same study has classified two further types of tourist who visit gastronomic destinations as part of an organized group:

- Organized coach tours. These tourists are generally not very knowledgeable about wine, visits tend to be brief and they have little inclination to make any purchases.
- Small groups of wine lovers. Greatly interested in all matters to do with wine, they expect to enjoy a detailed visit and a professional tasting session with an expert guide.

It must be said that tourists who regard food as being inextricably linked to culture approach the food and wine experience in different ways according to their degree of 'alimentary education'. In other words, their response during a tasting session, their expectations of a guided tour and of a region's resources will differ depending on their level of gastronomic culture:

- Cultured users. They are perfectly informed about organoleptic characteristics, they know all about the land and regional production, cultivation, livestock breeding, food and wine pairing, etc. When they are on a visit, they have no wish to lose time on matters with which they are already familiar. They do, however, like to be able to confirm personal knowledge on the subject and have the possibility to extend their expertise, particularly when a visit is totally involving and offers a unique, memorable and emotionally stimulating experience. They prefer to enjoy these visits alone or with the privileged few who have the same cultural and gastronomic background. Being able to enjoy a glass of fine wine in the same place where the wine has been produced has the same emotional impact on these visitors as experienced by an art connoisseur who visits Federico da Montefeltro's studio in the Ducal Place in Urbino, in that a beautiful example of Renaissance art is to be found in the very place it was conceived for.
- Culture vultures. They hope to become better acquainted with the world of gastronomy. Their interest in visiting a production region is real and tangible and they are open to making new discoveries and experiences. They like to feel involved in a visit and appreciate

being given clear and precise information, but are not keen on having too many technical details. They enjoy interacting with whoever is leading the tour or tasting session and will participate in 'fun' activities if they are intelligently organized and can learn something from them. They absorb new ideas during a food and wine tour in the same way they would do if they were being guided around a museum or visiting an exhibition with richly informative interpretive panels.

- Friendly types. Although not particularly interested in food or wine, they are willing to tag along with family or friends on a visit to a winery, olive mill or dairy farm. They prefer to stay with the group rather than on their own and are happy to go along with whatever the group decides to do. Once involved in a visit however, if their senses are truly awakened, they may discover a real passion for the subject. An unexpected liking and interest in a product may well arise from the tasting session and be an incentive to explore the area and region further. As a result, they are open to purchasing produce/products in the destination and will go on to develop their newly found interest in gastronomic culture.

Research published by Tourism New South Wales (2000) partly confirms these findings. Australian wine tourists are classified as:

- Accidental. They see wineries as a tourist attraction of the region visited, a cellar door visit is an opportunity for a social occasion with friends or family, have below average knowledge of wines but are moderately interested in wine, their interest and curiosity aroused by drinking wine/road signs/brochures or general tourism promotion, have moderate income and education, may purchase at winery but are unlikely to join mailing list.
- Interested. The cellar door visit is an enhancement to their trip but not the prime motivation for visiting the region, they have moderate to high interest in wine, moderate to high income, are usually tertiary educated, are likely to have visited other wine regions, to purchase wine at winery and to join mailing list.
- Dedicated. They are wine lovers who visit wine regions frequently as an integral part of a trip, have above average knowledge of wine, are extremely interested in wine and winemaking, mature, with high income and high education level, are likely to purchase wine at winery and to join mailing list.

The challenge therefore is to transform accidental wine tourists into interested wine tourists by making the experience of the visit a memorable one. Furthermore, 'international visitors who travel to wineries have a higher interest than other visitors in cultural attractions (museums, art galleries, wine festivals – particularly those reflecting local customs and heritage) and proportionally more winery visitors also went to national parks and botanical or other public gardens than did other visitors'.

As can be seen in Fig. 3.1, a further breakdown of the market has been made by looking at the following variables: the degree of awareness about the food and wine sector, the specialization of interests and knowledge, and the integration between cultural experiences and those of different types of tourism. In the pyramid diagram, three very different profiles mark the extreme points, while the inside area contains virtually all the different segments of the food and wine sector, each one displaying the characteristics that mark their position in relation to the three vertices. The profiles have been created by the authors of this book on the basis of observations and direct surveys carried out in numerous international gastronomic destinations, with visitors, operators, communicators, producers, businesses and public and private organizations.

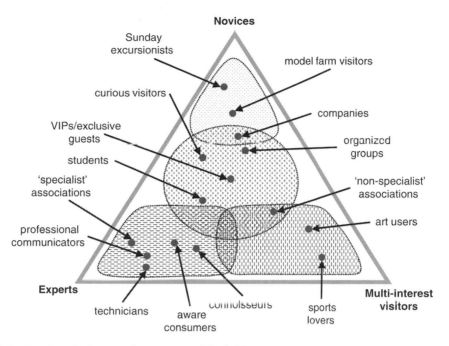

Fig. 3.1. Food and wine tourists: a pyramid of different types.

Tourists who rarely visit places where food or wine is produced, who have little or no curiosity beyond the confines of their own experience, who are suspicious of any technological innovations and who firmly believe that only those products with which they are already familiar are worthy of attention, have not been classified. They also tend to believe that 'authentic' food can only be produced following 'traditional' methods, ignoring the fact that sometimes this can mean that production is carried out without adhering to official food safety regulations.

The extreme points of the pyramid can be explained as follows.

- Novices. These are visitors who do not have any specific gastronomic knowledge or culture; they are often unaware of the opportunities offered by a multifaceted tourism experience, are not particularly driven to making independent discoveries and tend not to have high expectations of a food and wine destination.
- Experts. They are extremely knowledgeable about gastronomic subjects; they have little inclination to combine their interest in food and wine with other activities, e.g. doing sport or visiting art exhibitions.
- Multi-interest visitors. This group particularly enjoys combining two or more different elements into their leisure programme, e.g. combining food with sport, art and/or technology. They may have some kind of expertise in one of the activities or subjects but not necessarily in food or wine.

Figure 3.1 also demonstrates certain characteristics which are common to all tourists, both Italian and foreign, who are regular visitors to food and wine destinations:

- Technicians. They have specialist knowledge and technical skills in the sector, e.g. wine experts, dairy farmers, olive growers and restaurant owners and managers (Fig. 3.2). They consider a visit to a farm business or wine estate as a fundamental way to learn more about

Fig. 3.2. A tasting room designed for technicians (Champagne, France).

production in the region and as an opportunity to discover more about competitors in their particular segment and to benchmark their activities. Above all, visits such as these help develop professional know-how and provide occasions for acquiring up-to-date information on technological innovations, machinery and production methods. Face-to-face meetings with the business owner and technical managers play an important part of the visit. Very often, more than one production centre in a given area will be visited in order to gather as much information as possible in the limited time available (they are, to all intents and purposes, business trips). They rarely have enough time to visit other enterprises operating outside the food and wine sector, even if they would like to. When staying overnight, they tend to opt for a high standard of accommodation, and they are more likely to choose restaurants that have a reputation for good local cuisine based on regional products; they are particularly interested in food and wine pairing. These 'information-gathering' trips are usually taken by individuals or by small groups of people who have got to know each other through working in the food and wine business. Very often, they organize small delegations to visit regions further afield or abroad. They sometimes establish a friendly rapport with their hosts.

- 'Specialist' associations. Members of this group belong to local tasting associations, often under the umbrella of larger national and international organizations (e.g. gourmet and sommelier associations). They are generally professionals operating in the food and beverage sector and have specialist knowledge and skills. They regularly attend professional tasting courses at all levels to enhance their expertise, particularly when organized locally. Other routes to personal and professional development include taking a day trip to visit other regions and production areas or going abroad on a longer visit to check on production in other parts of the world. International trips are planned down to the last detail and there is generally a full programme of business visits and meetings, organized tastings and meals. Business owners and producers may also involve representatives from local associations and regional organizations and invite them along to meet the visiting 'experts'. The places chosen to visit generally have a reputation for excellence and there is a certain cachet attached to being able to enter the very heart of a prestigious production centre normally closed to the general public. Any other cultural aspects of the destination remain relatively unimportant. They expect to be greeted by highly trained personnel who are able to respond to technical questions and supply detailed information when necessary. While there is genuine interest in learning about new approaches and production methods, information given can also serve to confirm a visitor's own knowledge of the subject. Travelling together and participating in these kinds of visits fosters a sense of group attachment and belonging.

- Connoisseurs. With an innate sense of *joie de vivre*, they enjoy the good things in life. They do not have any particular specialist knowledge of the food and wine sector, but are well-informed about quality products, know which ones represent the very best that a region can offer and regularly buy these products for normal, everyday consumption. They have a lively and multidisciplinary interest in culture, enjoying anything to do with the arts. They tend to work in professional sectors/be white-collar workers. They keep themselves informed by reading guides and specialist magazines and publications with a popular approach. They often attend short, informal tasting courses and regularly do research on the Internet to discover more about food and wine products. They are happy to spend money on eating well, although they are not particularly interested in exclusive or formal restaurants; they are much more attracted to places that offer good, regional cuisine. When choosing accommodation, they are not that interested in having luxurious facilities, they tend to prefer to stay somewhere comfortable and characteristic of the destination that is able to offer them an authentic experience. While on holiday, even when the main focus is on discovering a region through its food and wine, they particularly appreciate having the opportunity to do other pursuits as well, e.g. enjoying open-air activities such as horse-riding or hiking, being pampered at health spas and visiting museums, galleries and art exhibitions. They tend to travel as a couple, as a family with older children or as a small group of friends. They are independent travellers used to making their own travel arrangements. If they are on a guided tour of a production centre, they enjoy listening to explanations and they appreciate being given professional but not necessarily technical information about a product.
- Curious visitors. Although without any specific knowledge about food and wine, they demonstrate a willingness to find out more even when their cultural knowledge and interests are not that wide. They are open to travelling outside their own familiar territory. People of all ages, with diverse social origins, fall into this group. They are happy to actively participate in new tasting experiences and to develop their sensory perceptions. They respond well to informative but entertaining explanations. Indeed, a well-conducted guided tour that has an element of fun in it can raise awareness about how a region is linked to its products, and be effective in creating more knowledgeable consumers and future customers (Fig. 3.3).

Fig. 3.3. Learning about wine (Alsace, France).

- Students. Generally high-school or university students studying scientific or technical subjects for whom a visit is a set part of their curriculum. Students from faculties of arts and humanities also take part in visits, particularly if they are studying communications subjects. Very often they do work experience or internships with a particular business in order to acquire professional skills, normally in the areas of management and administration or production. They may very well already have some specialist knowledge but this often tends to be purely theoretical. By being given interesting and responsible tasks during their work placement, students are stimulated to go deeper into a subject as well as developing technical and professional know-how. Classroom input is also extremely important in making a visit or work experience worthwhile. Students need to be well-prepared beforehand about what to expect during their visit and how to behave appropriately. A multidisciplinary approach is particularly effective in stimulating student interest.
- Model farm visitors. Mainly school groups or families, they usually have very little or no experience of rural life and production, but are curious and open-minded and have a natural inclination towards learning, particularly when a multidisciplinary approach is used (e.g. exploring a subject through science, art, open-air activities and games). Children, ably assisted by qualified educators, learn about farm life and production through a variety of hands-on activities, such as feeding the animals, milking the cows, and picking and selecting fruit to be made into jam. Encouraged to discover and explore their senses through active participation in farming activities, it is hoped that they will grow up to be educated consumers, able to appreciate the quality of farm produce, the beauty of rural surroundings and the importance of using sustainable practices to safeguard these areas.

- Companies. These include corporate clients who enjoy networking and socializing over lunch or dinner. A company may treat successful employees to a day trip as a reward for their business performance or organize incentive trips, where colleagues are encouraged to focus on company mission and share company values through training workshops and seminars. Companies are increasingly turning to food and wine producers and agritourism enterprises to organize these kinds of trips and events, particularly when there is a small group of participants. Choosing a destination that can offer a totally new experience compared with the more mainstream choices of a dining at a famous restaurant or holding a conference at a seaside resort can result in creating a greater sense of team spirit between colleagues and awareness that they are part of a 'privileged' group. Corporate clients cover all age ranges and have diverse interests; some may already have some knowledge of gastronomy, others may be less experienced. A producer who wishes to welcome company clients must therefore be aware of the different components of a visiting group, and be able to respond to their different needs. This can be done, for example, by planning tasting sessions for beginners and alternative sessions for the more experienced. If the group is staying for several days, a number of different activities can be programmed to suit all tastes and interests, e.g. sightseeing excursions and trips, museum and gallery visits, sports and open air activities such as country walks and, when appropriate, role play and simulations. The person responsible for dealing with corporate clients may very well find that they must also take on the role of entertainer and activity organizer.

- Sports lovers. Keen on sports and open-air activities, they follow a healthy diet and choose high-quality products. Although they are willing to visit food and wine destinations, their choice of where to go depends more than anything on whether the destination can offer them the possibility to pursue their interests, such as mountain-biking or hiking (by exploring the vineyards on a wine estate, for example). During the day, they particularly appreciate visiting the natural resources of an area, admiring the landscape while hiking or cycling and seeing where food and wine is produced. In the evenings, they like to relax in selected accommodation, dining on regional specialities. On the whole, this group has little interest in discovering more about the technical aspects of running a food or wine business and production methods; on average they spend little time inside the production centre, although they will treat themselves to a 'tasty' souvenir from the farm or wine shop. Local arts or crafts usually tend to be viewed quickly and briefly. They are usually interested in eating a varied, well-balanced diet and following a regime dedicated to enhancing physical performance, but without renouncing the pleasures of the palate. At breakfast or at snack time after a period of physical activity, they enjoy trying local products such as cheese and cured meats and home-baked bread and cakes. Used to organizing their own travel arrangements, they travel with small groups of friends, or they may choose to go on a trip with others, organized through specialist tour operators or with fellow members of their sports club.

- Art users. Cultural tourists in the strictest sense, only the most discerning among them are open to integrating different experiences while on holiday and to considering food to be an expression of a region and a way to discover regional identity. As such, they view the oenogastronomic experience as a necessary complement to visiting museums and monuments and other cultural treasures. They enjoy itineraries that use an interdisciplinary approach, proposing different activities based around a common theme. They expect to be treated with professionalism, demand detailed and accurate explanations, take pleasure in a didactic approach and appreciate the ability to be able to converse with ease on a wide range of subjects.

- Sunday excursionists. Independent travellers, generally travelling with family or friends, they occasionally choose a gastronomic destination for a day trip. They may already be familiar with aspects of food and wine, but their main aim when choosing a destination is to enjoy a relaxing day out in the country away from the noise and stress of city life. They do not expect detailed or technical explanations about the business and production methods during their visit, but they are interested in trying, tasting and buying products (Fig. 3.4). Visitors to country fairs and festivals also fall into this group.
- Aware consumers. They dedicate an enormous amount of time and energy (almost verging on the maniacal) to choosing food products that are part of their everyday diet. Aware of their rights as consumers, they read food labels thoroughly, check place of origin, often have a preference for organic foods and, when possible, try to buy their food supplies directly from producers, by visiting the place of production in person, ordering online or through cooperatives and consumer groups. They regard a visit to a farm business or winery as a useful opportunity to check on the quality of production and whether it conforms to food standards regulations and codes of practice. They are less interested in the didactic or leisure aspect of a visit.
- 'Non-specialist' associations. These are members of different types of associations, very often cultural clubs or societies whose main interest or reason for being a member is not to do with food or wine. These associations regularly offer programmes of organized activities

Fig. 3.4. Whiskey tasting session after the tour (Ireland).

for their members that may include conferences, courses or seminars dedicated to food and wine products and tasting. A farm visit or trip to a production region could be the culmination of a series of meetings on a particular food or wine theme. The aim of a visit could be to reinforce or consolidate concepts about food or wine production introduced during the course, or it could simply be a good excuse to go somewhere different and discover a new place in the enjoyable company of fellow members. In the first case, if visitors have already been exposed to notions about food and wine production, the person responsible for leading a guided tour must keep in mind that the group already has a basic knowledge of the subject, while in the second case the tour guide must able to recognize and respond to the different needs and experiences of the various components within the group.

- Organized groups. The visit is part of an all-inclusive holiday when the destination also happens to be famous for its food and wine production, e.g. in the case of wine regions like Chianti, Champagne, Rioja, Jerez de la Frontera, the Duoro Valley, Napa Valley, Canberra District, Barossa Valley, Stellenbosch and Franschhoek. Not having much technical knowledge about food and wine production, they often find themselves having to participate in activities that have already been pre-programmed by non-specialist tour operators. The all-inclusive package is an inevitable mix of activities planned around no particular theme except that there must be 'a little bit of everything' thrown in. The mood and inclination of a group of tourists depends very much on how well the tour operator has planned the various activities and visits included in the package. If tours are well-conducted by professional personnel, the degree of interest and level of satisfaction will obviously be raised even when visitors are exposed to totally new concepts about the business of food and wine production.

- VIPs/exclusive guests. These include politicians, artists and celebrities, VIPs and lesser mortals such as honeymoon couples, who decide to treat themselves to an off beat or exclusive experience, often at great expense, by having an individual guided tour of a winery or farm outside normal visiting hours. They may very well already have some specialist knowledge in gastronomic matters and they certainly expect to be given special treatment. Their visits therefore need to be planned down to the minutest detail and conducted with a high degree of professionalism. They particularly enjoy being given an unexpected surprise or gift and appreciate being put at their ease by efficient but discreet personnel.

- Professional communicators. Journalists specialized in the food and wine sector. They become 'taste tourists' when attending particular events or familiarization/press trips. They come into contact with the area, regional production and producers under atypical circumstances, in ad hoc situations where in a short, concentrated period of time they experience the very best that the market has to offer. They are therefore privileged unpaying guests and often work on the assumption that they should be given preferential treatment. They do not always have an objective view of the reality of a situation. They are regarded as being very similar to VIPs/exclusive guests by visit organizers. Their visits need to be conducted by experienced guides with specialist knowledge. It is more difficult for organizers to deal with non-specialist communicators as they may have only a basic knowledge of the sector. In this case, it is up to the guide to instil in them an awareness and sensitivity towards new ideas and topics linked to the world of gastronomy so that they will pass these ideas on correctly to the general public.

Each member of these segments has their own set of values, needs and expectations. Being able to distinguish who the target is facilitates supply-side actors in creating customized products that, as we will see in the following chapters, have all the necessary features to satisfy even the most demanding visitor. It must be remembered, however, that whatever form the tourism product takes, it must be designed to respect the values, identity and sustainability of the region and place of production.

ETIQUETTE FOR FOOD AND WINE TOURISTS

As we have already said, tourism can be a doubled-edge sword: if it is planned and managed according to sustainable criteria, it can be a contributing factor to economic growth and to the well-being of the resident population. Only sustainable practices will safeguard and protect a destination's identity and its resources for today's tourists and for those of future generations. Sustainable tourism also stimulates cultural exchange and enriches the lives of both visitors and residents by fostering reciprocal understanding. However, if tourism planning fails to incorporate sustainable practices, it can spark a process of cultural impoverishment, impacting visitors as well as residents, and be responsible for damaging the host destination beyond repair. Various international bodies have, at different stages over the years, developed guidelines to encourage all stakeholders, including tour operators, tourists, residents and destination managers, to adopt sustainable codes of practice for all phases of the holiday experience (WTO, 1985, 1997; World Conference on Sustainable Tourism, 1995; Associazione Italiana Turismo Responsabile, 1998).

By taking and re-contextualizing some of the general criteria outlined in the documents, it is possible to draw up a series of recommendations that food and wine tourists could also put into practice. When tourists treat the land and its resources, producers and products, the destination and its residents with respect, they will enjoy a fulfilling, authentic experience. Here, then, are some useful guidelines that producers and managers, tour organizers and visitor coordinators could pass on to prospective food and wine tourists.

Before leaving

Before setting off on a food and wine trail, tourists should:

- Explore their reasons for the trip and reflect on their expectations of the destination so as to make an informed and coherent choice.
- Seek information not only with regard to the logistics of the trip (transport, transfers, hotels, meals, etc.), but also about the spirit of the place they intend to visit. They should find out as much as they can about the cultural and social aspects of the area as well as the natural environment, resources and alimentary production.
- Verify the quality and sustainability of the holiday from an ecological, social and economic point of view, and make a conscious choice to visit only those destinations that operate in total respect for the environment, including whenever possible places on their itinerary that have been awarded official certification for tourism and environmental quality.
- Reduce their carbon footprint by opting for environmentally friendly modes of travel such as cycling or going on foot, or group travel by train or coach.
- Show interest in meeting the tour guide and their fellow travellers before setting off on the trip (e.g. by attending a tasting course). By being prepared before the holiday, tourists will be able to enjoy the gastronomic experience even more.
- Try to plan their visit during off-peak periods or when production is not in full swing (particularly if large groups are involved), also they should seek out itineraries that take them well away from mass tourism destinations.

During the visit

Visitors should:

- Carefully observe their surroundings and try to immerse themselves in the spirit of the place, giving themselves enough time to be able to understand the context of the visit. They should be actively open to cultural exchange.
- Modify their behaviour to conform to any rules or regulations with regard to visiting the host destination and the production area, and respect the underlying philosophy of the business, the personnel working there and the products.
- Be conscious of their role as visitor-consumer of the tourist product, as the quality of supply and the destiny and well-being of people living in gastronomic destinations depend partly on how they fulfil this role.
- Minimize any damage that their presence in the destination and production areas may cause. This is particularly important when carrying capacity is not very high and production could be put at risk.
- Regard the opportunity to participate in and share everyday experiences as a privilege and not expect special treatment or do anything that could have a negative impact on people or the environment, including being offensive about local customs or practices.
- Check with people first, particularly if they are working, if they mind being filmed or having their photograph taken.
- Seek out products, either to consume while in the destination or to take home as souvenirs, that reflect local culture (e.g. gastronomic products and local arts and crafts). Doing so will help safeguard the destination's cultural identity.
- Respect the environment at all times and also the destination's cultural and gastronomic heritage. Always use non-renewable resources in a responsible manner and limit waste production.
- Politely give personal judgement on situations or events that may or may not respond to the principles of 'responsible tourism', in terms of environmental respect and any legal, ethical and aesthetic issues to do with any aspects of the trip.

After the visit

Once home, tourists should:

- reflect on whether they were able to establish good relationships with the people they met and with the destination itself, building on those relationships perhaps by supporting the local economy through the purchase of gastronomic and other local products;
- evaluate their experience and give critical but constructive feedback to the person responsible for organizing the visit;
- share their experience with friends and acquaintances in an objective way, avoiding banal descriptions; and
- report back to the visit organizer or supply-side actors on any situations with which they were not entirely happy, e.g. problems to do with organization or if there were instances when the trip or visit did not correspond to sustainable criteria.

Finally, it must be said that it is not always necessary to travel very far: there is often much to be discovered in places that are nearby and with which we think we are familiar. Taking a trip, going on a journey or organizing a visit must not become something routine.

chapter 4

Transforming a *Terroir* into a Tourist Destination

A region and its food or wine production may not in themselves be sufficiently appealing or attractive to warrant visitor interest. In fact, before a *terroir* can be transformed into a tourist destination, research into the area's resources must be carried out and a critical analysis made of the findings. Once this has been done, resources and attractions can be linked together and organized in a thematic way, so that together they form a complete, coherent and competitive tourist product.

FROM PRODUCTION REGION TO TOURIST PRODUCT

If we observe Fig. 4.1, we can see that it gives us a breakdown in numbers of all the elements that make up Italy's vast heritage. The sheer volume and variety of resources that together form such a rich cultural mosaic make Italy an ideal model for didactic purposes. In fact, it would seem virtually impossible to find such an array of resources elsewhere. However, other countries may find themselves in very similar situations. Their cultural heritage and their social, environmental and economic contexts may differ, but in many cases, they also possess interesting resources with the potential to attract visitors.

Going back to Fig. 4.1, we can make a number of observations. The first and most obvious point is the abundance of resources that puts Italy among the world's highest-ranking tourist destinations. But if a tour planner takes a closer look and critically analyses the volume of data, they would surely question why a tourist might decide to visit an isolated country parish church without any notable works of art, when there are 95,000 churches to choose from. Or they might ask how one goes about making a medieval walled town a more competitive tourist product than its better-known neighbour. How do you convince a gastronome, visiting Italy with the express intention of finding out more about the process of making Parmigiano Reggiano cheese, to visit one production dairy rather than another, when they all operate within the same 'protected denomination area of origin' (PDO) and enjoy a reputation for top-quality cheese? What kind of stratagem can be used to convince a wine tourist that a little-known or little-visited DOC wine region does in fact offer plenty of

---

Culture (Dec. 2009)

95,000 historic churches	40,000 castles
20,000 old towns	30,000 historic palaces/manors
4700 museums	3000 archaeological sites
1500 abbeys	60,000 archives
12,300 libraries	4000 historical gardens

44 sites included on UNESCO World Heritage List

more than 700,000 cultural events (theatre, music, dance, opera, etc.)

more than 100,000 conferences and meetings

Nature (Dec. 2009)

24 National Parks (almost 5% of the national territory), 147 National Reserves, 141 Regional Parks, 326 Regional Reserves, 28 Protected Marine Areas, 46 Wetlands + dozens of other protected areas (local, WWF, LIPU, Legambiente; in total, almost 11% of the national territory)

Food products and produce (Dec. 2009)

Wines: 48 DOCG, 320 DOC, 118 IGT

Other products and produce: 128 PDO, 75 PGI, more than 3500 Traditional Products; 177 Slow Food Presìdia

---

Tourism supply – accommodation establishments (Dec. 2008)

Hotels: 34,155	Others: 106,108
5-star and luxury: 315	Campsites and resorts: 2595
4-star: 4623	Self-catering accommodation: 6000
3-star: 15,160	Farmhouses: 15,465
2-star: 7196	B&Bs: 18,189 Alpine huts: 993
1-star: 4299	Youth hostels: 427
RTA (Residences): 2562	Other: 2439

Fig. 4.1. A breakdown of Italy's tourism resources.

surprises in terms of the quality of its products and the beauty of its landscape? The answer to all these questions does not lie in making loud noises about being market leader. In fact, very often product claims tend to lack objectivity and do not give a realistic idea of a product's true market position with regard to competitors. It should also be borne in mind that what some tourists think about a product does not necessarily coincide with how that product is perceived by residents or by people working in the sector, even when tourists already have some pre-knowledge of an area and its resources. The only solution is to transform a region and its resources into a complete tourist product by first identifying the attractions and then linking them together by theme. This is no easy task, as it requires a lot of hard work, long-term planning and a professional approach, and also takes time to reap results. However, the drawing together of resources into an identifiable and appealing tourist product gives a *terroir* a distinct identity and marks it out from its competitors. In order to be able to do this successfully, it is essential that public and private operators in the sector cooperate to create a tourist offer that reflects the distinctive elements of a region, in all their complexity and variety. And all these separate parts need to be assembled, organized and managed in a coherent and logical way.

From a more practical point of view, if we shift our attention to focus exclusively on tourist activity, the challenge is to create holidays that can be positioned in the market, that attract tourists to the destination, that give a true representation of the region and that are sustainable in terms of business and the environment.

What does the term 'tourist product' actually mean? In order to understand the specific nature and characteristics of a tourist product, it should be said that a true definition should not be limited to describing it as simply a way of communicating the name of a destination. In fact, the tourist product is to do with consumer needs, wants and expectations. It offers a series of benefits that consumers should be able to derive from their holiday experience. The tourist product is therefore an instrument by which the supply side aims to wholly satisfy clients' needs. In food and wine tourism, client satisfaction will be based on how well the chosen region or area can respond to their needs and if the tourist product respects the region's essential characteristics and identity.

A renowned food- or wine-producing region with a good number of relevant tourist attractions may not necessarily on its own give visitors a satisfactory experience. Transforming a place on a map into a tourist destination is not easy. First, the area itself has to be considered as an essential component of the tourism system. Operators on the supply side should work towards convincing the host community, and as a result potential tourists, that their place of residence is a precious resource, to be enjoyed on a deep cultural level and not taken for granted or used and consumed in haste. If the host community lives well in a destination, it will automatically become more attractive in the eyes of potential tourists. They too will want to become residents of the destination, even if temporarily, and to experience first-hand the host community's culture. Visitors' satisfaction with their experience will create a sense of attachment and an emotional bond with their holiday destination.

If, as we have said, the tourist product is the instrument by which actors on the supply side satisfy consumer demand, it is clear that two essential points need to be made:

- tourists will translate their demand into a set of tangible and intangible elements that ideally will satisfy their needs and wants and offer a series of specific benefits; and
- tour operators/travel agents will seek to prepare and organize a tourist product (made up of tangible and intangible elements) that will respond as closely as possible to the demands of real and potential clients.

The tourist product therefore acts as a bridge between the needs of the demand side and the organizational factors offered by the supply side, taking into account current and potential environmental features and characteristics.

In order to transform an area and its resources into a tourist destination, a strategic marketing approach, following the steps below, needs to be adopted:

- The area and its resources should be assessed and appraised and potential tourist attractions singled out. The level of professional competence necessary for receiving visitors in the area also needs to be evaluated.
- Visitor needs, wants and expectations must be identified and linked to the area's resources. If the resources of a given destination are varied enough, the focus should be on responding to and satisfying a wide range of target consumers.
- The project/product has to be constructed by choosing the best actors, implementing the most suitable strategies and having a clear set of objectives. Other factors to be taken into account include: timing, resources, business methods, technological innovations and support, monitoring and control, results analysis and eventual improvements/modifications.
- A wide range of options and services must be developed in order to offer a rich and varied product. Every single component of the destination should be distinct but linked together by a coherent theme to form an integrated tourist product, able to differentiate itself from other destinations in the market.

Being able to identify and organize a product while at the same time respect the region's unique identity is extremely important. In fact, it should always be borne in mind that tourism is a service industry and is not a producer of goods; as we have said before, for demand to be satisfied therefore, the consumer must go to the place where the product is made. In tourism, it is the market (i.e. the tourist) that has to move to the tourist destination in order to be able to use the product (a holiday, a sightseeing tour, a winery or farm visit). As a destination takes on the role of tourist product and becomes a main source of attraction, it is clear that it must be treated with respect, otherwise there is a risk that the product will become used and abused and eventually lose its appeal.

The construction of a tourist destination does not only follow the premise that the offer must respond to demand: dismantling a region to create a product that responds to every single need or expectation on the market is dangerous and counterproductive, particularly when those demands have absolutely nothing to do with the spirit or potential resources of the region.

Figure 4.2 illustrates how a destination becomes a tourist product. Each of its separate components is clearly identified and is organized and managed by public and private operators working in synergy. It is not a closed or static system, providing us with a fixed model. On the contrary, the tourist product is in a constant state of flux, interacting with both internal and external elements. The depth of interaction obviously depends on being able to identify new components and single products and on the richness and variety of their offer.

So far, we have spoken in general terms about how to construct a tourist destination product. But how do we go about relating this to a single product offered by an individual operator or by a producer based in the destination? As can be seen in Fig. 4.2, potentially, the specific tourist product is made up of all the elements provided by an individual company, and that characterize the operator's business; furthermore, the regional tourism system in which the

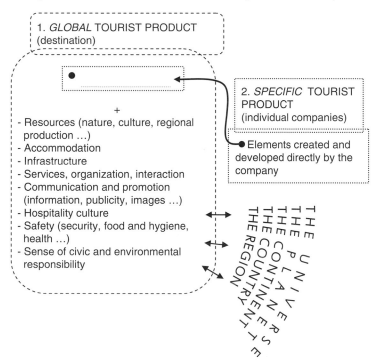

Fig. 4.2. The tourist product: essential elements.

company operates becomes part of the specific tourist product. This regional aspect must be considered as a strong component of every company's tourist product.

The business activity of a single operator inevitably communicates and reflects the environmental characteristics of the region within which it operates. In food and wine tourism, the connection between operator or producer and the environment is not only natural, it is a necessity.

It is clear, therefore, that the region must also play a central role in the specific tourist product created by a single producer or company. It would be unthinkable that a business involved in either food or wine production and open to receive visitors would completely ignore the area in which it operates. The specific tourist product (in this case gastronomic tourism) has two undeniable strengths: the territorial significance of the agro-alimentary resources and the environmental context of its offer; as a result it must share as many of the area's components as possible.

In the light of the above, imagine that the task is to create a brochure to welcome tourists to a winery. In order to appeal to potential visitors and give them an idea of the destination and its produce/products, this communication tool (together with attractive images) could be developed along the following lines:

- one section dedicated to the business itself (family and company history, traditional methods of winemaking, tools and equipment, etc.), the immediate surroundings, a description of the wine cellars, etc.;
- another section dedicated to the winery's products (brief notes on each of the wines, presentation of any other products such as olive oil and jams, traditional regional recipes to accompany the wines); and
- a further section dedicated to the region, its geographical characteristics, history and culture (archaeology, art, crafts, local customs and traditions, etc.).

To be able to include the greatest number of the destination's different components within the specific tourist product, some operators in the wine sector make use of the techniques below to communicate their businesses to potential tourists:

- enrich their brochures by adding land or geopedological maps;
- add panoramic views of their property and its surroundings;
- include photos of local crafts (e.g. lace);
- include pictures of their workers (e.g. the expressive face of a master winegrower); and
- attach small, transparent, plastic envelopes containing samples of soil from the winery's vineyards.

The tourist product therefore needs to be extremely well-planned and developed. Another point to make is that, because the supply side has a different perception of it compared with the demand side, it can be read in two ways:

- The user (the tourist) views the product according to a horizontal perspective, putting together all the different elements that make up the holiday experience and attributing the product with an overall estimation of its worth.
- The tourism operator tends to view the product according to a vertical or hierarchical perspective. In other words, giving their business (and those of their business partners involved in the supply of tourist services) an almost exclusive significance or value and paying little attention to the other elements or components that are not directly connected to their business (even when the nature and success of the tourist holiday product depend on these components as indicated by consumer demand).

Looking at the tourist product from a purely vertical point of view can lead the operator to make a number of serious strategic mistakes. If, as we have seen above, the tendency is for tourists to make an overall judgement of their holiday experience, just one single negative experience within the global tourist destination product (even when not attributable to an individual activity such as a hotel, restaurant or gastronomic business) will have negative repercussions on each operator involved in the supply of the tourist product. For instance, if a tourist catches a cold after visiting a cured meats factory and is later treated in an off-hand manner at the local chemist where they go to buy some medicine, this unpleasant episode will perhaps have a negative influence on the tourist's overall judgement of the holiday experience in the destination. And one single unpleasant encounter could be enough to cancel out all the happier and more positive experiences such as the hotel receptionist's warm welcome, the delicious risotto enjoyed at the local *osteria* or the interesting tour of the brewery that ended happily with a beer-tasting session of an extraordinary, traditionally made brew.

The more influence a single operator has on external elements and services (including those not directly connected to their business), the more chance they will have in providing a satisfactory visitor experience.

The following chapters will go on to look at the construction of the specific tourist product in more detail. The question now is what model should be adopted to plan a general tourist product, one that is equally valid for a destination as well as for a single business, whether a winery, farm or gastronomic production centre?

The model proposed by Normann (2001) is a useful example. It defines the tourist product as being a set of variable services with a core business that is characterized by the product and type of tourism organization responsible for its planning and production, together with a set of ancillary components that define/complete/identify/differentiate the product from its competitors.

What happens when there is a need to move away from the central core (in other words, away from one's own specific business activity) in order to increase the range of the tourist product and satisfy consumer demand? As we can see in Fig. 4.3, as individual operators gradually extend their field of action and increase their offer by incorporating other elements that add value to the visitor experience, so they have more chance of differentiating their product from the competition. However, it also means that they have less control over the tourist product as a whole. The further an individual operator ventures, the more likely it becomes that organizational aspects must be left to external operators, and therefore business relationships with other producers or suppliers of tourism services need to be established. This can often create complications, as business practices and professional competencies in different contexts vary and may very well clash with those of the individual operator.

Finally, it is desirable that a comparison be made between the 'public' and 'private' aspects of the tourist product. To do so, an external analysis needs to be carried out, examining the region's characteristics and resources and the market from both the supply side and the demand side. Particular attention needs to be paid to evaluating the strength of the competition and identifying market position so that it corresponds perfectly to the role that the organization plays within the destination as a whole and the overall tourism offer. Furthermore, the process of planning the tourist product requires an in-depth look into the internal aspects of the business or organization: the availability of financial resources, human resources and necessary professional skills; the state of the infrastructure and level of technological support. The analysis and comparison of external conditions outside the organization and its internal elements provide a structure for successful project planning, so that subsequent marketing actions are consistent with product identity and image, and that the presence of the product within the destination is persuasive and effective.

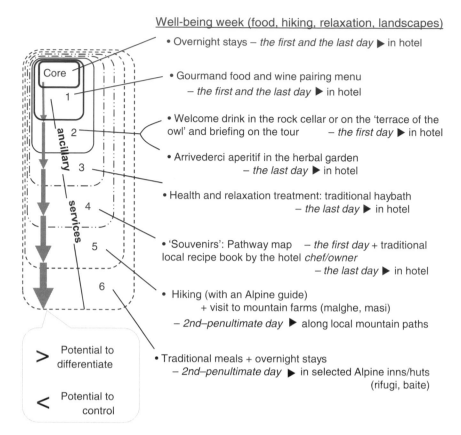

Well-being week (food, hiking, relaxation, landscapes)

- Overnight stays – *the first and the last day* ▶ in hotel

- Gourmand food and wine pairing menu
  – *the first and the last day* ▶ in hotel

- Welcome drink in the rock cellar or on the 'terrace of the owl' and briefing on the tour   – *the first day* ▶ in hotel

- Arrivederci aperitif in the herbal garden
  – *the last day* ▶ in hotel

- Health and relaxation treatment: traditional haybath
  – *the last day* ▶ in hotel

- 'Souvenirs': Pathway map   – *the first day* + traditional local recipe book by the hotel *chef/owner*
  – *the last day* ▶ in hotel

- Hiking (with an Alpine guide)
  + visit to mountain farms (malghe, masi)
  – *2nd–penultimate day* ▶ along local mountain paths

- Traditional meals + overnight stays
  – *2nd–penultimate day* ▶ in selected Alpine inns/huts
  (rifugi, baite)

Core

1

2 ancillary

3

4 services

5

6

> Potential to differentiate

< Potential to control

Fig. 4.3. An integrated tourist product for a hotel in the mountains (source: the authors' own adaptation of promotional material from Romantik Hotel Turm).

The model suggested by Kotler *et al.* (2009) can be adapted by supply-side actors working in the food and wine tourism sector and applied to any of their tourist products, as long as they include the following:

- A core product. Designed to satisfy real needs and being the goods/service benefit required by the tourist (e.g. in our case, on-site wine or oil tasting, overnight accommodation in a charming inn located in a food/wine-producing region/area).
- Facilitating products. Goods and services necessary to facilitate access to the core product (on-site facilities, dedicated visitor spaces, optimal use of visitor spaces, equipment, signs, parking; check-in desks, telephones, web sites).
- Supporting products. Created specifically to add value to the business product, to differentiate it from competitors and to position it in the market (e.g. through initiatives like food and wine pairing, itineraries inside the farm premises/wine estate with panoramic stops illustrated by interpretive panels, farm education tours; the comfort of well-designed tasting rooms; dedicated libraries, free books for bedtime reading).

If we observe the breakdown of the tourist product in Fig. 4.4 carefully, we can see that the distinctive product is not completely closed or self-sufficient. We therefore have to study the

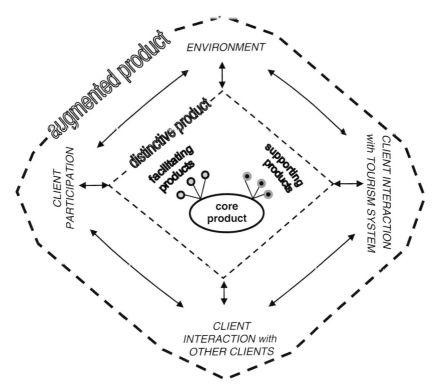

Fig. 4.4. The augmented tourist product (source: the authors' own adaptation from Kotler *et al.,* 2009).

way it relates to its two main components: the environment (of which the distinctive product is a part) and people (clients, other operators, residents, etc.).

We need to look at the wider picture and include and integrate the following elements, so that they interact with the distinctive product:

- The interface between the internal environment/atmosphere and the external environment/ atmosphere. In food and wine tourism, tourists perceive and appreciate the atmosphere and environment of the place/company they are visiting through their five senses. Visual (colour, luminosity, shapes and forms), auditory (volume and tone), olfactory (perfume, intensity, complexity) and tactile dimensions (consistency, texture, plasticity, temperature), together with taste, all contribute to attracting clients, to making a product statement, and to stimulating visitor reactions. They are also responsible for setting the mood of the visit. Some examples of how the five senses enrich visitor experience are: the unmistakable smell of must during the grape harvest; windows looking out on to the vineyards from the tasting room, the characteristic architecture of the wine vaults; the flower boxes at the entrance, the rustic or minimalist style of the décor and furnishings; the colours of the walls reflecting the colours of the landscape, the relaxing silence of the countryside; guided tours to explore the environs.
- Client participation. There could be services in place that encourage clients to participate as co-producers, e.g. interactive tasting sessions, individual personalized or self-guided

visits; the possibility to personally select and try wines at the bar; joining in and cooperating with working life on the farm, e.g. taking part in the wine harvest; attending cookery courses; following the transformation of raw materials into a finished product.

- Client interaction with other clients. The way a visit is timed and planned determines the quality of the experience. Dedicated visitor spaces need to be managed and used to enhance visitor experience; using the same space at the same time for groups who may be incompatible should always be avoided. For instance, groups composed of different target customers with different needs and expectations, such as a group of journalists on a familiarization trip at the same time as paying visitors, individual clients at the same time as tour groups, professional experts in gastronomy with a group of high-school students, a group of senior citizens at the same time as families with very young children.

- Client interaction with the internal and external tourism system. The visitor's experience of internal services goes through three distinct phases. The first is on arrival (the first sip of wine at the bar; the basket of fresh fruit from the garden placed in the guests' bedroom to enhance their sensory experience of the destination); the second is the consumption phase (the strategies used to make the holiday/visit memorable: the way technical information about a product is interspersed with moments of light relief or practical activities; the professional approach by the people dedicated to leading the tasting sessions and the welcoming, family attitude (or not) of the personnel); and finally comes the separation phase (presenting clients with a parting gift such as merchandising with the enterprise's logo or a small collectable; help with carrying guests' luggage to their car; a final handshake with the owner; a follow-up newsletter, etc.). If the operator/producer can also succeed in projecting their image and creating links over a wider area with external operators, organizations and resources and stimulate visitors' interest in exploring the region further, this will also have the effect of increasing visitor satisfaction with the overall holiday experience.

Given all the different elements that go into making up the augmented tourist product, it would be an impossible task for an individual operator to have direct control over each and every single component. The extended tourist product therefore needs to be considered as a system or network of different parts. By network, we mean a series of interlinking relationships between different regional companies or enterprises, all operating in the same business sector or even within completely different sectors. The fact that these businesses are all members of the same network means that there is an explicit agreement to share the same values, objectives and standards, to adhere to the same rules and to adopt the same criteria towards business practices. Membership can offer a series of advantages, such as greater visibility on the market, technical support in areas such as management or training, sharing promotional costs and gaining financial support through regional and national funding. A network of businesses working together in this way also guarantees that consumers will enjoy the same level of services right across the board, that prices are consistent rather than erratic, that information about potential services is easily accessible and that consumers ultimately are given a much wider choice. To sum up, in order to give tourist value to a production region or destination, regional operators (including those outside the tourism sector) need to work together. And what is more, policies and strategies for tourism management should also take into account the needs of the host community and try to involve them as much as possible, e.g. by organizing events, by inviting them to seminars on tourism development in the area and by offering economic benefits through employment opportunities.

TOURISM MODELS: THE GASTRONOMIC PRODUCT AS A CORE RESOURCE OR AS AN ANCILLARY COMPONENT?

It can happen that the main motive for travel is to seek out and enjoy a gastronomic experience; in this case food will be the core product and the main attractor and the organization of the overall cultural tourism experience will revolve around it. On the other hand, a tourist may view the gastronomic experience as being just one of many elements to be enjoyed during their holiday. In this case, the gastronomic product is an ancillary component rather than a core resource. However, it is not only the amount of visitor interest that determines the central or accessory role of a gastronomic product; indeed, the most decisive factor is the productive role of the destination. In fact, there are many regions that are not appropriate for food and wine tourism, or at least not all in the same way. Whatever the case, certain characteristics must exist in order to appeal to potential visitors and inspire in them a desire to travel to a specific place with the aim of discovering and tasting a specific product.

The transformation of a food or wine product into a tourism resource depends on whether it possesses the following characteristics:

- Exceptional organoleptic quality as a result of particular growing or breeding methods, the quality of the raw materials/breed/species, transformation processes, traditional or highly innovative technological methods.
- Uniqueness and originality also as perceived by the consumer, so that there should be no chance of the product being confused with another.
- Rareness or limited production increases appeal on the market and gives the product a reputation for being rare and exclusive, so that a tourist-consumer perceives the gastronomic experience of tasting the product directly in the place where it has been produced as something special and out of the ordinary.
- Points of sale mainly confined to place of production so that the consumer is forced to travel to the destination in order to purchase the product; although it can sometimes be useful if the consumer already has some knowledge about the product thanks to good communication strategies or retail opportunities outside the region. However, being able to enjoy a product in its place of origin, that has not been stored or transported over long distances, enhances its organoleptic qualities and offers the tourist-consumer an exciting sensory experience in a privileged atmosphere.
- Traditional and cultural roots, particularly if in a geographically limited area that is easy to define and identify.

It can happen, however, that the combined presence of the above characteristics is not enough to give a gastronomic product enough appeal or tourist pull. Even when the quality of a product is high and there are traditionally strong links to the area of production with limited distribution, it somehow still does not manage to become a core tourist product.

In Fig. 4.5 we look at examples of holidays in two different destinations, each known for their high-quality gastronomic resources. Both destinations lie in the same area (Emilia, Italy), a region that is famous not only in Italy for being one of the nation's richest in terms of gastronomic production but also whose products also enjoy an international reputation: *tortellini Bolognese*, fresh home-made pasta, Parma ham, Parmigiano Reggiano cheese, traditional balsamic vinegar from Modena and Reggio Emilia. As we can see in Fig. 4.5, the much-fêted Culatello di Zibello Pdo (cured meat) is placed at the centre of the core tourist product whose holiday proposal is strictly related to offering a gastronomic experience. Coppia Ferrarese Pgi bread, a special type of bread baked in Ferrara and so-called because it is made from two small spiral cones joined in the centre, serves as an accessory to a holiday that has a much stronger cultural element. In fact, tourist appeal in both cases depends not just on the products themselves but also on the environmental contexts of their places of origin. In the case of Zibello, a small town situated on the banks of the Po River, with just a few thousand inhabitants, the main attraction is without doubt the local gastronomy, of which Culatello di Zibello, a sweet-tasting, salt-cured 'ham', is the perfect symbol. The meat can be produced only in a very restricted area of just eight villages, well-known in Italy for its extremely foggy winter months, when the hams are left to mature in cool, ventilated cellars, with the fog filtering in (Fig. 4.6). The historic Renaissance centre of Ferrara, on the other hand, is one of Italy's most renowned and most important. Visitors are therefore attracted to the city because of its art and culture, rather than because of its bread (unless, of course, they have a professional interest). However, having the opportunity to enjoy freshly baked Coppia Ferrarese while visiting Ferrara will certainly add to tourists' appreciation of the atmosphere and distinctive identity of the city.

It is also interesting to note that in some areas where there is more than one quality gastronomic speciality, the tourist product can be developed around a single core product, with

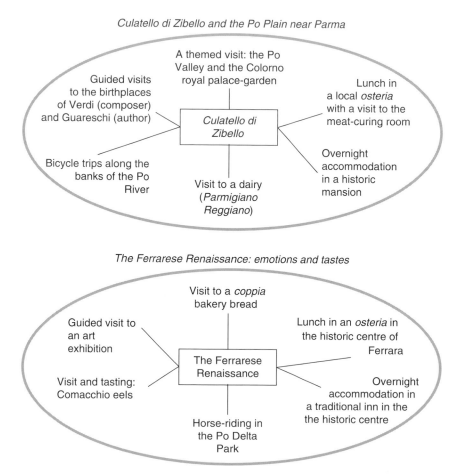

Culatello di Zibello and the Po Plain near Parma

Guided visits to the birthplaces of Verdi (composer) and Guareschi (author)

A themed visit: the Po Valley and the Colorno royal palace-garden

Lunch in a local *osteria* with a visit to the meat-curing room

Culatello di Zibello

Bicycle trips along the banks of the Po River

Visit to a dairy (*Parmigiano Reggiano*)

Overnight accommodation in a historic mansion

The Ferrarese Renaissance: emotions and tastes

Guided visit to an art exhibition

Visit to a *coppia* bakery bread

Lunch in an *osteria* in the historic centre of Ferrara

The Ferrarese Renaissance

Visit and tasting: Comacchio eels

Horse-riding in the Po Delta Park

Overnight accommodation in a traditional inn in the the historic centre

Fig. 4.5. Examples of tourist products: gastronomy as a core product or as an ancillary component.

Fig. 4.6. A Culatello di Zibello ageing room (Italy).

the others being accessories to it. We can observe this in Fig. 4.5, where Parmigiano Reggiano cheese has been made an accessory to a tour that has Culatello as its main focus. A different tour, dedicated to discovering cheese production within the same geographical area, would naturally put Parmigiano Reggiano at the centre.

Product appeal often depends on other factors too. As these tend to be linked to individual interests and to personal judgement on the part of the tourist-consumer, they are extremely difficult to control:

- Perceived value. Linked to the cultural level of the consumer and the way the production process is carried out. According to personal and/or preconceived ideas, the process may be considered an appealing factor, or it may even be thought of as boring or too complicated, or even too costly. Consumer opinion is also influenced by the media and opinion leaders, who may spark interest in a product by bringing it into the public eye.
- Occasions for consumption and degree of satisfaction given by the product. Sipping a good wine or savouring a bar of chocolate in good company or while reading a book can be a very pleasant experience; at an olive mill, olive oil experts or professionals will want to participate in a panel tasting session, while the less-experienced visitor will probably appreciate more the chance to eat crusty bread on which extra-virgin olive oil has been poured.
- Shape, consistency, perfume, colour, etc.; for example, the roundness of plump mozzarella cheese or the sinuous shape of a bottle; the perfume of drying grapes or the colour of a fruit.
- Emotional response. Difficult to classify as it is the result of a number of very different factors; it can partly be explained by consumer response to product image, by the type of company the visitor is in at the time of the tasting experience, the atmosphere and the appeal

of the site/*terroir*, the context in which the product is tasted and bought, the price, whether the visitor has felt welcome or not, opinions expressed by others (e.g. critics/friends), etc.

One more aspect remains to be examined: a product on its own is not sufficient. As we have said above, for a gastronomic product to become a tourist attractor, it has to be supported by regional resources and attractions, by the host community, by well-organized infrastructure and effective management. A food-producing area or region can only become a tourist destination once a tourism system has been put in place.

The positioning analysis in Fig. 4.7 is based on comparing two variables: the level of tourism organization and the quality of the agro-alimentary resources. As we can see from the map, not all of the sites (Italian extra-virgin olive oil-producing localities/villages) are ideally placed to become gastronomic tourism destinations in that they are unable to offer contemporarily a high-quality product and an adequate standard of tourism services (accommodation facilities, restaurants, etc.). If a product is to have appeal and be a tourism attractor, it must possess exceptionally high organoleptic qualities (perceived and recognized by the consumer) and have strong links with the land and the surrounding area. A potential tourism destination that already has a consolidated gastronomic tradition is naturally better placed to develop growth strategies, if it only needs to concentrate on creating suitable tourism services. Before making any decision with regard to system strategies, the area and its tourism potential need to be carefully analysed and appraised. Once this has been done, strategies can then be put into place to rectify any gaps in the system, e.g. by improving existing tourism services and/or creating conditions for new ones to be set up. Unfortunately, policies and strategies only aimed

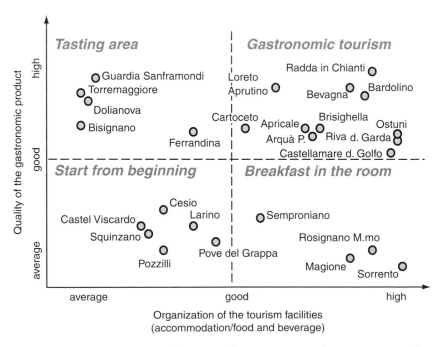

Fig. 4.7. Tourism positioning: a possible approach to mapping Italian extra-virgin olive oil production areas (source: the authors' own adaptation of field research and analyses of reviews in tourism and gastronomy publications, e.g. Slow Food, Michelin, Gambero Rosso, 2005–2007).

at increasing the number of bed places in an area or at constructing expensive infrastructure networks are often destined to fail if interaction between the destination and its tourist activities is not constantly and specifically monitored.

COMMUNICATING THE IDENTITY OF A GASTRONOMIC DESTINATION

The difficult task of communicating information or images of a region, its resources and its tourism products in order to appeal to possible food and wine tourists, can only be carried out successfully if there is an awareness of the potential risks posed by a post-modern approach that may, as we have already seen, generate a number of problems:

- The progressive elimination of reference frames for time/space. In other words, giving a geographical definition to a tourist destination that has no reference to its actual physical surroundings. This leads the tourist-consumer to view the tourist destination as being an area unto itself with no ties to the real environmental context of which it is part.
- Confusion between reality and how it is portrayed. An excessive use of images (and as a result, overwhelming possibilities of choice) leads to a lack of interest or indifference towards true regional identity and geographical reality, as they tend to be judged and interpreted according to the value and visual impact of the image.
- The tendency by tourists to collect places and landscapes that are not contextualized and that represent only a fragment of the real geographical identity of an area. For instance, all the complex and rich aspects of a destination are reduced to a single image confined within the pages of a holiday brochure. As a result, the tourism experience becomes an examination of how well the destination and the holiday relate to the promise made by the image and is not an objective assessment of the experience within the actual destination.
- The overwhelming desire to enjoy at all costs (or make clients enjoy) every aspect of the holiday by removing any negative factors from the visitor experience. This includes modifying or 'cleansing' elements of an area that are deemed unattractive, even when they are an integral and authentic part of that region.
- The consequences of giving a superficial or glossy image to a destination (by policy makers within the destination), that inevitably leads to the destination losing its identity, becoming isolated from its surroundings and falling into a cultural, social and economic vacuum: sustainable policies need to be put in place to protect and manage gastronomic tourism destinations.

The very nature of food and wine tourism means that there has to be a strong compromise between the economic aspects (the need to generate value) and the richness and range of regional resources (agro-alimentary product, the *terroir*, the milieu, etc.). Communications strategies must therefore:

- underline and reinforce the importance of environmental protection policies within the region (and as a consequence raise awareness of environmental issues in tourism);
- attract tourists; and
- give a sense of belonging to the region or destination on the part of the host community.

In fact, even when food and wine tourism communication strategies fall into the trap of being rather banal or unoriginal by projecting an attractive but stereotyped image of a destination, the visitor experience, although possibly limited to a single tour of a winery or farm, is nevertheless authentic (both in a symbolic and a practical sense): seeing the raw materials, observing production methods and participating in a tasting session give a real feeling for the spirit of the place and contribute to giving visitors a more intimate knowledge of the *terroir*. An individual experience such as this can act as a springboard to explore the region and its resources even further. A catalogue photo that depicts a beautifully laid-out picnic on a hillside surrounded by gently sloping vineyards is much more telling (although perhaps less persuasive for the average consumer) than a photo of a deck chair and a beach lounger on the shores of a tropical beach. Gastronomic tourism must therefore take on the symbolic load of its *terroir*, just as other tourism sectors reflect symbolic images of their destinations; but in the case of gastronomic tourism, the region's natural and socio-economic characteristics must also be projected.

Developing communication strategies for a gastronomic product, whether it is a destination, a one-site holiday or a tour, means having to transmit a very strong message with regard to regional spirit and identity. By making explicit links between leisure/holiday activities and agro-alimentary production in the *terroir*, it is possible to arouse visitor interest and evoke a desire to discover something out of the ordinary. The risks generated by post-modern tourism can be avoided and the tourist-consumer can be spurred into making more informed choices. Aware consumers are much more likely to be responsible visitors in a gastronomic destination and more inclined to enjoy the overall experience. It is up to the region and individual producers/operators to communicate the product's ethics and aesthetics and guide the visitor towards a full and complete understanding of the destination.

As we know, it can happen that a tourist product, in spite of its excellence, just does not manage to appeal to the demand side's needs and expectations. What is more, giving the destination a self-referential image often does not correspond to how the host community or tourists perceive it, nor does it coincide with a tour operator's proposal of a holiday in the area or how it is portrayed in the media.

Communication planners must therefore come up with ideas and strategies that:

- promote a true and consistent image of the *terroir*, defining its unique characteristics and giving a sense of the spirit of the place, and inform potential visitors about the real and significant benefits to be enjoyed by staying in the region;
- give visitors an overall perception of the area while making them aware of individual components/resources such as the physical environment, food/wine production and cultural aspects;
- make tourists aware of the fact that the gastronomic product, thanks to its sensory aspects and the way it lends itself to giving visitors an emotional, educational or entertaining experience, only really fully emerges when the consumer interacts with all the resources in the area;
- underline the fact that the destination's gastronomic product is a precious resource and it would be extremely difficult to find anything similar elsewhere;
- inform visitors about all the different possible options or choices available in the tourist offer, e.g. line, range, potential and current alternatives that can be supplied/chosen, degree of participation by the consumer in the design and construction of the product; and
- create different communication threads (in style and content) to reflect the different types of offer in the area and/or to appeal to different targets.

Before being able to plan appropriate communication strategies for a destination or producer/operator, the following points need to be checked and verified:

- The suitability of the *terroir* within the tourism system. In other words, evaluating potential in the area to utilize and develop resources and professional skills, to be innovative and forward-looking and to cultivate external business relationships.

- Destination image. This entails carrying out market research to verify consumer perception and to check whether the projected image corresponds to the real characteristics of the destination.
- Destination identity. This entails verifying how the host community perceives the destination.

Action plans that are commonly used in destination branding also provide us with a useful set of guidelines for effective communication strategies:

- Generate wealth.
- Guarantee widespread recognition of the tourist product.
- Clarify destination identity so that it corresponds to both how visitors and the host community perceive it.
- Take a straightforward, simple approach to communicating destination personality/identity, rendering it attractive and significant for the market and ensuring that the name/symbol/logo/image of a product matches the characteristics of the production company or the region in which it operates (product names/symbols/logos/images must have immediate impact and be easily memorized and recognized).
- Reduce to a minimum any perceived risks or uncertainties that potential clients may have about choosing or visiting the destination.
- Stimulate differentiation between competitors in the area.
- Present intangible aspects of a holiday as being tangible, enjoyable and valuable by creating a direct association between visitor expectations of a memorable holiday experience and the specific characteristics of the host destination.
- Facilitate, reinforce and personalize the visitor's emotional relationship with the destination before, during and after the holiday experience (by informing, persuading, reminding).
- Filter target markets to select the most appropriate target customers.

Let us look at a selection of slogans or images that have been used to welcome visitors to different wine-growing areas. On entering Napa Valley (USA), visitors are greeted by signs that read 'NAPA VALLEY. WELCOME to this world famous wine growing region. ...*and the wine is bottled poetry*' (Fig. 4.8). The phrase in italics is a quotation by Robert Louis Stevenson, who in 1880 spent his honeymoon in an abandoned house on the site of the old Silverado Mine on Mount Saint Helena, overlooking Napa Valley. His experiences in Napa Valley are retold in his travel memoirs, *The Silverado Squatters*. The symbol for Chianti Classico wines in Tuscany, Italy, is a black rooster. In France, the wines of Alsace are promoted by the slogan 'the art of surprising you', while in Burgundy the slogan is 'the art and joy of living' accompanied by its famous symbol of a snail. In Australia, the Canberra Wine District has chosen to emphasize the strong bond between its wine and the *terroir* with: 'Wine with diversity in variety and style found nowhere else. Wine that is Liquid Geography.'

The communication of an area or one of its products must be a metaphor or synthesis of what the destination/product effectively offers. A good example can be found in the communication strategies adopted by both public organizations and private individual producers to promote southern France's famous Roquefort cheese. The strategies emphasize the karstic *terroir*'s particular geomorphological features as the cheese is ripened inside rock caves by natural ventilating faults (*fleurines*). But they also focus on history, passion and traditions, and stories and legends about the origins of Roquefort cheese, as well as giving more precise and technical information about the specific breed of ewe and production methods.

Fig. 4.8. Welcome to Napa Valley (California, USA).

When communicating a gastronomic tourist destination, three strategies can be adopted and modified according to the specific characteristics of the destination. Attention should be focused on the following:

- Tradition. By highlighting the positive elements and the natural vocation of the destination, and concentrating on coordinating or reinforcing competitive, thematic or distinctive factors.
- Evolution. By highlighting the mix of factors responsible for change beginning with the current situation, in order to illustrate how the original vocation of the destination may have changed.
- Radical innovation. By highlighting the complete and absolute change in vocation of the destination (this is more likely to be the case in areas that do not have any particular traditional resources or where food and wine production is not particularly important or significant).

Whatever the case, the tourism system that has been put in place needs to be communicated along with the desire to grow and any factors that bring added value to the destination. There is also a need to support and reinforce links between internal components within the system and external forces.

Other important factors to decide on are which spatial communication approach to take and what level of the product to communicate. In order to influence consumers' mental geography, cognitive behaviour and opinions, it is necessary to:

- Identify the main characteristics of the area/product, its limits and perceived value.
- Utilize communications strategies to underscore the distinctive bond between the product and its *terroir*, and to give the region a well-defined geographical area, creating in the mind of the consumer clear associations between the region and its resources (Fig. 4.9).

Fig. 4.9. Landscape as identity: vines in the land of Cathars (Languedoc Roussillon, France).

As a result it is possible to make a strategic purchasing choice based on the relationship between 'product distribution and identity/homogeneity of the tourism space'.

It is important to point out that even when communication strategies have not been explicitly constructed for a destination/product/business, communication takes place all the same. The way in which a particular region, business or tour operator is perceived in the public domain may not necessarily be attributable to controlled marketing strategies. A number of factors can contribute to the construction of product image, e.g. the host community's attitude to tourists in the destination, the adoption of sustainable policies, the way the destination is maintained, the upkeep of its buildings and infrastructure, the professional way in which visitors are treated, the organoleptic qualities of the gastronomic resource. Even the way a tour guide at a winery is dressed will make a difference to the overall image of the destination. Every single aspect, including factors over which there is no control, counts. For this reason (and as we shall see again in Chapter 5), it is simply not enough to just focus on constructing a tourist product. Attention must be given to the way in which it is described and presented in terms of offer, services, visitor welcome, architecture, décor and furnishings, and physical surroundings.

This is even truer if we consider that the main objective is to communicate a strong message to the external actors (tourists or potential investors) as well as to the internal ones, such as residents or operators in the destination. With the external actors, the message helps to:

- create recognition of the destination/product through the spreading of information;
- stimulate consumer choice and willingness to buy through persuasion;
- evoke and recall memories and experiences; and
- lead to consumer loyalty.

With internal actors, the message helps to:

- create trust, shape identity and reinforce a sense of belonging, quality of life is raised;
- provide information;
- stimulate active participation; and
- foster good relationships between different parties with different interests.

It is often necessary to stimulate the host community into having the right sort of approach towards tourists. In low season, some local tourism organizations do make some attempt to raise awareness about the forthcoming season, usually through poster campaigns. The aim is to stimulate the local art of hospitality and to reinforce in residents the idea that they can boast about living in an area that is appealing and attractive to outsiders. In some cases, training courses in tourism subjects that would normally only be open to operators in the sector are also open to residents.

In conclusion, the successful communication of a *terroir* or a gastronomic product requires effective information dissemination, coherent images and the confirmation that benefits can be derived by the life experience offered by the destination/product, their identity and value.

Box 4.1. Case Studies.

There are many different ways to communicate an area's vocation to become a gastronomic destination. Much depends on the target (whether tourists, residents, operators in the sector or opinion leaders) and much depends on the inherent characteristics of the region and the product. However, if policy makers and destination managers move with professionalism and foresight, they can have an equally significant impact on the successful outcome of the communications campaign.

- A film that is a box-office success and features an area of food or wine production is bound to influence consumer choice and lure potential tourists to the area. *Sideways,* directed by Alexander Payne and nominated for five Oscars and awarded Best Adapted Screenplay in 2005, is a perfect example. Tourists from all over the USA and beyond flocked to the wine-growing Santa Ynez Valley, just a little to the north-west of Santa Barbara in California, to see where the film was made. From a tourism point of view, the film's success was due to a number of well-planned actions that put together became a winning combination. First and foremost, the plot of the film (in which the real protagonist is the wine-growing area of Santa Ynez) revolves around a journey. This in itself makes it very easy for the audience to identify themselves with the actors. The Film Commission and Conference and Visitors Bureau in Santa Barbara worked together with the film's director and production team, well before the film came out, to establish helpful and mutually beneficial relationships with the local Chambers of Commerce. When the film did come out, it was accompanied by a well-planned and well-timed marketing campaign aimed at increasing success with both the general public and film critics and translating the film into an 'animated' account of the area. The Conference and Visitors Bureau, for example, published a downloadable map on its web site (www.santabarbaraca.com). 'The map, which has been re-printed three times due to demand, highlights 18 locations from the film. To date, 120,000 maps have been distributed and over 65,000 people have downloaded it from santabarbaraCA.com' (Motion Picture Association of America, 2006). In another well-calculated

(Continued)

Box 4.1. Continued.

move, tour operators and travel agents were encouraged to come up with holiday packages based on the leitmotiv of the film. All these actions had an incredibly positive impact: they included the creation of 50 holiday packages, dozens of articles in the national and international press, eight familiarization trips for journalists and a consistently high number of tourist flows to the area (Rocco, 2005). In the year after the film came out, some wineries in Santa Barbara County were reporting a 300% increase in visitor numbers (Motion Picture Association of America, 2009). The Santa Barbara Conference and Visitors Bureau web site, which is packed with useful information and suggestions for where to go and what to do, still has a section entirely dedicated to *Sideways*. It also has a rich and detailed section given over to Culinary Tourism, further highlighting the gastronomic vocation of the destination.

- There are a number of instruments or tools that can be used to communicate the different resources of an area, that combined together shape a gastronomic destination's unique identity. One of the most effective is thematic mapping. Cisternino (Italy), a small town in Puglia, attracts food and wine lovers as well as outdoor enthusiasts. They are drawn to its tiny historic centre with its charming whitewashed buildings and the surrounding countryside dotted with *trulli, masserie* (old farmhouses), dry-stone walls, Indian figs, almond trees, vineyards and olive trees. But above all, people come to the area to enjoy its magnificent Mediterranean cuisine. Some of its most renowned dishes include *orecchiette* pasta with broccoli sprouts and Cacioricotta cheese, broad bean puree, potato bread, *tarallini* (small, ring-shaped bakery products) and almond cakes. Cisternino's butchers also offer a quite different gastronomic experience with their '*fornelli pronti*'; in other words, they have ovens on their premises and customers at the counter can choose raw local meat specialities (*gnummered', bombette,* mixed-meat sausages) that are served oven-roasted in a short space of time at the table, either inside or outside in summer. Over the last few years, tourism promotion campaigns organized by the City Council have mainly concentrated on exalting the region's culinary resources. Aside from the usual information material that is given out to tourists and operators in the sector (a leaflet about the town and its surroundings marked with hiking, cycling and horse-riding tracks), a new map, *Map of Agro-alimentary Produce in Cisternino, Itria Valley* (*Carta delle produzioni agroalimentari di Cisternino in Valle d'Itria*), has been produced which illustrates where all the products and producers in the region are located. The map represents the municipal region and lists all the local producers and anyone involved in transforming raw produce into finished products, dividing them into the different categories in which they operate: dairy farmers, breeders, oil producers, bee-keepers, fruit and vegetable growers and manufacturers, cheese makers, wine producers, butchers who transform meat using local recipes, pastry chefs who bake traditional almond cakes and biscuits, fresh pasta makers and coffee producers. Prior to the construction of the map, each business activity was visited by the map's designers and each operator individually contacted and interviewed. The businesses or activities on the map are accompanied by symbols representing the category they belong to, their business characteristics, their product focus and production methods (e.g. if product transformation happens internally or if the raw product is purchased from an outside supplier) and whether organic or conventional farming methods are used. Practical information is also listed, e.g. whether the

(Continued)

Box 4.1. Continued.

business is open to visitors, if tasting sessions are organized and if products are available for purchase. If a thematic map is well-researched, well-planned and gives accurate, reliable information, apart from being attractive to look at, it can be the first step towards creating a complete, coherent and competitive tourist product for a gastronomic destination. The map offers opportunities to integrate leisure tourism with seaside tourism (the Adriatic coastline is nearby) and gives visitors the chance to be more aware of the possibilities the region holds for them, enriching their holiday experience. In addition, the actual planning and construction of the map meant charting all the producers, businesses and individuals involved in gastronomic production in the area. This resulted in greater awareness among the actors of other operators in their particular sector, in understanding the stages that products go through in the supply chain. This process has the potential to stimulate business ties and form the basis of a network of cooperation and reciprocal respect, the premise for guaranteeing product quality and launching new ideas (e.g. adopting innovative farming methods based on the concept of biodiversity or taking steps to obtain a denomination of origin certificate). When business and regional interests find a common ground through initiatives such as this, there is greater stimulus to work together and improve all aspects of production and supply throughout the entire region, rendering gastronomic production more efficient and sustainable and reinforcing regional identity. Furthermore, a thematic map not only gives increased opportunities to visitors and producers, it also reminds the host community of its rich gastronomic heritage, composed of products, recipes, people and landscapes.

Information in the distribution process

So far, we have seen how the communication of a product is centred around effective information dissemination and the projection of an accurate, authentic image. We have also seen that in food and wine tourism, the function of a communication campaign is not just to reach potential consumers in the market; it must also communicate a strong message to residents and operators in the sector. Among these are the people responsible for communication distribution. Their task is to create appropriate communication channels, in the right place and at the right time, to inform the general public about the product.

Choosing which distribution strategies to use and selecting the most effective communication channels depend on a number of internal and external factors. For example, in the case of a food or wine business enterprise, the type of product would need to be carefully considered, as well as the resources and characteristics of the business in question, the resources of the region in which it operates and an analysis made of possible costs and potential earnings. Once this has been done, possible distribution partners will need to be selected on the basis of the following criteria:

- ability to view and treat the product appropriately, so that it is communicated in an apt manner;
- suitability with regard to reaching the right target (potential conflict of interests should be avoided, e.g. the distributor may represent other clients/products that are incompatible with the producer's own product);
- business approach being professional, flexible, efficient;

- effectiveness in the market, and
- financial solvency.

Communication is, however, one of the main functions of distribution policy. It means the sharing or gathering of information with regard to the market, the product or its competitors. It includes communicating persuasive messages about the tourism offer, establishing relationships with real and potential clients, interpreting and evaluating the suitability of a product to respond to market demand, advising how to make the product more appealing to target markets, negotiating prices and conditions, etc., regardless of whether distribution channels are direct or indirect, short term or long term. Different types of distribution strategies can be adopted according to different business means and objectives, from intensive strategies aimed at reaching the widest possible market through numerous intermediaries to exclusive channels of distribution aimed at reaching niche markets. In the latter case, the number of intermediaries is reduced to a minimum, perhaps even to just one or two highly experienced operators in the sector.

One of the greatest problems with communication in indirect distribution channels is asymmetric information that is often responsible for compromising product success in the market. This happens when the product's defining characteristics and essential values are not communicated down the producer–intermediary–client/tourist chain; product identity is lost along the way and as a consequence it loses its importance in the distribution channel. This presents a huge risk for gastronomic tourism, because as a product, its essential features are experience and emotion. The success of communication strategies for food and wine tourism depends on being able to stimulate potential visitors' senses and inform them about the unique characteristics of a given area and its products. The problem of asymmetric information therefore needs to be tackled. Very often, it can be put down to lack of awareness about the cultural or environmental aspects of a destination or not having enough information about resources and facilities. Above all however, it is the lack of specific knowledge about gastronomic matters on the part of communication distributors or intermediaries (travel agents and tour operators, but also local tourism representatives and incoming tour operators) that puts the product's success at risk.

The reality is that many operators, including those working in the destination itself, are insufficiently prepared about a product and consequently fail to communicate it successfully. All too often there is little interest in the idea of bringing together different resources in the area, linking them together by theme and then integrating them into a unique tourist product. This failure to realize the full potential of an area/product means that opportunities to create holiday packages offering a variety of experiences are often missed. The problem of asymmetric information is probably best tackled at source (from small producers of gastronomic products to destination policy makers) by developing more effective communication with distribution partners. This will then lay the basis for greater:

- understanding;
- involvement (also for those who earn a commission for their services);
- pleasure in sharing the tourism experience with visitors (planning, staying, departing); and
- incentive to communicate the holiday as a unique opportunity to enjoy an original (technical and emotional) experience.

The food and wine tourism industry is characterized by a wide cross-section of different business activities and many of its principal operators are not exclusively linked to tourism. A case in point is a wine producer who makes the decision to open up his cellars to welcome visitors and then later expands his offer to include overnight accommodation. Because of these wider business interests it can sometimes be a good idea to look beyond the tourism sector to open up new communication channels. Trade fairs and business conventions can provide excellent opportunities to meet possible project or distribution partners. In the tourism sector, some of the major international events are: 'Pow Wow', 'Bit Milano', 'Salon Mondial du Tourisme' in Paris, 'ITB Berlin', 'Fitur Madrid', 'WTM London', 'JATA World Travel Fair of Tokyo' and 'ITE Hong Kong'. Participating in major food and wine fairs can result in interesting business opportunities.

In fact, there are also many international fairs and exhibitions where food and wine are the main protagonists. The choice is vast: in the USA, we have the 'Fancy Food Show', 'Natural Product Expo', 'United Fresh Marketplace'; in France, the 'Salons des Vins et de la Gastronomie', 'Salon International de l'Agriculture', 'Natexpo', 'Marjolaine', 'Salon des vins et des Vignerons Indépendants'; in Spain, the 'Club de Gourmets', 'Vinoelite', 'Salón del Vino', 'Alimentaria'; in Italy, the 'Salone del Gusto', 'Vinitaly', 'Cheese', 'Cibus', 'Merano International Wine Festival', 'Salone del Vino'; in Germany, 'Anuga', 'IGW', 'Salon Gourmet', 'Weinmesse', 'Forum Vini'; in Australia, the 'Good Food & Wine Show'; in Japan, 'Foodex Japan'; in India, 'World of Food India'; and then there are 'Wine and Gourmet–Asia' in Macau, 'Thaifex' in Bangkok, and so on.

There are also other operators in the sector who have chosen a different route to communicate their products. Take, for example, some *vignerons indépendants* in France. They have made a conscious decision not to invest in traditional marketing strategies, e.g. through the media or magazines; instead, they use the money they would have otherwise spent on advertising and promotion to finance their own personal travels. Their annual trips serve to promote their products personally, to seek out potential project partners and new ways to market. They pick up on new market trends by meeting with importers and networking with others involved in the sector at specially organized meals and events. They come into direct contact with restaurateurs, owners of wine bars and wine shops, other distributors and end customers by visiting points of sale. On top of all this, they invest a certain amount of their time to personally invite and accompany journalists on tours of their vineyards and wine cellars.

Integrating tourism successfully into the food and wine sector is an extremely complex operation. It involves individually identifying every single business partner, from suppliers and distributors to external project partners. This selection process is important in guaranteeing that products and their characteristics are properly communicated and that any financial investment is properly channelled and gives good returns. Producers must also select what criteria they wish to see reflected in their marketing strategies.

Organizing a familiarization trip

Consumers would no doubt be enthusiastic if they had the opportunity to experience a product first-hand before making a purchasing decision. In tourism, familiarization trips give tour participants the chance to discover a destination for free in the hope that they may eventually publicize it and bring it into the public eye. Fam trips, as they are commonly referred to, function as a communication tool and usually involve strategic partnerships between private and public operators.

What exactly is a fam trip? As we have said above, it is essentially a promotional trip aimed at giving participants as full experience of the destination as possible or to introduce them to a specific aspect, e.g. local food and wine products. Fam trips are generally organized by public or private tour operators operating in the destination as well as other stakeholders who have a vested economic interest in the success of the destination as a tourist product. Journalists, opinion leaders (e.g. TV and sports celebrities, politicians, artists) and intermediaries are given free trips in the hope that they will influence potential clients to buy the product. Ways that they can directly impact consumer choice include: providing travel agency clients with information in the pre-purchasing phase about possible holiday packages or hotel stays in the destination, writing tourist guides and articles for tourism magazines. Indirectly, they can influence potential buyers through articles or interviews in the media that are not specifically to do with tourism, but perhaps by discussing other aspects of the locality or its surroundings inspire interest in the destination on the part of the reader or listener. Given the importance of familiarization trips in terms of destination image and information dissemination (and potential earnings), it is clear that the successful outcome of a fam trip is significant for the host destination.

Organizing a fam trip is a complex and delicate task, needing particular attention. This form of communication is a direct dialogue with 'privileged' guests who will go on to transmit their impressions of the trip and destination with unforeseeable results. Fam trip organizers may find the guidelines below helpful in planning and managing these types of trip.

- The trip should preferably be organized to coincide with a special event to launch (or re-launch) a destination or a food/wine business, before the beginning of the tourist season.
- Participants should not have to pay for the trip; occasionally a financial contribution may be asked to cover travel expenses to the destination, but in the case of journalists, travel expenses are usually covered by the newspaper.
- Guests (journalists in particular) should be selected according to their specific professional interests, compatible with the destination and with the rest of the group.
- Invitations or press releases should be sent out in good time; contacting people just before an event is inappropriate and unhelpful.
- The right journalists should be invited at the right time, perhaps by contacting the news editor directly. Monthly magazines plan their issues over a much longer time span compared with weekly or daily papers; for instance, there would not be much sense in waiting until the beginning of September to invite journalists on a fam trip about the October grape harvest. If the journalist works for a monthly magazine, it would be most unlikely that an article would be written and published immediately on their return.
- The trip programme needs to have a specific, coherent theme; this also helps the editorial office decide which journalist would best cover that particular subject.
- The programme sent out with the invitation should be respected. For instance, a travel agent may only have accepted an invitation for a fam trip lasting several days because they had a special interest for their clients in visiting a particular hotel and spa centre, offering treatments based on olive and citrus oils. If the programme promises them the chance to try these treatments personally but they do not actually have the opportunity to do so, this will obviously have a negative effect on the way they view the trip organizers and on the destination/hotel itself.
- Contacts need to be set up between the guests and several operators in the area; it is important that trip participants get a sundry but complete vision of a gastronomic destination, by including visits to producers, accommodation facilities, restaurants, local tourism representatives, etc. Meeting fam trip guests personally is an excellent way to get across the destination's unique and varied characteristics and the nature of services offered; although meetings can be relaxed and informal, they should always be conducted in a professional manner and should not be too long or spun out.
- Guests should experience the spirit of the place; the trip may be 'technical' but that does not mean they should not enjoy a satisfying cultural encounter with the destination.

- Guest facilities should reflect the theme of the trip and be chosen according to the quality of their services and their professional approach; accommodation can be varied to give participants a taste of what the destination can offer, e.g. spending one night in a five-star luxury hotel, followed by a night in a country mansion.
- Meals need particular attention. On gastronomic fam trips, the organizers must check beforehand the quality of the food and make sure it represents the best of regional production; table service must be impeccable; menus need to be planned ahead to make sure that there is an appropriate number and variety of dishes each day and for the duration of the trip; food and wine must be paired to enhance the tasting experience and reflect regional products.
- Trip escorts and guides must be friendly and open, flexible and professional. Above all, they must know the area well; they must be prepared to respond to individual questions concerning the destination and its resources, especially if a journalist is covering a particular aspect and needs further information for an article. This could be in the form of a recipe, details about the history of food and wine production in the area, a description of how climatic factors have influenced the region's food/wine production, a list of characteristic B&Bs or farmhouses serving organic produce, exclusive restaurants, etc., the names of people in the area who can organize outdoor activities such as horse-riding or mountain-biking.
- Guests should be given free time to relax or to pursue personal interests.
- Each guest will need to be presented with a press kit; materials obviously need to be of good quality, interesting and attractive. They could include brochures, CDs with professional, high-resolution images of different aspects of the destination that can be used for publication (e.g. the changing landscape over the seasons, traditional dishes, gastronomic products), merchandising that reflects the trip's theme (e.g. a bottle of wine or extra-virgin olive oil), a book about the producer and the family business, an example of local handicraft, etc.
- Contact with the guests should be maintained once the trip is over. A recall service is essential to verify whether articles have indeed been written and published; future contacts can also be assured by sending an occasional newsletter, giving details about upcoming events and new initiatives in the destination.

In order to inform the media about an up-and-coming familiarization trip, a press release needs to be issued. Indeed, any new initiative needing to reach the attention of the media and/or general public should be communicated by this means, for example:

- conferences on food and wine tourism;
- the inclusion of a food or wine business in a new gastronomic guide;
- change of management;
- new product launch;
- special offers (e.g. limited editions of prestigious wines available for a restricted time on the market);
- vertical tastings and specially organized dinners for a limited number of participants; and
- special activities (e.g. trekking in the hills of a wine-growing area; participating in a cattle drive event at the end of the summer season, as cows are brought down from their mountain pastures).

Set out below are a number of suggestions to help draw up an effective press release:

- Only issue a press release if you have something of import to communicate.
- Language should be journalistic in style (following the 5W rule: What, Why, Who, Where, When) and be clear and straightforward.

- The title needs to be brief and simple and attract attention, a good title can then be used for any eventual article published in the press.
- The first paragraph should be a synthesis of all the information contained in the document.
- Any personal judgements or comments should be avoided – keep it brief and simple and easy to read (e.g. 1.5 spacing, 12 lines).
- Highlight key words (e.g. in bold or in italics).
- Include contact details (of the person responsible for press relations within the organization).
- Make it clear that any low-resolution photographs contained in the document are also available digitally and in high resolution for eventual publication.

Box 4.2. Case Study: a Themed Food and Wine Familiarization Trip.

A hotel in Velturno,[1] in the South Tyrol, Italy, needs to update and relaunch its image. It is located in the Valle Isarco, on what is known as the 'chestnut path'. It has been run by the same family for generations and has a loyal group of affectionate clients who return year after year, particularly during the chestnut season. They tend to be mainly families or middle-aged couples. The hotel, which has been awarded four stars, is now in the hands of the 'new generation' and has been completely restored and redone utilizing the local chestnut wood. It now offers elegant and stylish accommodation and a new spa centre 'Castanea', where treatments are based on the use of oils and creams made from horse chestnut extract. Hotel cuisine is creative and uses regional produce. The hotel is part of a chain called 'Tuttomontagna' that organizes a wide range of sporting activities. For example, the hotel organizes Nordic walking or snowshoe excursions for their clientele. The management now feels it is time to target a different market: young Italian couples who enjoy good food, spa treatments and sports, wishing to discover in a thematic way localities in the lower mountain areas.

In order to raise visibility in the market, the hotel decides to organize a fam trip for journalists:

- The occasion is a gourmet weekend during *törggelen*, an autumnal event during which it is possible to savour roast chestnuts, traditional home-made dishes and nouveau wine, arriving directly on foot at the winery or farm where the gastronomic stop is organized.
- Organizations involved are both private and public operators in the tourism system, i.e. local members of the 'Tuttomontagna' hotel chain, local farmers, apple and fruit producers in the area, local artisans and wood carvers, the town tourism information office and the tourism boards of Valle Isarco and the South Tyrol.
- The press office is run by an external organization that has contacts with all the leading Italian newspapers.
- The guests comprise a group of about ten journalists and photographers from daily, weekly and monthly publications (all contacted well ahead of time), who regularly write about gastronomy and the art of good living or sports and outdoor activities.
- The programme is organized as follows:
  - Day 1. Afternoon arrival of guests at the hotel and welcome by hotel management before being shown to their rooms. Brief meeting before dinner with those responsible for marketing tourism in the South Tyrol who have been involved in the organization of the fam trip. Dinner is a gourmet meal based on a tasting menu with chestnuts as the main theme. Meeting with the chef.

(Continued)

Box 4.2. Continued.

- ○ Day 2. After breakfast, excursion to Velturno Castle and a visit to the local farmers' and crafts market. Guided hike along the 'chestnut path' for about 5 km, stopping off on the way to visit two local fruit producers to enjoy a break and try their products. Lunch in a mountain refuge (*canederli*, stale bread balls with speck, chives, etc., and *schlutzkrapfen*, ricotta and spinach ravioli). Walk continues to the town of Chiusa. Afternoon free. Optional chestnut-based beauty treatments in the hotel spa (already booked via e-mail through the press office before departure). Evening *törggelen* meal at a *maso* (local farmhouse) with traditional music organized by the 'Tuttomontagna' group of hotels.

- ○ Day 3. Short course on Nordic walking organized by hotel staff (equipment also provided by the hotel), followed by a visit to a local wood carver. Optional spa beauty treatments. Lunch in the hotel (same menu as hotel clients). Check-out after lunch. Hotel management remains at the disposition for those who would like to ask further questions or view the hotel facilities again.

- The press kit contains: the hotel brochure with detailed description of the spa; a copy of the chestnut-inspired tasting menu; information leaflets about Velturno, Chiusa and Valle Isarco; a guide and map of the hiking paths in Valle Isarco; a CD with photos of 'Autumn in Valle Isarco'; informative material about farms, mountain huts and producers involved in the fam trip; the business card of the Valle Isarco marketing director; the business card of the South Tyrol Tourism Board's marketing director; a copy of the fam trip's programme; an explanation and description of *törggelen*; a copy of the Italian Touring Club magazine and a road map of the South Tyrol; and a memory stick containing labelled, high-resolution photographs of the South Tyrol with a special dedication.

[1] The familiarization trip on which this case study is based was organized by Hotel Taubers Unterwirt together with the tourism organizations mentioned in the text.

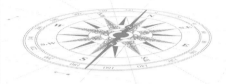

chapter 5

The Supply Side: the Actors Involved in Food and Wine Production

WHY WELCOME TOURISTS?

Opening up to food and wine tourism can present a wealth of interesting opportunities for both producers and visitors. Guided tours, if carefully planned and organized according to sustainable criteria, are invaluable when it comes to maintaining and safeguarding regional production and identity.

Some of the benefits that can be gained by welcoming visitors on a guided tour are listed below. For example, a well-run tour can:

- give visitors the opportunity to discover what the producer really does and also clear up any misconceptions or misunderstandings they may have about food or wine production;
- act as a communication tool, providing a clear and coherent image of the business and the region in which it operates;
- educate the visitor to appreciate the taste of a product and learn the best way to enjoy it;
- increase sales;
- increase income as a result of diversifying the offer;
- provide a useful database through the collection of data on clients, visitors and the market in general, and supply feedback on many different aspects relating to a product, e.g. how visitors rated the product from a sensory point of view or how much they enjoyed their visit to the area (general atmosphere, visitor welcome, facilities, staff, etc.);
- be pivotal in building and fostering ethical and transparent relationships with customers and clients;
- stimulate market competitiveness through continuous product improvement (e.g. by adapting traditional methods of production or implementing cutting-edge technology to improve product taste);

- create opportunities for employment and business development;
- be responsible for establishing horizontal and vertical connections with regional bodies and enterprises;
- communicate regional identity through its products;
- reinforce regional identity (the way local residents and the people involved in food and wine production perceive their region) and image (how tourists view the region);
- maintain and develop rural production methods and local craftsmanship; and
- increase visitor appreciation of a region and the beauty of its landscape.

Not all producers are in a position to welcome tourists on to their premises: sometimes bureaucratic obstacles may be the cause (e.g. the infrastructure does not meet health and safety requirements); others may not have sufficient personnel or perhaps the quality of production is not considered to be such as to merit a visit. There are, of course, producers who are simply not interested in opening their doors to visitors. This may be for a variety of reasons: they may not have much faith in the potential of food and wine tourism or they do not want to run the risk of being overrun by disinterested groups of tourists. In some cases it could even be reluctance to reveal what they consider to be the 'secrets' of their craft.

Francesco Paolo Valentini, a highly respected wine producer operating in Loreto Aprutino (Italy), explains why his winery remains firmly closed to tourism: 'We don't open our wine cellars to visitors, because at the end of the day what counts for us is the final result of our labours: our wine. Showing off our wine cellars would be a bit like a painter showing off his paints and brushes – it really doesn't mean anything. Many visitors just go out of curiosity to look at old wine barrels without having any real interest in the wine itself.'

Before a business takes steps to extend the core product (which remains centred around agro-alimentary production) and open up to tourism, it is essential that a series of key factors are taken into consideration:

- Is it really in the producer's interest to have on-site visitors?
- What aims or objectives does the producer have in mind?
- What benefits will the producer derive from tourism?
- Are economic, human and technological resources sufficient to provide the necessary facilities and services?
- Is the infrastructure suitable for hosting visitors?
- Is the producer open to taking on new business tasks, which, while undoubtedly enriching professional experience and expertise, will require a whole new mind set and a rethinking of his traditional managerial role?

HOW TO WELCOME VISITORS: CREATING THE TOURIST PRODUCT

Taking as given the high quality of its core product, any agro-alimentary enterprise wishing to open up to tourism must first of all make an objective evaluation of its offer by identifying its strengths, weaknesses and unique selling points. A well-constructed SWOT (strengths–weaknesses–opportunities–threats) analysis, conducted with a critical approach, can be an extremely valuable instrument in helping the producer to make this assessment. For the venture into tourism to be successful, the producer needs to take into account a set of criteria that includes the type of infrastructure available, the number of personnel, whether the atmosphere is congenial to welcoming visitors, and how the visitor experience will be planned, organized and managed.

The guidelines below will be useful not only for producers who are thinking about entering the food and wine tourism sector for the first time, but also for those who have already started a business venture and would like to compare their business practices with our model.

Providing the right type of welcome

A successful, rewarding tour for both the producer and visitors needs to be planned extremely well. The first step is to create a user-friendly web site with all the essential information a visitor might need. This should include, for example:

- Contact numbers and address.
- A map to scale and clear directions of how to arrive.
- Opening hours.
- A description of the business and the philosophy behind it.
- Whether groups can be accommodated (a designated section for tour operators would be useful in this case).
- Booking conditions and prices.
- A detailed description of the visit so that visitors already have some idea of what to expect. For example, a visit to a winery could include a tour of the cellars, followed by a conducted wine-tasting session with accompanying food to complement the different wines.
- Advice about what to wear. For example, wine cellars can be chilly places even in summer so visitors would be advised to bring a jumper, and wearing rubber soles will prevent slipping on wet floors, while sturdy walking shoes may be necessary if the tour involves a hike to a mountain dairy farm or a trek along the country roads of Chianti.

All information published on the site needs to be clear and accurate and only a limited number of relevant top-quality photos or images should be used. The site should also be easy to navigate, a pleasure to look at and display up-to-date information.

The next step is to ensure that potential visitors have already seen an image of the outside of the structure beforehand, either on the web site or in printed form (e.g. on a leaflet or brochure), so that it is immediately recognizable to them on arrival. This serves to create excitement and expectation even before the tour begins. Promotional material describing the place to be visited and the type of tours available needs to be widely distributed. Tourist Information Centres are an obvious starting point, but up-market delis, grocers, restaurants and wine bars (both local and further afield) are also good places to catch the public's eye. Tourists should be able to pick up leaflets about the visit at hotels or B&Bs in the area and at all the main tourist attractions. Other communication strategies could include direct mailing or having stands at cultural events and food fairs.

Activating an efficient direct communications policy with the public is also important. There should always be someone available to answer the phone during office hours, responding to enquiries in a polite and friendly manner. An answering machine service can provide information about opening times and how to book outside office hours. Responding promptly to e-mail enquiries either on an individual basis or by using an automatic reply system helps to create and maintain good public relations.

Adhering to fixed opening hours during the week and weekends will also make the experience more accessible to the general public. Opening times should be displayed at the entrance together with a brief description of how the visit is organized, e.g. the possibility of having guided tours for groups or single visitors, whether the tour also includes product tasting and what kind of facilities or services are available on-site, e.g. refreshments, restaurant, gift shop, children's playground, etc.

Clear road signs with the name of the winery or farm prominently displayed should guide visitors for at least the last few kilometres until they reach their destination. The area in and around the farm should look well cared for, as first impressions are all-important. Indeed, the whole environment needs to be meticulously presented, communicating to visitors the underlying philosophy of the business and the individuals who work there, whether this is based on family tradition and craftsmanship or innovative, cutting-edge production.

A decision also needs to be taken on whether visits will take place even when farm production or machinery is at a halt (e.g. olive mills during the summer months). If so, explanations given during the tour need to be informative and involve the visitors in a lively and stimulating way to avoid disappointment or boredom.

Outside and inside lighting should be efficient and in keeping with the buildings. A car park area with plenty of shade and space for coaches or minibuses to manoeuvre needs to be created, but sensitively designed and positioned so as not to spoil the visual impact of the farm itself. Parking spaces or parking lots should display eco-friendly features and be built with environmentally friendly materials whenever possible.

Visitors will need to gather together at an easily identifiable spot before the tour starts. Depending on the layout of the farm, this could be in a large courtyard or entrance hall or even in the farm shop, if space allows. Visitors will be happy to look around and perhaps buy farm produce while they are waiting for the tour to begin. Wherever it is, the meeting or welcome point should reflect and reinforce business image and identity.

It is also a good idea to provide some form of entertainment for waiting groups. This could be a video of life and work on the farm or at the winery, background music, books and guides for people to leaf through, and games or toys for the younger visitors. A few seats and fresh drinking water will be greatly appreciated by most visitors. Lavatories must obviously be kept impeccably clean. All in all, the space set aside for visitors must be welcoming and attractive, cool in summer and warm in winter.

Easy access to the farm must be provided for the disabled or physically challenged, and their needs taken into account when planning the tour route. It is best to call in an expert to get advice with regard to structural requirements and facilities and services necessary for a smooth and enjoyable visit.

The outside and inside of the building should at all times reflect the business philosophy of the enterprise.

Finally, an enthusiastic, friendly, polite and professional team of personnel has to be on hand to guide, inform and help tourists get the most out of their visit.

Organization and presentation

People will certainly have a more rewarding visit and come away more knowledgeable if they are able to tour all the areas of the farm and get a complete overview of what happens at each stage, following the exact sequence of production (although there are numerous exceptions to the rule). For example, on a wine tour, the visit could begin with a stroll around the vineyard and finish at the winery shop where people could then browse the wine-related products and accessories at leisure. If the product happens to be extra-virgin olive oil, at the end of their visit to the olive groves, visitors could be invited to view where the tasting panel meet to try out and test the different types and qualities of oil produced on the farm. An explanation of the production cycle of cheese could begin with a tour of the pastures to see the dairy herds and end in the farm shop. However, in many cases a complete tour is not always practical or easy to organize. For example, the olive groves may be too far away or the grapes for wine production may come from a different producer. The farm management may have to limit the visit to the final stages of production if practicable, and give visitors the opportunity to taste and purchase farm produce.

Whatever the approach, farmers must adhere to government or local authority regulations with regard to all the areas included in the tour. In addition to providing a welcoming atmosphere and easy access for all visitors including the physically challenged, all spaces must be well-lit, impeccably clean and odour-free (within the limits of what is possible on a working farm!). Attention should also be given to making sure that visitor numbers can be accommodated comfortably. Areas that look run down, or, even worse, poor hygienic conditions, are totally unacceptable and will only have the effect of keeping people away. What may be considered characteristic or atmospheric in one context (e.g. hanging cobwebs in the ancient wine cellars of a noble château) may have a totally adverse effect in another.

Different types of equipment and accessories will need to be ordered, according to the type of product and tour organized. For example, visitors may be required to wear shoe covers or even protective clothing. Other items concern the product itself. Vacuum-packing machines and sealers for cheeses and meats or specifically designed wine cartons or other packaging will be needed, so that products can be bought directly from the farm shop or delivered by courier to customers at home and abroad.

The tasting room

Tasting rooms can vary enormously in style, from elegant salons furnished with antiques to state-of-the-art, dedicated areas for serious tasting and testing. Whatever the case, all rooms must be:

- well-lit, using only natural or white light and neutral décor to enhance the colour of the product;
- odour- and perfume-free to facilitate sensory analysis of the product;
- temperature- and humidity-regulated for the comfort of visitors and for optimal tasting conditions;
- spacious and comfortable;
- well-furnished and equipped with tables and chairs, white napkins or paper serviettes, a tasting assessment sheet on which to make notes, and pens and paper;
- supplied with product-specific equipment, e.g. appropriate glasses for the type of wine served, a spittoon, plastic beakers, paper napkins, special glasses for professional oil tasting, plates for cheese, cheese knives, plates and cutlery, corkscrews;
- furnished with suitable storage equipment for the correct conservation of food and wine products (e.g. a fridge, equipment to preserve wine from becoming contaminated once the bottle is opened); and
- fitted out with the appropriate equipment for the washing and drying of glasses, plates and cutlery, etc.

The list could also include other items such as sparkling or still mineral water, bread or crackers, fresh fruit; indeed anything that might serve to cleanse the palate between one tasting and the next.

Architectural style

Apart from conforming to public laws and regulations, and being welcoming and comfortable, the different areas visited on a tour, if cleverly designed and planned, have further potential to enhance the visitor experience. A recognizably uniform architectural style with harmoniously designed buildings and landscaped green spaces provide the backdrop for a pleasant, agreeable visit. An architect-designed visitors' centre or tasting room, built with precious local stone or innovative materials, will have an immediate positive impact on the visitor.

Combining art and design with food and wine tourism gives added value to the visitor experience:

> as can be testified by the current trend to not only utilise wine vaults or cellars to house exhibitions and art shows (a trend set many years ago by the Mouton-Rotschild chateau when it invited various artists including Picasso, Chagall and Mirò to design their wine labels), but to transform them into tourist attractions in their own right through specifically commissioned works of art. Giving tourists the opportunity to enjoy not just an oenological experience but also a cultural one creates an even more enticing offer.
>
> (Chiorino, 2007)

To use the wine world again as an example of current practice, there are already a number of wineries where the use of architecture and design is practically a eulogy to contemporary art. For instance, at Ca' del Bosco in Erbusco (Italy), the visitor's experience of the art world begins the moment they pass through the winery gate designed by world-famous architect Arnaldo Pomodoro. In the grounds of Castello di Ama in Chianti (Italy), visitors can enjoy an annual art exhibition set in the harmonious scenery of the Tuscan hills.

Some buildings or interiors are so cutting-edge in their design, construction and use of materials that visitors are mesmerized by the sheer fantasy of the creations before them: transparent globes which seem to float in the air, soaring towers and majestic sails or abstract forms, exemplifying the work of architects such as Botta, Piano, Calatrava, Ghery, Bo, Casamonti, Hadid and Gonzalez. In contrast, castles and stately homes evoke the magic of bygone eras. The Castello di Brolio in Gaiole (Chianti) is a case in point; a visit here makes history come alive. A wine cellar that began its days as a bunker in wartime serves to remind visitors of other times and hardship.

Each and every winery has its own distinctive personality. Some have become known for championing the use of bio-architecture and raising awareness about environmental issues; others are inextricably linked to the geological and geomorphologic formation of the land. Good examples are the Italian Cantine del Notaio in Rionero, literally carved out of volcanic tuff; or the great vineyards of Champagne that lie on a thick stratum of chalk; or even the sinuous roofs of Bodega Ysios (Alava, Spain), which reflect the geomorphological features of the surrounding landscape (Fig. 5.1). And in tune with the latest sustainable practices, adaptive reuse of abandoned factories and warehouses for the food and wine sector is creating an exciting mix of gastronomy and industrial archaeology.

The importance of a distinct architectural style that reflects business practices and philosophy is not confined to wineries. It is true for any enterprise involved in food and wine production. Something as simple as a particular architectural detail or design object, or even a beautifully carved antique chest, can be enough to create a suggestive atmosphere and extend the visitor experience to beyond simply tasting the product. The careful choice of appropriate lighting and background music, e.g. in the farm shop, can also contribute to creating the right type of atmosphere.

In most cases, farms and wineries are surrounded by beautiful countryside. Stunning scenery provides a suggestive backdrop to any visit and it is worth considering offering tourists the chance to explore the immediate environs. For example, a visit to the gentle, rolling hills of the Crete Senesi, just south of Siena, will render a tour of the vineyards and *cinta* pig farms in the area even more stimulating and interesting for the tourist. Further south, visitors on a tour of the olive mills of Puglia will be intrigued by the cone-shaped roofs of the *trulli*, the traditional, whitewashed stone houses that are found only in this

Fig. 5.1. Architecture reflecting geomorphology (Alava, Spain) – © Photoservice Electa/ Photoshot.

region of Italy. Over in Ireland, a sip of Irish stout has a completely different taste if it is enjoyed from a viewpoint overlooking the roofs of Dublin while inside the brewery. And the vast vineyards that can be admired through the huge glass windows of the tasting room at the award-winning Evelyn County Estate, in Australia, are more than just a breathtaking backdrop: they are part of the tasting experience itself. What is important is that a food and wine enterprise should make the surrounding scenery part of its offer and incorporate it into the tourist product.

Informative literature

Attention also needs to be given to the type of informative literature provided for visitors. Supplying them with technical sheets about the products is useful but rather limited; farm managers need to consider other support material such as flyers, brochures or even digital software that portray their enterprise in an appealing and attractive manner. Apart from information about the farm business and its products, other material could include leaflets giving details about the surrounding area and nearby attractions, local tourism information and descriptions of museums and other places of cultural interest. Information about places to stay in the area and where to go to eat will also be useful, particularly if these are in keeping with the ethos of the farm and specifically cater to visitor needs.

Whatever the case, all information material put at tourists' disposal should:

- convey the true spirit and essence of the farm and its region;
- give a realistic description;

- attract tourists by giving a clear overview of the offer and describe how a visit to the farm will enhance their vacation experience;
- be clear and easy to understand, with accurate, up-to-date information about the farm's activities (always remember to go through and correct drafts before going to press);
- communicate to the target audience in captivating language;
- be translated by native speakers with experience of the food, wine and tourism sectors, whenever possible;
- be attractively designed with high-resolution images;
- be printed in sufficient numbers to satisfy visitor needs; and
- be completely up to date (this is particularly important when the quality of a product varies from year to year) – it is not necessary to use expensive support material, it is the high quality of information that counts.

The staff

A professional approach

The staff who are responsible for receiving and welcoming tourists on a tour obviously play a fundamental role in making the visit a success. A food and wine enterprise offering a well-planned tour in architecturally striking surroundings, with state-of-the-art equipment and high-quality products, could still turn out to be a disappointment to visitors if personnel are incompetent or unsuitable for the task.

According to some producers who have extended their offer to include charming B&B accommodation and eating facilities, even the people who are responsible for room service must already have had some experience of working directly with the product (e.g. grapes in the vineyards); in this way, all the staff, regardless of their individual roles within the enterprise, have a working knowledge of what the farm has to offer in terms of production and are able to talk about it to the guests. However, the people who really need to display professional competence are those involved in guiding visitors on the tour and during the product tasting. The problem is that this can only be a full-time job when tourist demand remains high all year round. On small farms particularly, the person who guides visitors around is usually responsible for other aspects of the business too.

Whatever the case, it goes without saying that the person who takes visitors on a winery tour, no matter what their professional role is normally, must be an experienced wine taster or a qualified sommelier. On a dairy farm, it is vital that whoever is in charge of conducting the cheese tasting knows the precise and exact order in which to present cheese in order to exalt the taste and flavour and educate visitors' palates. A visit to an olive farm must be led by someone with experience of oil tasting, who can immediately identify the extra-virgin olive oil's characteristics, being able to distinguish between defective oils and the type of defect (e.g. mouldy taste) and the fragrance of an extra-virgin olive oil. They should also be able to identify the peppery, bitter taste of one oil and the milder, more delicate flavour of another.

However, technical knowledge on its own is not enough to guarantee a successful visit. The guide must also try to give visitors a bigger picture by putting the product into a wider context: retelling the history of the farm, describing farming traditions and implements, narrating the fortunes of the generations of families who have worked there, will make a visit come alive for tour participants. The history and development of the region can be explored, along with any connections with art and literature. An explanation could be given with regard to how geology and landscape have shaped the nature and quality of the product. And this is not all. A personal knowledge of dishes prepared by local chefs, restaurants, museums, hotels and other attractions in the area is essential, in order to be able to inform and guide visitors as thoroughly as possible.

In the case of foreign tourists, effective communication also depends on having a good working knowledge of at least one foreign language. Other essential qualities include being open to new experiences and having a readiness to learn, particularly with regard to new developments in farming and in the food and wine sector as a whole. A highly motivated person with good interpersonal skills, capable of firing enthusiasm and sensitive to visitor expectations, not only can make a tour satisfying for everyone but also turn it into a memorable occasion. Drawing on personal experience, a successful tour guide will develop strategies for dealing with difficult or dissatisfied clients and see these occasions as an opportunity to learn and grow professionally. It is not always easy to maintain the interest or attention of large groups, but if handled correctly, using appropriate verbal and body language for the target audience, visitor response will be positive and enthusiastic. Finally, the most important objective for anyone concerned with the visitor experience is that they truly represent the ethos of the farm business.

Internal communications and in-house training

The implementation of an effective internal communications policy is an essential business objective for any enterprise. Everyone involved, from administrative staff to farm workers, needs to have the right information, in the right way, at the right time, in order to function effectively. Coordinated, transparent and shared information that allows people to carry out their individual responsibilities efficiently creates a sense of common responsibility towards the enterprise and a shared commitment to its success. An internal community which believes in and supports company values will project a positive and powerful image of the business to the outside world.

For example, everyone on the staff needs to be informed about the different types of offers available, and to pass this information on to visitors. At the end of a winery tour, visitors should be informed if they can sample wines at the bar, if they can purchase wine and if there is a possibility to have it home delivered. If there is a restaurant in the vicinity owned by the same proprietors, then visitors need to be informed about this as well.

Finally, all personnel should be given the opportunity every now and then to develop their professional skills through in-house training or externally organized courses.

Style of welcome

A visitor to a *maison de champagne* in the Champagne region of France, which is part of a global luxury brands conglomerate and only produces bottles of premium champagne for the high-end market, will enjoy the gracious welcome of an impeccably dressed guide. With her dark suit, discreet jewellery and just a hint of make-up, she is the epitome of professionalism and elegance. Cordial, but never overly familiar, articulate and self-assured, she is the perfect guide for both individuals and small groups. At wine-tasting sessions, she serves the simple tourist with the same charm and courtesy as she would a foreign ambassador (Fig. 5.2).

A family-run business, even when it produces prestigious wines, will obviously have a more informal approach. Visitors may often be greeted by the proprietor of the estate. In this case, the added value is that a personal detailed, informed description of wine production can be given without the filter of any intermediaries.

It makes no difference whether the business is rooted in tradition and craftsmanship or if its focus is on innovation and creativity; what is important is that the welcome to visitors is personalized and coherent with the ethos and image that the enterprise wishes to communicate.

Fig. 5.2. A formal approach in a *maison de champagne* (France).

Organizing the visit: a general guide

Planning ahead

In order to plan a successful guided visit, a number of decisions need to be made beforehand. These include making decisions about:

- The policy to adopt with regard to guided visits. Should they be for individual visitors only, or just for groups, or both?
- Whether to accept only pre-booked visitors.
- Whether visits should only take place at fixed times.
- Whether to offer individual visitors the chance to tour the premises independently.
- Fixing a minimum and a maximum number of visitors, according to carrying capacity, so as to ensure that everyone has a pleasant visit, particularly in the tasting room.
- How long the visit should last. The length of time people will need to walk from one area to another, the length of any talks or videos and the amount of time dedicated to the tasting experience all need to be carefully calculated.
- Whether to accept visitors even during the most critical stages of work and production on the farm (e.g. during grape harvest time); creating difficulties perhaps for the workers but extremely exciting for visitors.
- Whether to organize tours even when nothing much is happening and there is not an awful lot to see in terms of farm activities (e.g. on an olive mill during the summer months). In this case, the tour needs to be particularly interesting in order to satisfy visitor expectations.
- The itinerary to be followed. It makes sense that the tour begins with the primary product before going on to look at the other phases of production, although some producers have

found that a more exciting approach is to begin in a more suggestive setting, e.g. in the wine vaults or in the maturing room for cheeses on a dairy farm. Visitors could then be taken on a tour of the production area so that they come into direct contact with the realities of life and work on the farm and their experience is not limited to a quick taste, followed by a visit to the farm shop (which, unfortunately, is often the case).

- Giving the itinerary a logical sequence, e.g. adopting the standard formula of tour–taste–purchase.
- Whether to charge an entrance fee for individuals and/or groups, and how to calculate the cost (according to what is included in the offer). Should it just cover the tour, or tour plus tasting, or even tasting and accompanying food? Issuing tickets makes it easier for the business to monitor visitor numbers and to calculate the financial impact of the tours on overall turnover. Charging a small entrance fee helps to cover the cost of the time, money and resources invested in creating and conducting the tours, as well as being an alternative source of income. At the same time, it gives 'value' to the visitor experience. Strangely enough, many producers operating in the food and wine sectors do not give much importance to or fully appreciate the positive financial contribution that comes from tourism, nor do they tend to monitor numbers or visitor typology. There is a real need to raise awareness in this area and to develop systems for data collection, analysis and interpretation, which would certainly help in defining long-term business strategies.
- Drawing up a basic text or outline of explanations that will be given during the tour, which can also be easily modified according to the target audience. Essential information should include technical details about the produce/product and production methods, if it is necessary to outsource for primary materials, distribution channels to market, etc. Visitors also need to know something about the people behind the business, its history, its buildings and architecture, its environmental and social policies, and any news or anecdotes that will arouse their interest. If independent tours are planned, appropriate materials need to be created and designed (explanatory leaflets, audio guides, etc.).
- Whether to prepare a surprise for visitors. This could be a meeting with a wine expert, with the producer, with the person responsible for looking after the vineyards or olive groves, with the cheese maker or the laboratory technician. It could take the form of a small gift or merchandising (a cheese knife or a cheese dish with the company logo, a wine drop stopper, a wine glass or a small bottle of extra-virgin olive oil); giving visitors the chance to taste a rare delicacy will render the tour even more memorable.

Conducting the tour

For a tour to be successful, the guide must:

- Fully explain the exact programme of the tour before it begins. This is particularly important if there are any problems or sudden changes to the usual schedule (e.g. one of the areas may be closed to visitors because of reconstruction, or perhaps stocks of the main product are temporarily sold out).
- Give visitors guidelines as to how they should behave during the tour so as not to interrupt or disturb people working. They need to be made aware of any potential dangers in the working environment (e.g. avoid touching machinery and equipment) and of the importance of treating their surroundings with respect. A polite reminder to visitors to keep together and not wander off, to keep pace and not slow things down, will also help create conditions for a smooth and enjoyable visit for everyone.

- Manage the time available effectively, adhering to the programme and maintaining everyone's attention by making sure there are no 'dead moments'.
- Speak clearly and effectively. Any explanations must be brief and to the point. Appropriate intonation and body language (maintaining eye contact, use of gestures, etc.) should be used in order to maintain interest.
- Have the technical knowledge to be able to give more in-depth information when required.
- Make sure that everyone understands a few basic concepts right from the very beginning. This will keep everyone interested, even those with little prior knowledge. The key is to modify language and content according to the target audience and to pause every now and then, checking to see if everyone has understood.
- Describe clearly and competently all the different phases of production, from the primary product to the finished one. For visitors to fully appreciate the relationship between production methods and the quality of the final product, they need to be informed about the roles that machinery and technology play. If traditional methods or craftsmanship play a part in production, visitors need to be told. But the same is also true if production methods are particularly innovative or creative. There is still a tendency for people to view traditional methods as being the only way to produce a 'genuine' product; being able to see exciting new machines and methods of production and then to finish a tour by tasting a premium product will go some way to help dispel the myth.
- Focus attention on the unique features that characterize the enterprise and give it its distinctive personality. This could be because of a particular or experimental production method, a commitment to sustainable or organic farming, or even workers' team spirit and dedication.
- Include information about other producers in the area and explain the strong connection that exists between food and the region, in particular the special partnership of food and wine.
- Provide information and documentation about all the products.
- Pick up on visitor satisfaction, getting feedback whenever possible and useful suggestions to improve the tour experience.
- Desist from giving banal or unnecessarily technical explanations. The guide must also avoid making false statements about the product to satisfy visitor expectations. In the same way, claiming to be the best on the market to the denigration of others is ethically wrong.
- Provide a memorable, enjoyable brand experience for everyone, instilling an indissoluble link in the visitor's mind between the tour and the product, creating a loyal customer base for the future.

The tasting session

A general guide

Perhaps the most important moment during a tour is the tasting session. By coming into direct contact with the product, the visitor is no longer a passive onlooker but becomes an active participant. The best way to appreciate the qualities of any food or wine product is through the five senses (e.g. in the sensory analysis of the characteristics of chocolate, even sound is used); the experience is further heightened by the knowledge gained about the product during the tour and having the opportunity to try it in its original environment. The characteristics or special features of a tasting room have already been described above. Generally, for non-professional visitors, a greater emphasis is placed on the pleasure of the experience. However, there are rules that need to be observed and tasting conditions need to be regulated (technical analysis, codes of conduct, specialized vocabulary).

Whatever the situation, the tasting experience will be more rewarding for the person conducting the session, as well as the participants, if the following steps are followed:

- Give useful advice to help people experiment with the five senses, encouraging them to use as many as possible when analysing a product in order to discover new qualities and characteristics.
- Teach visitors the correct techniques for carrying out a sensory analysis (or at least explain the basic rules to get started).
- Invite people to draw on their own personal experiences and memories of colour, sound, taste and smell – as their senses reawaken, visitors will learn how to have a more 'technical' appreciation of the product and discover its range of sensory characteristics.

A sensory profile of a product will emerge, even when an analysis is carried out by amateurs, if certain codified techniques are carried out. These techniques obviously vary from one type of product to another. Specific publications and guidelines are available outlining which techniques should be adopted, together with evaluation and testing sheets, from a number of organizations. For example in Italy, for wine tasting: AIS (The Association of Italian Sommeliers), ONAV (The National Association of Wine Tasters), for cheese tasting: ONAF (The National Association of Cheese Tasters); for oil tasting: ONAOO (The National Association of Oil Tasters); for cured meat tasting: ONAS (The National Association of Salumi Tasters).

Visitors who have never had any previous experience of sensory analysis can easily participate if they are given a clear set of guidelines. Regulations or techniques will vary according to the type of product undergoing the analysis; however, there are some procedures that are common to most tasting sessions. These are that the analysis is conducted:

- in favourable conditions with appropriate lighting, temperature and humidity;
- in places that are well-aired and are not contaminated by extraneous smells or odours;
- only on products that are well-preserved and in optimal condition;
- according to a coherent sequence (e.g. in wine tasting, one should begin with a dry *spumante* or a young, dry white wine before passing on to a mature, dry white, followed by a rosé, a young red wine, a more mature, full-bodied red wine, ending with a sweet *spumante* and a dessert wine; in cheese tasting, the milder, younger cheeses should be tasted first before going on to the stronger, more mature and fuller-flavoured ones);
- by a taster who is in good physical and psychological health, aware of the importance of conducting the analysis in the appropriate and correct manner (e.g. with a clean, prepared palate, having avoided rich or spicy food, coffee, cigarettes, etc. beforehand, and not wearing perfume or after-shave lotion);
- at an appropriate time of day (e.g. wines should be tasted in the morning after a light breakfast while cheeses are best tasted late morning or late afternoon);
- beginning with a visual examination of the product before going on to smell and to the olfactory taste analysis;
- with an appropriate number of samples in order to appreciate the different characteristics of the product without being too overwhelmed, particularly when there are less-experienced tasters; and
- with suggestions (perhaps even experimenting *in situ*) regarding possible food/wine partnerships to accompany the product, and advice about the ideal occasions to enjoy it (this is important for less-experienced tasters or when tasting is conducted during a meal or a food and wine pairing session on a wine estate or farm, see Fig. 5.3).

Fig. 5.3. Food and wine pairing (Sonoma Valley, California, USA).

Wine
Details given to visitors during a wine-tasting session should cover the following points:

- name and denomination (AOC, Grand Cru, DO, DOCG, DOC, etc.);
- vintage;
- typology (red, white, *spumante*, etc.);
- variety and blend of grape;
- origin (area of production, geographical location, soil composition, altitude, exposure and climatic conditions, etc.);
- agronomic information (vineyard management and work periods, grape production per hectare, etc.);
- production methods (harvesting, crushing, fermentation, ageing, bottling, etc.);
- chemical/scientific information (fermentation, temperature, sulphites, etc.);
- number of bottles produced a year;
- information on organoleptic properties (sight, smell, taste);
- conservation and storing methods; and
- pairing.

Cheese
Analysis during a cheese-tasting session would concentrate on:

- a visual examination of the appearance and consistency of the outer rind of the cheese (aspect, colour, thickness, etc.);

- a visual examination of the body for colour and texture;
- stage of mould growth;
- presence of eyes (holes);
- consistency to the touch;
- the quality and intensity of aroma during the olfactory test;
- flavour, structure, texture, retronasal olfaction, palatability, sweetness and mouthfeel attributes during the tasting test; and
- general product information (quantity, typology, dimension, distribution methods, etc.).

Further information could also be given with regard to origin and denomination, the type of pasture, the type of herd (ewes, cows or goats), the type of milk produced, production techniques, correct conservation, correct serving methods (e.g. what type of knife to use, how to cut the cheese), the use in cooking, accompaniments to complement the flavour (e.g. which particular wine, beer, bread, jam, honey or fruit best exalts the taste).

Olive oil

An olive oil analysis should begin by first identifying the presence of any defects. According to the official evaluation guidelines set down by the IOOC (International Olive Oil Council), the main defects are wineyness, roughness, a metallic taste, mould, muddiness, mustiness and rancidness. When there are no defects present (as in extra-virgin olive oil), the tester must use the senses of smell and taste to identify fruitiness (grassiness or nuttiness), bitterness and pepperiness; and then if the olive oil is sweet and if it tastes herbaceous or 'green' (leaves or grass), or of dried fruit, artichokes, apples, almonds, tomatoes and so on. Unlike wine and cheese, a visual examination is not called for, as the colour of olive oil is not considered to be a relevant sensory descriptor.

Beer

A beer analysis begins with a visual examination in order to evaluate the clarity, the colour, the richness of head or foam and the degree of carbonation. The olfactory test serves to identify the beer's aroma. A sensory analyst will able to distinguish if the dominating scent is the sweet smell of malt or the lighter, more citric scent of hops, and if there are fruity undertones, etc. The olfactory taste analysis concentrates on the beer's flavour (acidic, sweet or bitter), its strength, drinkability and mouthfeel attributes.

Cured meats

Using the senses of sight and touch, an analysis is made of the external appearance of the meat (hardness and darkness of the skin, colour, homogeneity, fat, marbling, sheen); odour (aroma, rancid odour, mould odour); texture (hardness, softness, crumbliness, fibrousness, pastiness, adhesiveness); and flavour (flavour, saltiness, rancid flavour, pungency, sweetness).

Coffee

An espresso should ideally be tasted from a small, half-filled coffee cup. Descriptors for a sensory analysis include: the intensity of colour, the thickness and texture of foam (this should be dense and compact, light brown in colour and laced with a few dark brown streaks), the intensity of aroma (lightly scented with an aroma of fresh flowers or fruit), flavour (initially acidic or bitter, but light and pleasant, then sweet), mouthfeel (full-bodied, smooth, not astringent) and retronasal notes like the aroma of freshly baked bread or pastry that is unique to Arabic coffee (Illy Università del Caffè, 2008).

Chocolate

All five senses are used in the sensory analysis of chocolate. A visual examination focuses on colour (from dark ebony to a reddish-brown). Attention is also given to the sound that it makes as it is broken into pieces (this should be a sharp, clean-cut sound), the dominating scent and secondary notes (flowery, green, toasted, malty, caramel, dried fruit, red fruits, spicy, wood, tobacco, etc.). The tasting analysis concentrates on flavour, whether it is astringent, bitter, sweet or acidic for example, and the mouthfeel attributes (e.g. smooth or grainy).

Involving the tasters

The person responsible for guiding a food and/or wine itinerary must demonstrate the same qualities during the tasting session as during the tour, namely: the ability to communicate and give precise and accurate information, be capable of synthesis, be able to involve everyone in the group, have an awareness of different target needs, be open-minded and flexible, and able to offer a personalized service to all visitors.

Furthermore, the tasting session is an opportunity to give visitors a multidisciplinary and synesthetic experience by integrating different sensory modalities. A professional and creative guide can provide visitors with an exciting new sensory experience by evoking the particular characteristics of the land from which the product has been crafted. Not only does this serve to emphasize the inextricable link between a product and its *terroir*, but it also stimulates visitors to explore and to experience the countryside further, to discover with their own eyes the region that has just offered them such a remarkable tasting experience. For example, the distinct flavour of a Vitovska wine (taste) could be associated with the salt-filled breeze (touch, smell) that ruffles the vines on the hills (sight) of the Carso Triestino, on the borders with Italy and Slovenia, the area of origin for that particular wine. This kind of experiment is only successful, however, if visitors can be led towards discovering their own ability to 'see with their mouth and nose'; in other words, during a cheese-tasting session on a dairy farm in the Dolomite mountains, the visitor should be able to visualize those very same cows, from whose rich and creamy milk the cheese is produced, grazing in their Alpine pastures.

The tasting session also offers other opportunities for visitors to enjoy a new or unexpected experience. A producer could, for example:

- treat everyone to a surprise by offering them something out of the ordinary (e.g. cracking open a bottle of the most prestigious wine produced on the estate, cutting open a whole parmesan cheese and immediately offering everyone a sliver, offering a spoon of warm, fresh ricotta cheese);
- propose wine tasting around a particular theme (e.g. vertical wine tasting);
- give everyone an evaluation sheet (even an informal one) with the correct descriptors and terminology for a sensory analysis of the product, but leaving enough space for participants to fill in their own observations; and
- create alternative itineraries that involve visitor participation.

At the end (or at the beginning, if visitors do not have their own evaluation sheets to fill in), everyone should be given a printed list of technical specifications for each product examined.

As can be seen in Fig. 5.4, welcoming tourists to a farm or winery signifies more than just giving them a tour and a description of production methods; it means sharing with them the twin pleasures of discovery and appreciation, and this is particularly true in the tasting session. By using the correct mix of techniques, implementing entertaining strategies for learning, and adopting a combination of different styles and ideas adapted for the target, it is possible to create a strong association between the technical data of the product and the local environment

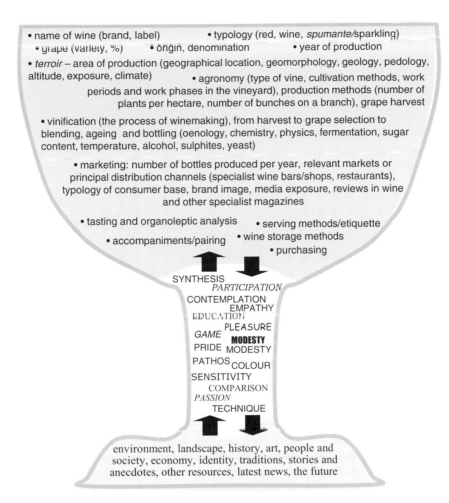

- name of wine (brand, label)
- typology (red, wine, *spumante*/sparkling)
- grape (variety, %)
- origin, denomination
- year of production
- *terroir* – area of production (geographical location, geomorphology, geology, pedology, altitude, exposure, climate)
- agronomy (type of vine, cultivation methods, work periods and work phases in the vineyard), production methods (number of plants per hectare, number of bunches on a branch), grape harvest
- vinification (the process of winemaking), from harvest to grape selection to blending, ageing and bottling (oenology, chemistry, physics, fermentation, sugar content, temperature, alcohol, sulphites, yeast)
- marketing: number of bottles produced per year, relevant markets or principal distribution channels (specialist wine bars/shops, restaurants), typology of consumer base, brand image, media exposure, reviews in wine and other specialist magazines
- tasting and organoleptic analysis
- serving methods/etiquette
- accompaniments/pairing
- wine storage methods
- purchasing

SYNTHESIS
PARTICIPATION
CONTEMPLATION
EMPATHY
EDUCATION
PLEASURE
GAME   MODESTY
PRIDE MODESTY
PATHOS COLOUR
SENSITIVITY
COMPARISON
PASSION
TECHNIQUE

environment, landscape, history, art, people and society, economy, identity, traditions, stories and anecdotes, other resources, latest news, the future

Fig. 5.4. A total experience: discovering wine and its region of origin through words and images.

(economy, art, culture, history, stories and interesting anecdotes, legends and facts, people and identity, and other regional products). By emphasizing the product's links with the region through words and images, visitors are given a complete and fulfilling experience.

Purchasing the product

It is not always possible to buy farm products directly from the producer. There may not be an on-site shop, or it could be a question of marketing and a conscious decision on the part of the producer to avoid entering into competition with its own distributors. However, the act of purchasing a product undeniably brings the visit to a close and is an extremely important phase for the producer.

There are some enterprises that have their own internal shops, operating on the basis of selling nearly all their production through direct sales. On the other hand, there are others who only make a very small percentage on what they sell to visitors. It is interesting to note, however, that many producers who sell only between 2 and 3% of their production in direct sales say that even this small amount is an important form of publicity. Nearly all producers who are involved in food and wine tourism declare that at least 50% of visitors who have enjoyed their tour will buy one or more products, plus the sale of tickets also makes an important financial contribution. The role the tour guide plays at this stage is again of utmost importance: with a friendly smile, alert and attentive to customer needs and an ability to advise customers, the guide's behaviour will have a direct impact on purchasing decisions.

Another important aspect to remember is that in order to appeal to visitors, the point of sale must look attractive and be well-stocked. As an integral part of the offer, it must mirror the image that the business wants to present to the outside world. The visual impact will be even stronger, and the image reinforced, if a common theme (e.g. style, use of colour) is used to link the décor and layout with the wine and food labels, boxes or containers, etc. It is also extremely important that the products tested during the tasting session are on sale, along with the principal or more popular products. If, for some reason, the shop is out of stock of a particular product, customers should be informed immediately and advice given with regard to alternative ways to purchase it.

Products need to be displayed attractively and samples must be replaced frequently to retain their organoleptic characteristics. Prices should be clear and easily visible, and ideally should not compete with local distributors. The producer may also decide to sell other local and regional products to complement the farm's own products. Additional merchandise could include wine drop stoppers, cheese boards, bags, T-shirts or other apparel printed with the enterprise's logo, books and guides, and examples of local handicrafts.

Customers should be able to pay by direct debit or credit card. They also need to be provided with appropriate containers (clearly marked with the logo) that guarantee the correct conservation and safe transport of any products they have purchased. Offering the possibility of home delivery, as we have already seen, certainly works to the producer's advantage. A visitor is much more likely to buy something, particularly if they come from abroad, if they know that they will not have to carry any extra weight or run into problems with customs and border police because of security regulations. Efficient and speedy home delivery (with perhaps a surprise gift inside the parcel) is ideal for impressing a new client and building customer loyalty.

Expanding the tourist product

Producers may decide to expand their offer even further by introducing other services or activities (Fig. 5.5). This means having the necessary economic, structural and technological resources as well as acquiring a new set of skills in the area of human resources.

For instance, a farm or food factory could organize events for both private and corporate clients (e.g. festive occasions, wedding banquets and gala dinners) and offer catering services, either on-site or in special locations. A winery, for example, could organize a buffet lunch in the wine vaults, or in the case of an olive mill, in the olive grove. Another possibility is for the farm or enterprise to offer health and beauty treatments based on the main company product and, if appropriate, using residue products. Creating an on-site restaurant or wine bar is another way to increase or improve the tourist product. Many producers choose to offer guest accommodation. Depending on the type of enterprise, this can range from simple B&B accommodation to luxury apartments furnished with antiques, or even architect-designed hotel rooms.

Fig. 5.5. Example of a potential oenogastronomic tourist product.

Herederos de Marqués de Riscal, a leading Spanish wine producer, is an excellent example of a winery offering numerous integrated services and facilities. Its 'Ciudad del Vino' ('City of Wine') in Elciego (Alava, Spain) is a specially designed complex that includes the most ancient wine cellar of Rioja (1858) and an exciting, new building designed by the architect Frank O. Gehry. The building houses a luxury hotel, a spa offering vinotherapy treatments, a restaurant, a meeting room and a conference centre.

Cultural events and gatherings, meetings and seminars organized by the company also serve to attract new clients or visitors. They present a perfect opportunity to put the company in the spotlight and raise company profile.

Some ideas that have already been tried out successfully are:

- conferences on art and wine, medicine and wine, literature and wine, on local handicrafts, on the creative cuisine of up-and-coming local chefs who use produce/company products in their recipes;
- classical music, blues, pop-rock and jazz concerts (the notes of the music evoking the tastes and sensations of the produce/products);
- art and photography exhibitions with the product as a central theme;
- journalism and literary awards;
- book presentations;
- menu-tasting dinners organized around a theme, perhaps restricted to club members;

- cookery and wine courses, oil-, cheese- and chocolate-tasting courses;
- sports or fitness events such as hiking or mountain-biking in the surrounding area, guided walks in the vineyards or olive groves; and
- fund-raising auctions where the most prestigious produce/products are sold to raise money for various charitable initiatives.

Club membership could also be added, entitling members, after the payment of a registration fee, to enjoy special privileges such as:

- home delivery of selected products like reserve wines, limited production or special label wines not normally available to the general public, along with other accompanying products;
- free wine tasting during company visits;
- discounts on company products;
- invitations to special events (lunches, dinners, special product tasting, trips);
- participation in company activities, for example the grape harvest;
- receiving newsletters via e-mail or direct mail and publications; and
- free access to the company web site containing recipes, product information, suggestions for food and wine pairing, etc.

Some wineries also offer a recorking service for vintage wine.

Museums can play a very important role in promoting a company's products, particularly if visitors have not had access, for whatever reason, to the production process. There are museums for all different types of products. To cite Italy as an example, there is the Museum of the Art and Technology of Sugared Almond Production of Pelino in Sulmona, the Olive Museum of Fratelli Carli in Imperia, the Lungarotti Foundation Wine Museum in Torgiano and the 'G. Amarelli' Museum of Liquorice in Rossano. Some producers have also set up exhibitions that are not strictly connected to production methods or techniques. The Glass Museum, in the Banfi Castle in Montalcino, which illustrates the history of the art of glass making from the 15th century to today, is a perfect example.

For a museum visit to be effective and meaningful, it must be educationally valid with well-displayed, clearly labelled exhibits and hands-on activities in order to foster visitor participation. An enthusiastic and well-prepared guide can also encourage tourists to interact and play an active role. For instance, in France, at the Moutarderie Fallot in Beaune, Burgundy, tourists discover how difficult it is to prepare the perfect mustard: a few volunteers are invited to make their own mustard from the ingredients available. Using a pestle and mortar each one prepares their own recipe (Fig. 5.6). The winner is the person who manages to select and combine the ingredients to make the closest resemblance, in terms of taste and consistency, to the company's own mustard, the prize being a selection of mustards.

Self-evaluation of visitor welcome quality

Once a business has formulated a clear policy with regard to the type of tourist product it intends to offer, it must then elaborate procedures to evaluate its performance, with particular focus on product effectiveness and visitor satisfaction.

One way of monitoring internal tourist product performance is to set up a self-assessment system, similar in a way to HACCP (Hazard Analysis and Critical Control Points), with which most businesses operating in the food and wine sector are already familiar. This type of system permits risk assessments to be made at each stage of the 'production line' and to put into place preventive measures; the focus in this case being on the successful outcome of the tourist

Fig. 5.6. Visitors getting involved into the production process of *moutard* (Bourgogne, France).

visit and client satisfaction rather than food hygiene and safety. Below are some suggestions of criteria to apply that could be helpful in formulating a self-assessment analysis:

- The people who will be making the assessment need to be properly trained.
- A protocol needs to be developed to define the ideal approach and actions to be taken for a tour to be successful.
- A flow chart could be used not only to identify all the different activities that make up the tour, but also to designate the best people to be responsible for those activities.
- Possible 'dangers' need to be identified and the type of risks which could affect the successful outcome of the tour analysed.
- Critical control points should be identified, with particular reference to the different activities or actions that take place at each stage of the tour and which are crucial to its success.
- Having identified critical control points, it is necessary to establish parameters so that visitor satisfaction is not jeopardized.
- Collected data should be reviewed on a regular basis.
- Once problems or drawbacks have been identified, appropriate strategies to rectify these must be defined and implemented.
- A decision must be made as to how the analysis will be conducted and carried out.
- A reliable system for recording and storing data needs to be set up.

One way of assessing customer satisfaction is to distribute questionnaires at the end of a visit. If clients also consent to provide personal information, this can be invaluable for building a customer database and profiling new consumer targets. The tour guide can also carry out an informal survey by inviting people to comment on how pleased they are with the tour or tasting session, or if they are happy with the choice of products in the shop, for example. Asking people to sign a visitors' book and express their opinion of their visit is another way to gauge customer satisfaction.

Whatever method is decided upon, the producer must:

- listen to people's opinions and treat even negative comments as an opportunity to take action and improve the visitor experience;
- analyse feedback and the effects that the visits have on the business itself in terms of infrastructure and production, economic gain, public image and on the surrounding area or region; and
- look for ways to constantly improve their offer, investing time and energy to make the experience memorable for everyone.

GASTRONOMIC TOURISM FOR KIDS: WHERE TO START[1]

Holidays are meant to be a time of fun and relaxation for all the family, young and old. If the holiday also offers opportunities to learn or try something new, all the better. Unfortunately, families are often let down because tourism operators do not always know how to respond to the diverse needs of their clients. Even those who offer child/family-friendly tourist products are not always up to the task, as they are unable to cope with offering simultaneous activities to visitors from a range of ages and backgrounds, with different tastes, needs and interests.

Cultural tourism is becoming a popular holiday choice for families with young children. They seem to be opting more and more to travel to cultural destinations rather than taking a traditional seaside or mountain holiday; rather than choosing to stay in just one place, many seem to be keen on touring and visiting more than one destination during their holiday.

Many parents are also having children later in life and, as a target segment, they have quite clear demands. They seek active holidays that can satisfy every member of the family, organized by skilled and professional operators who can offer stimulating experiences in safe, secure environments.

A well-planned gastronomic tourist product can respond to all these needs and offer excellent opportunities and experiences for all the family.

Guidelines for welcoming children (and their parents) on a gastronomic tour

There are of course many model farms and botanical gardens already in existence that welcome young visitors. The majority of these tend to be children and adolescents on a school trip and they will probably have already done some kind of preparation in class before the visit. Food or wine production enterprises can however organize tours that will appeal to both children and parents.

Nevertheless, there are some important considerations to make:

- Being outside in the open air, and being able to experiment through hands-on activities, is enormously important for a child's cognitive and psychological development (Fig. 5.7). Children should be given the opportunity, therefore, to be actively involved through travel, play and manual activities in some part of the production process, so they feel that they have directly contributed to creating the produce they will later get to eat.

Fig. 5.7. Young tourists at work in a model farm (Piemonte, Italy) (credit: Elisabetta Cane).

- A child's sense of taste needs to be educated and stimulated in exactly the same professional manner as an adult's.
- Even for children as young as 3–4 years old, it is possible to organize simple activities to involve them in the tour. However, 5-year-olds and upwards will be much more interested in travelling and seeing the different stages of production and the type of manual work that it involves; they especially enjoy having the opportunity to imitate and 'work' like grown-ups.
- Children grow up: a responsive, sensitive child, who learns more about the agroalimentary chain through stimulating activities and experiences today, will be tomorrow's aware consumer.
- Understanding the story of a product from its very beginnings to the time it arrives on the dinner table can foster a greater interest in different types of food (not just focused on calorie content as so often happens) and an appreciation of what goes into transforming a raw product into a finished one.
- Coming into direct contact with the world of production and learning something about nutrition can help eliminate bad eating habits.
- Children can be extremely curious and attentive, but they can also be restless and impatient. They are not the easiest of public audiences, although working with them can be incredibly satisfying. Tour personnel need to be professional in their dealings with them, open and firm, enthusiastic and capable of engaging the children's attention.
- Children can be captivated by even very small things.

To ensure that a gastronomic tour for young visitors is successful, there are a few ground rules to be followed:

- They need to feel involved, and discover exciting new things that are flavoursome and good to eat.
- Children's attention spans can be very short. If tours are too long or explanations too difficult or detailed, they will quickly become bored (after all they are on holiday). Information should be tailored to explaining concepts that children can easily understand and assimilate.
- An inductive, active approach to activities will be more successful than a deductive one.
- Manual activities such as mixing ingredients to make a cake or actively helping on the farm are good ways to excite children's natural curiosity.
- Language must be kept simple and direct.
- During tasting sessions children's taste memories need to be awakened so that familiar tastes and experiences can be applied to new concepts, colours and flavours.
- Children should be invited to give an opinion about a product freely, in a relaxed atmosphere, without feeling under pressure or judged by others in the group.
- Any explanations or questions should lead to the acquisition of new concepts.
- The gastronomic tourist product must always be tailored to the age of the participant.
- Learning through playing is the best way to render children protagonists of the tasting experience.
- It is important to help children understand, by keeping their attention focused, explaining in simple language the relationship between cause and effect, between the act of production and the act of consumption, between the raw material and the finished.
- Children need to have a visual idea of quantity, so they need measuring instruments like ladles and spoons.
- The theme or topic of the visit is more important than giving a detailed explanation of all aspects of the business. At a dairy farm for instance, it is sufficient to explain the product cycle of just one cheese without trying to give information about all the other farm products.
- Product and production methods can be linked to the lives of the people who work the land; stories and legends can be retold, customs and traditions explained.
- Support materials such as paper and crayons should be on hand, as well as simple toys and games connected to the theme of the visit; a simple, attractively illustrated information leaflet with basic information about the product could be given to all the young tour participants.
- Children on a tour should also be given a simple map of the layout of the premises so that they can construct a mental plan of the geography of the place and its surrounding area (Fig. 5.8).
- Activities should be organized to involve the younger visitors as well as the older ones.
- The aim should be to educate children's sense of taste and stimulate the other senses in a professional way but using clear, direct language and simple, easy-to-understand concepts.
- A multidisciplinary approach should be adopted.
- Explanations involving new concepts or instructions for manual activities should be repeated slowly and clearly, but without being too insistent.
- Every effort should be made to learn the names of the young participants, to involve them in the activity by calling them by name and using a tone of voice that is reassuring and engaging.
- Children need to be praised for their efforts.
- Group work and collaboration should be encouraged in a supportive, uncompetitive atmosphere.

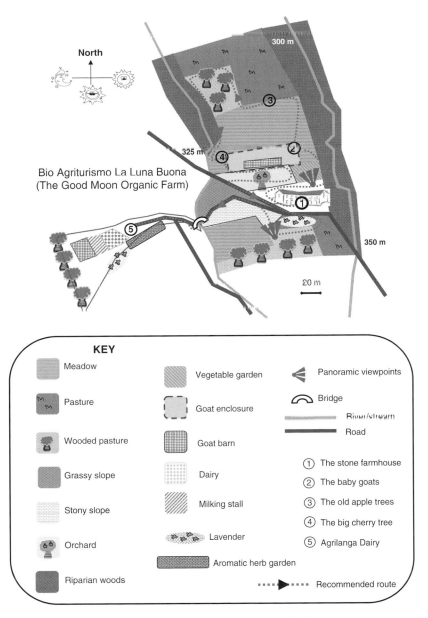

Fig. 5.8. Down on the farm: illustrated map (source: Cane, 2010).

- Giving the children an easy-to-read, attractively illustrated programme of the planned activities beforehand will excite their curiosity and interest.
- Parental presence should be reassuring and not intrusive.
- The carrying capacity of the building/room/space used during group tours should always be calculated beforehand, taking into account the kind of activity planned, and the age and needs of the participants.
- Whenever possible, permanent spaces or areas should be set up with materials and equipment already laid out for the planned activities. Attention needs to be paid to the children's

comfort and safety, so furniture and equipment should be appropriate for the targeted age group. Any possible dangers or risks (e.g. in handling machinery or tools) should be clearly communicated orally and visually, through well-displayed, easy-to-understand signs and posters.

- Children should not have direct contact with dangerous machinery or handle potentially hazardous materials.
- Parents need to be told before the visit if their children need to be dressed in particular clothes for their own safety; e.g. they may need to wear sturdy, non-slip shoes, or wear a jumper inside a chilly wine cellar, or a sunhat and T-shirt to protect them from the sun if they are working outside.
- Outdoor activities are ideal as children have the space and freedom to move as well as getting idea of the important role the environment plays in food production, as long as they are not distracted by their surroundings.
- A take-home gift at the end of the tour connected to the theme of the visit will be greatly appreciated and will serve to remind children of their 'gastronomic experience' once they return home, e.g. a colouring book with games; simple illustrations outlining production methods, stories and recipes; a small jar of jam, a piece of cheese or even a bread roll.
- At the end of the visit, the tour participants could be given a short questionnaire to gauge their satisfaction with the tour and/or activities. For younger children, illustrations reminding them of what they have seen during the tour or the activities they have taken part in would be helpful and encourage them to fill in the questionnaire.

In the same way that a group of adults would use a tasting score sheet during a tasting session, children will also enjoy learning about the different characteristics of a product and compiling a record of their sensations on a specially designed tasting sheet (Fig. 5.9). Using colour and printed illustrations, they can depict or record the colour, shape, texture, taste and smell of a product. This kind of concentrated activity helps the children to focus on and remember their sensory experiences.

Each tasting sheet should contain the main characteristics of the product. At a cheese tasting for example, the score sheet should ask the children to observe the aspect and colour of the cheese, its structure, if there are any holes in the cheese, the texture and tonality, the smell of the rind and the olfactive and taste sensations. In other product tastings, children could be asked, for example, to compare and evaluate the crumbly consistency of biscuits, the crustiness, firmness and moisture in bread, the persistence of taste in honey, the coarseness of flour, etc. Another exciting sensory experience is to try to combine the same product with a number of different ones, e.g. tasting the same jam but on different types of bread.

Again, as in an adult tasting session, the physical characteristics and the organoleptic sensations that the children will need to identify in a product need to be clearly described, as well as explaining the meaning of the different terms used. Explanations should be straightforward but not over-simplified. The use of correct terminology, accompanied by simple and practical examples to illustrate new concepts, is recommended. At no time should any of the participants feel uncomfortable or inadequate to the task. Asking the children for their help during the tasting 'game' will help maintain interest and make them feel more involved in the activity. Appealing to their memories also helps them to develop their sensory ability, e.g. they can be asked to associate a familiar organoleptic sensation (pleasurable or disgusting) with the memory of a certain object, event or routine. Drawing out their sensations and experiences in this way helps them to become more articulate and develops their ability to express themselves.

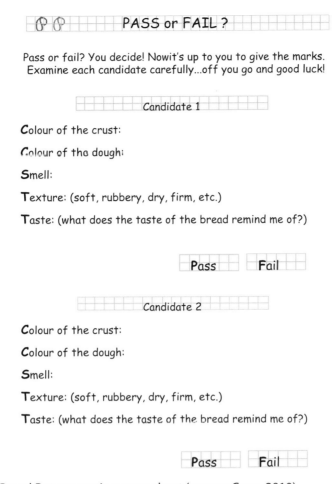

PASS or FAIL ?

Pass or fail? You decide! Now it's up to you to give the marks.
Examine each candidate carefully...off you go and good luck!

Candidate 1

Colour of the crust:

Colour of the dough:

Smell:

Texture: (soft, rubbery, dry, firm, etc.)

Taste: (what does the taste of the bread remind me of?)

Pass   Fail

Candidate 2

Colour of the crust:

Colour of the dough:

Smell:

Texture: (soft, rubbery, dry, firm, etc.)

Taste: (what does the taste of the bread remind me of?)

Pass   Fail

Fig. 5.9. The Bread Report: tasting score sheet (source: Cane, 2010).

It can also serve to explain why children like some products more than others, or even why they refuse to eat certain products.

The layout and atmosphere of the tasting room is extremely important. The lighting and temperature need to be just right, the décor needs to be neutral and the room needs to be odourless so as not to interfere with the organoleptic qualities of the product. If the weather permits, the tasting session can also be organized outside in the open air, as long as there are not too many distractions. Participating in a cheese tasting while being able to see the animals grazing in the meadows will render the experience even more stimulating and gratifying for a child.

Children do, however, have different perceptions of size and space compared with an adult. A large room will appear much larger to a child. It is important therefore to come up with some stratagems that will make a tour seem shorter than it really is. It is obviously almost impossible to create a space that is totally in keeping with children's needs (unlike nursery school, where everything is built on a small scale so that the children do not feel dwarfed), but small gestures can make a difference: putting leaflets explaining the day's activities at a height that is easily accessible can make a child feel valued and independent.

Box 5.1. Case Studies.

- The Maison Champy, one of the most famous wine cellars in Beaune, Burgundy (France), also offers a tasting programme for younger visitors: 'A la recherche des arômes'. The programme has been specifically devised for 4- to 18-year-olds. The children (mainly of primary school age) can attend a mini-course lasting about 2 hours in which they discover tasting techniques and how to develop their sensory ability. As future consumers and potential wine tasters, they learn how to select, place, recognize and memorize the perfumes and aromas of plants and essences (e.g. lemon notes in the melissa plant), and to associate tasting sensations (sweet, savoury, bitter, acidic) with foods that they are already familiar with (salt, sugar, lemons, unripened fruit, or vanilla and ginger in home-made *pain d'épices*, etc.). The final tasting is managed exactly like a technical tasting session, except that the panel tasters drink orange juice instead of wine.

- Guido Pastor is a unique bee-keeping enterprise in Cisterna d'Asti, Piemonte, Italy: unique in the sense that the young visitor learns all about keeping honey bees through role play. For a few hours, the children are transformed into bees, search out the flowers that they need to produce honey and protect the queen bee who coordinates and commands life inside the beehive. The role play helps to keep the children's attention focused and creates an atmosphere of quiet concentration. Even more importantly, however, it brings home to children the type of care that bees need, the problems that bee-keepers face, how important a clean environment is for the well-being of the bees, and just how difficult honey production is. At the end of the activity, the children are taken on a tour of the working environment, where they can see the bees at work and the quantity of honey produced. There is also a small laboratory for wax transformation. At the end of the tour, there is a tasting session and participants get to try honeys from all over the world. They are encouraged to observe differences in colour and to identify the different tastes in order to understand how honeys made from bees in different parts of the world have a totally different sweetness; some can even have a slightly salty taste. The children begin the workshop by closing their eyes and associating a past experience with the honey taste on their palate. Before going home, each child receives a jar of honey as a present.

Other ideas for children's activities connected to the world of food production and transformation include:

- Simple cooking classes (perhaps led by a celebrity chef); children can be given a special bag or box to take home a sample of what they have made.
- Guided tastings of jam, vegetable, cheese, bread, oil, cured meat, etc.
- Fruit picking.
- Visiting a flour mill to understand how a grain of wheat is transformed into bread or biscuits; the visit can be rounded off with a bread-baking session and tasting.
- Visiting a dairy farm or cheese factory, where they can follow every step of the product's journey from pasture to table; at the end of the tour the children can be given the opportunity to make a small cheese.
- Joining in the activities on a farm such as milking or helping with the honey harvest.
- Learning to identify and catalogue aromatic herbs in a herb garden.
- Guided nature walks across farmland or woodland; storytelling workshops on a gastronomic theme, etc.

Mealtimes, especially during the holidays, hold a particular significance for children. When they sit down to eat they have exactly the same right as an adult to enjoy the food in a pleasurable atmosphere. Some ideas for getting restaurants to be more child-friendly include:

- Offering menus specifically created for young diners where they have a selection of dishes to choose from. An illustrated menu will facilitate them in their choice.
- Avoiding offering children just one course, such as a smaller portion of pasta with tomato sauce or hamburger and chips, usually accompanied by a fizzy drink and a chocolate dessert. Children's menus should offer a carefully selected choice of tasty local produce or specialities.
- Creating designated spaces with low tables and chairs and unbreakable china. Some children will enjoy having the opportunity to sit down with others of a similar age under the expert guidance of an adult, giving their parents a little time to themselves and allowing them to enjoy their meal tête-à-tête in an adjacent room.

NOTE

[1] This section of the chapter has been written in collaboration with Elisabetta Cane.

chapter 6

Food and Wine Tourism Best Practice: Case Studies from Around the World

Studying the theory behind what constitutes good business practice is fine, as long as its application brings concrete and effective results. Therefore, this chapter is entirely dedicated to looking at a selection of food and wine enterprises that have successfully incorporated tourism hospitality into their product. The case studies set out below range from large international brands to small producers and have been selected by the authors based on their own personal experience of the producer's professional approach and efficient organization. Within the following pages, food and wine producers in particular (but also students of gastronomic tourism and other operators in the sector) will find many new ideas to help them plan, develop and organize tours to welcome visitors to their wineries, farms and other food or wine enterprises. For those who already organize and manage gastronomic tours, it is hoped that the cases below will serve as a valuable benchmark.

In the analyses, each production sector is represented by at least one case study with an explanation of how each different phase of the tour is organized. In some cases, alternative ideas for tours have been added to increase tourism potential and to give a more complete idea of possible visitor management and organization.

AT THE WINERY

Californian wineries have always been the leading edge as far as tourism hospitality is concerned:

> As way back as the beginning of the 1990s, in a country considered by Italians as being totally lacking in gastronomic culture, American winemakers were already demonstrating their great

skills in welcoming visitors to their cellars and estates. Because they found themselves having to popularize a wine culture in a country that knew very little about the product (unlike France or Italy where wine has always been part of everyday life), they had little option but to open their doors to visitors in order to make their product known. Not only did they fling their cellar doors open, they already had restaurants on their premises, gadgets in their gift shops and all kinds of events going on.

(Petrini and Padovani, 2005)

One winery in particular stands out for its commitment to reaching out to the general public: the Robert Mondavi Winery in Oakville, Napa Valley, California. They have been welcoming visitors almost since the first day they opened in 1966 and over the years they have developed a rich and lively education programme. Their approach is clearly stated on their web site:

Educating the American public about wine, food and the arts has always been part of the philosophy behind Robert Mondavi Winery. The winery was one of the first to present educational tours and programs, culinary events, concerts and art exhibits and its visitor programs have become world-renowned.

(www.robertmondaviwinery.com)

The visit

Organization

- The Mondavi winery can be visited and experienced in a number of different ways: visitors can choose to go on a straightforward tour of the wine cellars followed by a tasting session, or those with more knowledge of wine can opt to do a technical tasting course. They can explore the nuances of food and wine matching over lunch or enjoy a sumptuous evening meal and vertical tastings of the winery's most prestigious wines in an exclusive and suggestive setting. The choice is extensive. Winery tours and tastings: 'Signature tour and tasting' (max. 15 persons, pre booking essential); 'Discovery tour' (max. 20 persons, children welcome); 'Wine tasting basics' (max. 15 persons); 'Exclusive cellar tasting' (max. 10 persons); 'Twilight tour' (max. 15 persons). Wine and food tours and tastings: 'The "Harvest of Joy" tour and lunch' (max. 10 persons); 'Al fresco lunch in the garden' (max. 12 persons); 'To Kalon vineyard trek and picnic lunch' (max. 10 persons); 'Wine and chocolate expression' (max. 10 persons); 'The "Four Decades" tasting and dinner' (for 6–10 persons). Wine education: 'Aromas and flavors of wine' (max. 10 persons); 'Wine tasting beyond basics' (max. 10 persons).
- The most complete tour of the winery, named 'Signature tour and tasting', covering every aspect of wine production, is extremely popular and pre-booking is highly recommended. An entry fee is charged and tours take place at fixed times.
  - The tour follows the grape's journey from vineyard to bottle:

    this renowned winery tour follows the path of the grape from the vineyard to the cellar to the finished wine. Guests view our famous To Kalon Vineyard and the inner workings of the winery, including fermentation and barrel ageing. The tour concludes with a seated educational tasting of three wines. (www.robertmondaviwinery.com)

  - Maximum number of participants: 15.
  - Children under the age of 13 are not accepted on this particular tour, but other child-friendly tours have been devised to keep younger visitors happy.
  - Tour length: about 75 minutes.
  - Groups are also welcomed during the grape harvest.

    ○   Information about the winery (original founders, company history, distribution and markets, etc.) is given during the tour but not in any particular order.

    ○   The wine educator's approach is friendly and informal.

Arrival and welcome

- The winery is immediately recognizable from a distance as visitors will already have visited the winery's web site to book the tour.
- The names of the tour participants are registered at the Visitor Welcome Center.
- Great attention has been given to the visitor areas: elegant and stylish interiors in keeping with the setting and atmosphere of a leading California wine estate; beautifully maintained lawns and vineyards, contemporary art pieces, fountains and shady trellises on the outside.
- As individual visitors arrive before the appointed time of the tour, the tour guide (in casual clothes) greets them and introduces himself and gradually gathers everybody together into a group.
- Once everyone is present, the group is formally welcomed in a small room furnished with a few chairs set in a semicircle and maps on the walls, clearly visible to all. The maps serve as a vital visual support to the opening explanations about the Californian wine-growing areas, focusing on the Mondavi estate. The geographic and climatic features that make it such an ideal territory for wine-growing are described, before going on to explaining the concept of *terroir*. The type of language used is simple and to the point, and only goes into more technical explanations once it becomes clear from tour members' questions that they would like to have more detailed or specific information.
- Winemaking is described as an 'outdoor sport' and wine is likened to a newborn baby that needs to be cared for, step by step, as it grows and matures.

FURTHER IDEAS

- Different meeting points around a wine estate can be set up for tour groups, particularly if they have booked in advance. One winery that was visited gathers people together under a centuries-old oak tree just by the winery entrance.
- Individual visitors might like to have the opportunity to visit a winery without a guide; this also frees staff from being explicitly engaged to accompany groups. Armed with an audio-guide, information leaflets and interpretive panels to guide them around the estate, tourists can enjoy an independent visit before joining a tasting session led by an expert from the winery. Individual visits such as these represent a great saving on human resources, but possible problems can arise when people have a lack of respect for their surroundings. Careless visitors have been known to damage buildings or equipment and some have even been known to steal things, in fact one of the tasks of a winery guide is to keep a discreet eye on visitor behaviour. Individual visitors are well catered for (audio-guides, information leaflets, etc.) at the Château de Meursault (Burgundy, France). In Calistoga, California, the Clos Pegase Winery offers visitors a self-guided art tour. The winery complex was designed by renowned architect Michael Graves in 1987, after winning an architects' competition sponsored by the winery's owners with the San Francisco Museum of Modern Art. The visitor, guided by a leaflet similar to a museum guide, can wander in the garden and admire the proprietor's personal art collection. The idea to build a 'temple to wine and art' was first conceived back in the 1980s. The garden, indeed the whole complex, including the fermentation area and wine tasting rooms, was created as a space for design and leisure: there are over 1000 pieces of original art works, with sculptures, paintings and

antiques, all celebrating the affinity between art and wine. There is also a Resident Artist programme giving artists the chance to stay on the premises and create. The architectural project:

> [...] responds in grand but playful splendour to the need to be showy and ostentatious. Even the name of the winery, the origin of which comes from a work in the collection representing the myth of Pegasus, was a symbolic choice on the part of the proprietors who wanted to create a connection between their wines and the Greek myths. In doing so, they have laid claim to a nobler and more ancient tradition than their main competitors in the market: French wines.
> (Chiorino, 2007)

Outside

- After the initial welcome and explanation, the group then goes outside into a small, protected area facing on to rows of vines. Visitors are invited to sit on the benches provided, for the second part of the talk.
- The vines in this area have been planted for educational purposes only and each row represents a different species of vine, all of which are grown on the estate. The guide picks a small bunch of grapes from the first row, hands it to one of the visitors and invites them to take a grape and pass it on so the others can do the same. This gives everyone in the group the chance to discover what that particular type of grape tastes like before being made into wine. In the meantime, the guide outlines some of the pedoclimatic features of the *terroir* where the grape is grown, before going on to describe the grape's characteristics, how that particular variety is used and the wines that are made from it. The same is repeated for each of the vines, so that visitors can sample the grapes at different stages of maturation and get an idea of the taste of each variety. The atmosphere is relaxed; people are obviously very involved, they ask questions spontaneously and begin to exchange comments among themselves. It is a moment of great interaction. This particular visit takes place around the time of the grape harvest, which is probably the most interesting season for wine tourists; however, it is still possible to give visitors a direct experience throughout the year. Tour guides can, for example, point out the phase of berry growth at that particular time, explain pruning methods and so on.
- Before the group enters the wine cellars they are invited to try a variety of grape that was brought to California by the first missionaries: this is a starting point for talking about developments in oenology over the centuries, describing the particular advances that have been made over the last decades and how consumer taste has gradually evolved.

FURTHER IDEAS

- Being able to visit the vineyards is an important feature on a tour for those who are seriously interested in discovering more about the estate's wines: unfortunately this is not always possible, particularly if the vineyards are some distance away from where the wine is actually made. If the vineyards extend over a large area, it may be worth considering using motorized transport (e.g. a jeep or a minibus) to take small groups around the estate, with a driver/guide.
- The Benziger family winery (Glen Ellen, Sonoma, California) offers six tours a day at fixed times, for up to a maximum number of 25 people. The tours are mainly for the mass market: the 'Biodynamic Vineyard Tram Tour' led by a driver/guide lasts 45 minutes and includes the chance to sample two of the estate's wines. The tram takes the visitors into

the vineyard with a couple of stops along the way. The first stop, at a panoramic viewpoint, is dedicated to a description of the pedoclimatic conditions and geological features of the area, with the guide using a model to help explain their impact on the soil and the terrain. The second stop focuses on the winery's biodynamic approach to wine-growing and, if visitors are lucky, the chance to taste some grapes.

- The panorama is an essential part of a successful visit: the 360° 'panoramic guided tour' of the vineyards and nearby villages conducted by visitor guides from the Cantina Sociale Produttori del Barbaresco, in Piemonte, Italy, not only gives tour participants an exciting visual experience of the stunning landscape, but is also educational and informative. Visitors are taken to the top of Barbaresco's ancient tower, originally built by the Romans and rebuilt in the 13th century, and from there they enjoy a visual tour of the countryside and learn more about the land laid out before them, one of the best and most productive wine regions in the whole of Italy. The sweeping view takes in the vineyards of Barbaresco, and towards the south-west, visitors can just get a glimpse of the town of Alba and the wine-growing area of Barolo. The plain and the rolling hills of Asti can be made out towards the north-east, while in the north-west, on the other side of the Tanaro River, the hills of Roero can be seen where the DOC wine Arneis is produced.
- Some wineries have created small botanical gardens where individual visitors can take a varietal walk and discover different species of vines with the aid of an auto-guide. Clearly labelled flower and herb gardens also give tourists the chance to learn more about plant extracts and essences. This kind of experience is very useful particularly if visitors later take part in a tasting session and undertake a sensory analysis of the wine.

The wine production areas

- The group then enters the production area. At the entrance, a short video, with a live commentary by the guide, shows work going on in the vineyard, the cellar and the barrel ageing room.
- The visitors are led along a walkway between wooden fermentation vats. While the winery workers get on with their different tasks, the guide explains the company's philosophy towards winemaking, why they have made certain technological innovations to their production processes and how the different machines work.
- The group then goes down to the level below, to where the bottoms of the wine vats are: there is a strong smell of must, the colour of the wine is studied and commented on. Visitors observe the steel vats and wooden barrels (Fig. 6.1). The guide is well-prepared and is able to answer even the most technical questions and explain what each of the workers is doing, without ever disturbing them or interrupting their work.

FURTHER IDEAS

- Some wineries have foreseen the possibility of having visitors tour their production areas and have installed raised walkways in their cellars right from the outset, so that tourists can view the vinification tanks without disturbing the workers; this is the case, for example, at the Braida winery (Rocchetta Tanaro, Piemonte, Italy). Where this is not possible, it is always a good idea to advise tourists beforehand on the best way to enjoy their visit without compromising the working conditions of the winery.
- Penfolds, an Australian winery, has designed a 'Make Your Own Blend Tour', which is an excellent way to get visitors involved in the art of winemaking. After doing the classic tour of the winery, participants are invited into the Winemakers' Laboratory to create their

Fig. 6.1. In the wine ageing room (Napa Valley, California, USA).

own personal blend of wine, using the same varieties of grapes that Penfolds uses for its wine production. At the end of the session, each person receives a customized bottle with their personal blend of wine as a souvenir of their visit.

- Other wineries have created rather unusual tours that combine viewing their wine production areas with brief 'lessons' in industrial archaeology. Maison Champy (Beaune, France), dating back to 1720, is the oldest *maison de vins* in Burgundy. Part of the building was designed by none other than Monsieur Eiffel himself. The tour includes a visit right to the top of the building where a machine, invented by Pasteur to accelerate the maceration and fermentation processes of must, is housed. Pasteur's experimental ideas had to be abandoned in the end, but being able to imagine such a great scientist at work here provides a uniquely evocative experience for the visitor. Pietrantonj is a small winery operating in Abruzzo in Italy. It has two enormous underground cisterns that can hold up to 1402 hectolitres. Visitors are invited to step inside the cisterns that are completely lined with Murano glass tiles.

- Some wineries may feel that they do not possess any outstanding features worthy of attention. However, a friendly, informative and professional approach on the part of the guide and/or other winery staff may be more than enough to render a visit a memorable one. A visit to a tiny winery, owned by Sylvie Spielmann, *propriétaire récoltant* and *vigneron indépendant*, in Bergheim, Alsace, France, deserves a special mention. The excellent lesson on the meaning of *terroir* and the concept of *cru/grand cru* was supported by maps of the area showing the geological features of the vineyards. Having the opportunity to then taste and savour the wine from this mineral-rich terrain remains a lasting memory.

Wine tasting

- The group then passes from the cellar to the tasting room. In the centre there is a large wooden table and enough chairs to comfortably seat everyone in the group. There are three glasses at each place.
- The visitors sit down and the guide hands each person three tasting sheets that will be used to analyse three different wines. Bottles of mineral water are also placed on the table.
- As the first wine is being tasted, the guide outlines its characteristics. They then move on to the second tasting and then on to the third. The different members of the group are encouraged to use their olfactory and taste memories to identify the aromas and flavours of the different wines and to comment on their organoleptic characteristics. Even the most inexperienced visitors are invited to pass comment; the atmosphere is relaxed and friendly and not at all competitive, with the guide making sure that everyone feels involved. The first two tastings do not have any accompaniments (e.g. no bread or crackers on the table), but the third glass of wine is accompanied by delicious savoury *tartines* influenced by Californian fusion cuisine. The *tartines* provide an excellent introduction to food and wine pairing; menu suggestions are made and advice given about which dishes would best accompany the Mondavi wines.
- The tasting session over, the guide thanks everyone for their attention and asks if anyone has any more questions. Visitors are invited to stay on should they wish, directions to the wine shop are given, as well as instructions for buying wine online and the advantages to be had by joining the Mondavi Wine Club.
- Just outside the tasting room, a lady is at work preparing *tartines* for the next group coming in, underlining the fact that each group is freshly catered for. A bowl of wine corks and wine labels (of the wines experimented in the tasting session) are placed on a side table; visitors can help themselves to these as they leave and take them home as souvenirs.

FURTHER IDEAS

- Food and wine pairing or matching is becoming ever more popular, with demand coming mainly from people who do not have much experience of the wine sector. Food and wine pairing sessions in the USA are enjoying enormous success, with some wineries basing their entire tour around this subject. There are many ways to integrate food and wine pairing sessions into a classic wine tour. At the Kendall Jackson Winery in Sonoma, California, tourists do not visit the areas dedicated to wine production. Instead, they are treated to a sophisticated five-course finger food menu (including dessert), each course accompanied by a glass of Kendall Jackson wine under the guidance of a wine educator and enjoyed in the informal atmosphere of a wine bar. At the Peju Province Winery (Rutherford, Napa Valley, California), visitors do get to visit the cellars, but far more importance is given to the three- or four-course tasting menus that small groups can enjoy in the winery's own kitchens. Here diners can observe the chef and the kitchen staff preparing the meal; the ingredients of the dishes are explained as they are served and suggestions made as to the best pairings. At Healdsburg, Sonoma, California, the Chalk Hill Estate 'Culinary Tour' includes a visit to the proprietor's private organic garden. The gardener, acting as guide, helps visitors to identify the different plants and essences. The formal food and wine pairing sessions take place three times a week. These have to be pre-booked and groups from six to 16 people (mainly couples or groups of friends) are catered for inside the elegant Estate Pavilion. An expert wine educator acts as host and an acclaimed chef is in charge of preparing the tasting menu. The Maison d'Olivier Leflaive (Puligny-Montrachet, Burgundy, France) offers a food and wine pairing programme entitled 'Table d'Olivier'. This consists of a fixed menu accompanied by 14 of the *maison* wines. An oenologist guides diners through the wines, while the proprietor pops in every now and then to see how the meal is progressing.

- In Riquewihr in the Alsace region of France, Jean Hugel (Hugel & Fils) created a tasting session that was almost an interactive game. Based on acquiring a few basic concepts, the aim of the session was to raise individual awareness about wine. The tasting was focused on four or five wines, beginning with a simple, everyday wine and ending with something more complex and prestigious. After the second wine was sampled however, the normal rules for wine tasting were overturned, and the first wine was tasted again. If the first wine was judged to be still pleasing to the palate, it meant that in terms of quality it was just as good as the second wine, in spite of its label and inferior price. The third wine was tasted and then, as before, attention focused on the first. If the latter still compared favourably, the same considerations were made, otherwise the third wine's superiority was agreed upon. This approach continued until the last wine was tasted. In just over 10 minutes, participants learned the basics for being able to appreciate and distinguish simple wines from more complex ones of the same grape variety. The company has also published several brochures. One of these contains suggestions for pairing their aromatic wines (the quintessence of Alsace wine production) with oriental cuisine. Different sections are dedicated to the dishes of northern and southern China, Indonesian and Thai cooking, and Japanese and Indian food. The brochure also describes how to match the different qualities of individual wines (e.g. roundness, body, sweetness, freshness) to the flavours of the dishes (e.g. sweet and savoury or hot and spicy).
- It may happen that a visit to a winery is limited to paying for a glass of wine and sipping it at the bar of the wine shop. This usually happens when the winery's aim is to attract passing customers who are not particularly interested in knowing more about the product itself, but would perhaps like to stop and buy some bottles as a souvenir of their holiday in the area. The layout of the wine shop plays an important role in attracting these types of visitors who appreciate being able to buy quality gadgets, wine accessories, design objects, etc. At the Imagery Estate Winery & Art Gallery (belonging to the Benziger family in Sonoma, California), the wine shop is set out like a permanent wine collection: the bottles are displayed under the same original paintings that are reproduced on the wine labels.

AT THE DAIRY FARM

Dairy farms have the great advantage that they can offer visitors a complete overview of the production process, from the raw material to the finished product, in a short space of time. Being able to see fresh milk transformed into mozzarella and taste the still-warm cheese at the end of the tour is an undeniably gratifying experience.

The visit

The Vannulo Dairy is located on the Palmieri family's organic farm and estate in Capaccio Scalo, Campania, Italy (Fig. 6.2). It has been chosen as a model for gastronomic tourism in that it combines a high-quality product with well-organized hospitality. An 18th-century manor house on the estate has been completely restored and provides two comfortable suites for overnight guests. The farm, situated just a few kilometres from Paestum, a UNESCO World Heritage Site, is an organic water buffalo dairy farm. The mozzarella cheese produced here can only be bought from the estate shop and is not on sale anywhere else. The strong bond

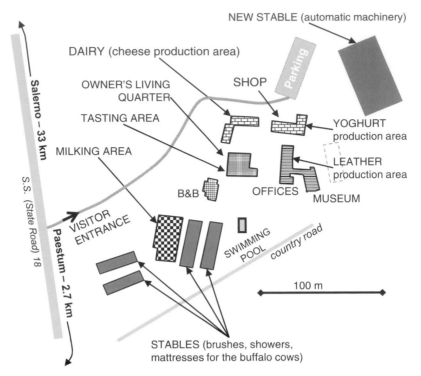

Fig. 6.2. The Vannulo Estate Map (source: the authors' own map; the layout is based on the original map supplied by the Vannulo Estate).

linking the land, the producer and the product is implicitly communicated and unconsciously assimilated by the visitor-customer. This is further reinforced when the visitors are taken down to see the buffalo herd. Visitors are stunned to see how the animals react when the tour guide calls individual buffalos by name.

Organization
- The tour must be booked well in advance and an entrance fee is charged.
- There are three tour options: farm and dairy tour, tour and light lunch, tour and full lunch. Lunch is served in the proprietor's private residence, dating back to the 18th century. Visitors who opt to have lunch are treated to a fixed menu and have the opportunity to sample some of the farm's products.
- The tour covers each phase of the production cycle.
- Groups are accepted (minimum number of participants: 10; maximum: 50).
- The tour lasts 75 minutes.
- Tours usually take place in the morning to allow groups to see the mozzarella cheese being made.
- The guide's approach is confident, friendly and informal.

The tour
- The tour begins outside the cheese factory. A large window looking on to the production area allows the group to look inside and observe the cheese being made. The fact that

visitors never enter the building itself means that working and hygienic conditions are never compromised. The guide explains each step of the production process: how the raw milk is first filtered and then coagulated, then the cutting of the curd and maturation (and the production of ricotta cheese from the residual serum); two people stretch and pull the obtained dairy product by hand and finally put it into brine to salt. Great attention is given to emphasizing the quality of the milk and to the fact that the cheese is made entirely by hand, resulting in a premium product (Fig. 6.3). The guide also gives a brief account of how water buffalo first came to be introduced to the Campania region, and the origins of mozzarella cheese, a fundamental ingredient of Neapolitan pizza, that is actually a by-product of Provola cheese.

- The tour then continues to see where the farm's yoghurt is made from pasteurized milk. The guide explains the functions and uses of the different machines, as well as giving a general description of all the farm's dairy products. The organoleptic characteristics of milk are also discussed.
- The next stop is the leather handicrafts shop. The shop was set up to complete the supply chain of buffalo products. In reality, the skins are bought from other suppliers.
- Visitors then move on to the farm museum where examples of farm equipment and everyday utensils from different epochs are on display.
- After this, the visitors finally get to meet the buffalo. There are about 300 adult female buffalos on the farm (although seemingly a large number, the quantity of mozzarella produced is relatively small). The group learns about buffalo behaviour and how the animals need to live in optimal conditions in order to produce milk of the highest quality (they are even given homeopathic treatments when necessary). Visitors watch while some of the buffalo cows pass under the showers and have their coats brushed. The buffalos are

Fig. 6.3. A plump buffalo mozzarella (Campania, Italy).

then allowed to relax on special mattresses in their stalls. A new stable has recently been installed for automatic milking. The guide gives more information about organic produce and the sustainable farming methods practised by the farm's owners. The expanse of estate land guarantees that there is a correct balance between the space given over to the buffalo herd and the area utilized for cultivating forage to feed the animals (each buffalo cow is given at least 25 kg of grass a day). The most exciting moment comes when those who wish to do so, are invited to stroke one of the animals. Being able to look a buffalo in the eye and come up against such docile grandeur is a truly unforgettable experience.

- In the estate shop, visitors stand and sample fresh mozzarella balls. The shop also sells yoghurt, ice cream and cappuccino, all made from the farm's own buffalo milk. Finally, the guide ends the tour by explaining the distinctive sensory characteristics of the product.

FURTHER IDEAS

- The Valtellina Dairy Group (Latteria Sociale Valtellina), in Delebio (Italy), offers alpine tours in summertime. Tour participants can hike up to the mountain pastures, watch the cows being milked, sample Bitto cheese (a PDO cheese, exclusive to mountain areas and only produced in the summer months), and should they wish to stay overnight in the high mountains, accommodation can be arranged.
- The Cooperative of Milk and Fontina Cheese Producers in Valle d'Aosta (Italy) runs a Visitor Centre in Valpelline. In order to give visitors a complete picture of how Fontina is made, the centre has been divided into three sections, focusing on the history, the *terroir* and the methods used to transform milk into the finished product. There is no strict viewing order and visitors can move from one section to another as they please, watch a video, or visit the small museum and photo gallery housed inside the centre. In food tourism however, the senses are all-important, so the cooperative has organized guided tours of the cheese maturing room, located beside the Visitors Centre. An enormous space that can hold up to 60,000 cheeses at any one time, the maturing room was once the entrance tunnel to an old copper mine, and even today the railway tracks that were once used to transport copper, are now used to move the cheese. The space is cold and damp, impregnated with an overwhelming smell of ammonia. Here, visitors learn how each cheese is individually stored and handled (in extremely difficult working conditions) until it reaches the correct stage of maturation (Fig. 6.4). The tour ends with a tasting of Fontina cheese.
- Cheese-tasting courses give gastronomic tourists the chance to discover and compare the characteristics of cheeses from different production areas and producers, at different stages of maturation or at different times of year. These short courses can be organized by individual *affineurs* (cheese agers) in their cheese ageing rooms or sales points. It can be very stimulating to participate in a cheese-tasting session in an unusual and evocative location such as an old community dairy: a memorable experience for the visitor.
- The Fromagerie Gaugry (Gevrey-Chambertin, Burgundy, France) receives raw milk from about 30 dairy farmers in the area. The milk is used to make seven different types of unpasteurized soft cheeses with a washed rind, including the renowned AOC L'Epoisse. The cheeses need to mature in cold, damp conditions and the original buildings were so cold and inhospitable that only small numbers of people could be accommodated for a very short space of time. The dairy has now constructed new buildings on the premises that allow greater numbers of visitors to comfortably view the whole production cycle (Fig. 6.5). Both individual visitors and groups are catered for. Independent tourists and guided groups follow the same route, along a walkway that runs parallel to the different production rooms and they

Fig. 6.4. Tools for brushing Fontina cheese (Val d'Aosta, Italy).

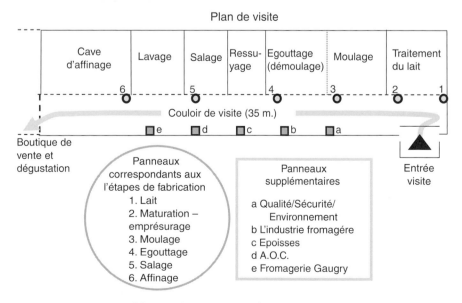

Fig. 6.5. Tour organization of the production areas of the Fromagerie Gaugry (source: the authors' own map; the layout is based on the original map supplied by the Fromagerie Gaugry).

can observe all the different phases of production through large transparent glass panes. Information panels and a simple leaflet printed by the company (that must be handed back at the end of the visit) help guide the individual visitor, while those on the guided tour are treated to a tasting of the company's products accompanied by a glass of Burgundy wine.

AT THE BREWERY

Breweries always have great appeal, whether they are small artisan breweries or large beer factories. Particularly in countries where it is the preferred drink to accompany a meal, beer lovers and connoisseurs get great pleasure from discovering new brews. There is something very satisfying about sipping a beer in congenial surroundings, served at just the right temperature, in just the right glass.

The tour

- The family-run Cantillon Brewery situated in the heart of Brussels (Belgium) has been making beer for over 100 years. Lovers of Lambic beer flock here to enjoy a drink in surroundings that have not changed since the brewery opened in 1900. Since 1978, it has been a 'living museum' informing visitors about the history of the brewery, their methods of production and the difficulties involved in producing a naturally fermented beer in such a particular microclimate. Opening their doors to visitors was the only way the family could keep the brewery in the public eye and their traditional production methods alive in a rapidly changing market. The tour naturally focuses on the artisan methods used to make the unique-tasting Lambic beer. Individual visitors are given a simple A4 sheet that guides them around the dimly lit production areas that have remained almost unchanged since the founding of the brewery. Groups of visitors, on the other hand, are given a guided tour and can watch the beer being made during 'public brewing sessions'. The tour does not follow the different phases of the production cycle in chronological sequence (clearly illustrated in the leaflet), but takes visitors through a number of production areas located on different floors of the building. The visit begins with the area dedicated to the brewing process before moving on to view the hot water tanks and the mashing and grinding room. The cereals (wheat and malted barley) used to make the beer are stored and displayed in the attic, along with the hops that are used to give the beer flavour. In the chilling room there is an enormous red copper container where the must is cooled by air filtering through the Persian blinds. This cooling process takes place from the end of October to the beginning of April and, as the blinds are opened and closed to create a draught, the air carries the wild yeast spores that set off the process of natural fermentation. It is here that the visitors begin to get an understanding of how the room's microclimate and microorganic balance create the right conditions to produce a spontaneously fermented beer. After this, the group is taken to the barrel room to view the fermentation and maturation phases, to see the bottles being washed and the beer being bottled. They may also have a chance to see how Gueuze or beers with fruit are made. A visit to the beer cellar is completed by sampling the brewery's products (Gueuze, Kriek, etc.).
- Just a short walk from the centre of Dublin and located in the heart of the St James's Gate Brewery, the Guinness Storehouse is Ireland's number one tourist attraction. Guinness is also one of the world's top brands (every year the brewery manufactures millions of litres of its renowned stout). The Storehouse, with over 100 employees, is also very impressive

from an architectural point of view. It was originally built at the turn of the 20th century in a style inspired by the Chicago school of architecture; it is an amazing structure supported by massive steel beams. The building was renovated between 1997 and 2000 and now covers an area of almost 16,000 m² distributed over seven floors. In the centre there is an enormous glass atrium shaped like a huge pint beer glass. On first impressions, the Guinness Storehouse tour would seem to be constructed according to the criteria of 'post-modern tourism'; actually, the tour's approach is deeply rooted in Dublin's history, culture and traditions. Visitors are not taken on a tour of the production areas. The tour concentrates instead on communicating some very clear messages, including the company's contribution to Dublin's economy, history and culture and the importance of responsible drinking. The guided tours, available in four foreign languages (French, German, Spanish and Italian), are for pre-booked groups only. Individual visitors can take a self-guided tour covering all seven floors, organized into different thematic sections with hands-on activities, interpretive panels, videos, interactive displays and so on. The different sections are divided into: How Guinness is Made (history, production methods, ingredients, art and passion), Global Dimensions (markets and transportation), The Story of Arthur Guinness (founder), 'My Goodness, My Gilroy' (75 years of advertising), The History of a Building (the story of the building's transformation from fermentation plant to top tourist attraction), and finally, on the seventh floor, the Gravity Bar. On showing their entrance ticket (in fact a souvenir drop of Guinness in a small plastic pebble), visitors receive a complimentary pint of Guinness and enjoy a 360° panoramic view of Dublin city. The first stop, halfway through the tour, is designed to give visitors the rudimentary basics of beer-tasting techniques and to explain the best conditions for drinking beer, with tastings of Guinness, Guinness Extra Stout and Foreign Extra Stout. Under-age visitors are served a soft drink. The Storehouse also has an independently run retail shop on the ground floor. Corporate clients are well catered for and designated spaces can be hired for meetings, conferences, workshops and training courses. The fact that the tour essentially attracts mass tourism means that there is a risk it could be just another 'theme park' experience. However, the visit is so well-organized and has been planned so carefully that it never falls into the trap of becoming banal or unoriginal. The strong link between the product and its city of origin is continuously emphasized throughout the tour; this is reinforced by the fact that the building itself is part of the city's urban landscape. With the aid of a specially produced panoramic guide on the window giving the names of Dublin's most important buildings, visitors can easily identify the city's most significant landmarks from the Gravity Bar on the seventh floor (Fig. 6.6). The names of the landmarks and quotations from Dublin's authors are etched on the glass windows.

AT THE OLIVE MILL

In spite of the fact that olive oil consumption is part of the Mediterranean tradition, the produce's organoleptic and sensory characteristics are relatively unknown to the general public. This is even truer for foreign visitors where olive oil is not part of their culture. A visit to an olive mill therefore can be an exciting revelation for both domestic and international tourists. Here they can discover what essential characteristics an oil must possess in order to qualify as an extra-virgin olive oil, the importance of timing and harvesting methods, how olives are cultivated, the kind of results obtained from continuous or discontinuous pressing cycles, stone grinders, hammer pressers or state-of-the art olive presses incorporating the latest technology.

Fig. 6.6. Enjoying the urban landscape while drinking a pint of stout (Ireland).

The sensory characteristics of olive oil change according to where it is cultivated and visitors can discover the defining notes of an olive oil from one mill and then go on to compare it with other locally produced olive oils.

Most people nowadays are aware of the health benefits of a Mediterranean diet, so they will be interested to find out more about the nutritional properties of olive oil and the best ways to conserve the product. If a tour takes place outside production time, the guide must make every effort to involve the visitor and try to give a clear and lively picture of the atmosphere and frenetic activity of life on an olive farm during the harvest.

Olive oil tasting sessions tend not to be technical, unless of course visitors already have some experience or are professionals in the field. Visitors generally sample the oil as it is used in local cuisine, e.g. poured on crusty bread.

Another point in favour for those who may be considering opening their doors to tourism is the remarkable variety of landscapes that are a feature of olive-growing areas. In Spain, for example, there are the olive groves and the picturesque whitewashed houses of the *pueblos blancos* of Andalusia where olive oil is often processed by large cooperative olive mills. In Italy, the geomorphological features of the land are so varied that olives are grown in an array of stunning landscapes: the terraced olive groves of Liguria; the centuries-old olive trees of Puglia; the olive 'woods' of Aspromonte; the new, regimented olive groves in the Sibari area (Calabria); the mixed-cultivated fields (olive trees and cereals) of the Marche; the contrast of the hills in the PDO areas of Abruzzo with the surrounding steep slopes of the Maiella and Gran Sasso mountains; the calm waters of Lake Garda with its olive groves and the alpine foothills; the rolling hills of Umbria and Tuscany dotted with olive trees that were the inspiration of so many Renaissance painters; and so on.

The tour

At the Galantino Olive Mill in Bisceglie (Puglia, Italy), the retail shop, on two floors, sells a wide range of the farm's products, from bottles of extra-virgin olive oil to a selection of olive oil speciality products and oil-based cosmetics. Also inside is a meeting point for visitors, a small conference room and a dedicated space for olive oil tasting. The guided tours around the farm's 18th-century olive mill where the olive oil is made are free. Already engaged on the farm in a variety of roles, the guides are familiar with the company's business philosophy and strategies as well as being specifically trained to welcome and guide visitors. The tour begins with an explanation of the functions of the machines inside the mill including ancient granite millstones. The characteristics of the terrain are described along with sustainable and organic farming methods, what happens during the olive harvest, the variety of olive plants, how the olives are picked and cleaned, storage, what happens when the olives are crushed into a paste and then sent to the extractor to remove water and other residue, bottling, the sensory characteristics of the product and suggestions for using olive oil in cooking. The guide spends some time explaining the *terroir* and describing the characteristics of Coratina and Ogliarola, olive plants that are native to this particular area north of Bari. The extra-virgin olive oil obtained from these plants has a distinctive spicy and bitter taste. The guide then goes on to recount the history of the Galantino Olive Mill that goes back 100 years. Each step in the development of the mill is retold, together with accounts of the people who were responsible for initiating change and progress: the purchase of the mill, the purchase of the land, the relationship with local farmers who still bring an additional quantity of their olives to the mill to be pressed, the prizes won and the achievement of international recognition. The guide then goes on to describe how there is increasing demand for high-quality olive oils with distinctive sensory qualities. The mill has had to respond to these changes in consumer behaviour by producing a wider range of products to suit more sophisticated tastes. The tour ends with a free tasting of some of the mill's products. Visitors can choose which products they would like to sample, ranging from traditional extra-virgin olive oil to organic, fruit- or herb-infused olive oils. The mill also receives large groups of tourists. They are offered tasting workshops in the showroom as it can accommodate a greater number of visitors. Another interesting point for visitors is to learn that different varieties of extra-virgin olive oil can be listed according to their *terroir* and sensory characteristics (similar in a way to a wine list), so that restaurateurs and gastronomes can choose which oil would best accompany and complement dishes on a menu.

FURTHER IDEAS

- Some olive oil companies have parallel production lines (often working simultaneously): the continuous pressing method, which is the most modern, running alongside the more traditional or discontinuous method, or two to three phased production processes. In this case, the tour experience is even more exciting as visitors get the chance to sample the end products and compare the differences between them.
- Tourists or professionals who already have some knowledge about extra-virgin olive oil production are usually fascinated by the changes that new technologies have brought to the sector. The Monteschiavo Olive Mill in Maiolati Spontini (Marche, Italy) is an excellent example of a company that has invested in cutting-edge technology for olive oil extraction and machines designed by the Pieralisi Group (who are also proprietors of the mill). Visitors to their web site (www.frantoiomonteschiavo.com) can watch the different phases of olive oil production on live webcam.

- Olive oil tasting sessions are much more satisfying and suggestive when they take place in buildings or spaces that have a characteristic style and architecture. In Puglia, for example, one of the largest olive-growing regions in the world, tastings can be held in some of the underground olive mills of Salento. The mills were traditionally built underground for safety reasons and to keep temperatures at just the right level for optimal production and storage. Also in Puglia, olive oil tastings are organized in the legendary *trulli* of Valle d'Itria. Short courses for those wanting to experience being on a tasting panel can also be organized on request.
- The area of Ferrandina (Basilicata, Italy), where the Lacertosa Olive Mill is located, is famous for a particular variety of olive plant called Maiatica. At the mill, visitors not only watch oil being extracted from the olive drupes, they are also invited to see the rather complex but traditional local custom of baking the Maiatica olives. These are delicious tasted on their own or are used as an ingredient in a number of local recipes.
- Diners at the Archibusacci Mill Restaurant in Canino (Lazio, Italy) can look out through a large window and see one of the olive mills while enjoying *bruschetta* (extra-virgin olive oil poured on to toasted bread) and other local dishes using the mill's own olive oil. A similar experience is reserved for tourists at the Fratelli Carli Olive Oil Museum in Imperia (Liguria, Italy). The vast production area is protected by an enormous glass panel so that visitors can observe what is going on as they walk past on their way to the museum.
- There is increasing interest in olive oil products, particularly in the health, beauty and leisure sectors. Many rural farms are combining their production activities with tourism hospitality, offering guest accommodation and on-site beauty centres, using their own olive-based cosmetic products and oils.

AT THE DISTILLERY

A guide in charge of taking visitors around a distillery needs to be able to explain the different phases that go into producing liquor or spirit and the function of a still. Visitors also need to know that distilled beverages are the result of fermented raw materials such as grapes, malt, fruit and herbs.

The visit

'The Jameson Experience' at the old Midleton Single Distillery in County Cork, Ireland, takes place inside the original industrial plant dating back to the 17th century. Unlike other big brand names in the whisky business, Jameson's tour does not include a visit to today's production areas. Instead, a smart guide in uniform, at fixed times throughout the day, accompanies visitors on a tour that is almost a 'history lesson' in industrial archaeology. The scope of the tour however is broad enough to captivate everyone's interest. It begins with a video about the production of Jameson whiskey, the main theme of which focuses on the history of the distillery, the buildings and factory life as it was in the past. Inside the old distillery the machines are no longer in use but they serve as an eloquent testimonial of production methods hundreds of years ago. The guide explains the similarities and differences in whisky production today, and the methods the company uses for storage and distribution. A great deal of emphasis is placed on explaining the differences between Irish whiskey and Scotch. Scotch whisky is made by first drying the barley malt over fires that have been stoked with dried peat. The result is a distinctive smoky flavour, quite different from Irish whiskey. Another difference is that most Irish whiskey is distilled three times. At the end of the tour, visitors can enjoy a glass of whiskey at the company bar (included in the price of the ticket). The old distillery also houses a restaurant that offers traditional Irish dishes and home-made cakes. The on-site shop is the only place in the world that sells bottles of Jameson's 'Reserve'. Customers can buy their own personalized bottle of 'Reserve' and have their name printed on the label. In spite of the fact that the tour is repeated over and over again during the day, the guide still manages to be friendly, communicative and engaging. The highlight of the tour is when the guide asks for three volunteers to come forward to take part in a whiskey-tasting workshop. The volunteers sit down at one of the tables in the bar and they are given five different whiskies to taste. Three of them are Jamesons' whiskies, one is a Scotch and one is a bourbon. The glasses are placed on a paper tablecloth specifically designed for the tasting workshop. The guide asks them for their impressions and sensations after each tasting, while also explaining the basic techniques for tasting spirits and how the sensory notes of the different drinks should help the tasters to identify them. At the end of the workshop each of the volunteers receives a tasting certificate. It is an enjoyable end to the tour, particularly for the three 'tasters' who feel that they have had a privileged experience compared with their tour companions who were there only as observers. However, even those who did not actually take an active part in the workshop come away entertained and much more informed about tasting techniques.

FURTHER IDEAS

- 'Bolle' (literally 'bubbles') is the name of the futuristic structure designed by Italian architect Massimiliano Fuksas for the Nardini Distillery in Bassano del Grappa (Veneto, Italy). It can accommodate groups of eight to ten people up to a maximum number of 50, on request. The tour lasts about an hour and includes a visit inside the auditorium, a short video and a grappa tasting workshop held inside the company's brand new shop. The Nardini family has been producing grappa since the 18th century and the quality of its products is renowned. However, many tourists come here not just because of the Nardini name; they come because of their interest in contemporary architecture and the work of Fuksas, who is probably one of the best known living Italian architects. His structure is intended to visually represent the process of distillation and the transformation of the raw material. Two transparent ellipsoid bubbles hang suspended between the trees, symbolizing the mercurial lightness of alcohol (the still and the beverage) and the tenaciousness of the earth (the grape vine rooted in the soil). The bubbles actually house the company's research laboratories, while the underground auditorium has been added to host events and receive visitors. There is a small pool of water at ground level.
- For those who cannot make the journey to Lynchburg, Tennessee (USA) to tour the Jack Daniel Distillery, the company web site (www.jackdaniels.com) provides detailed information about the original founders, its history, location, products and production as well as ideas for recipes and the possibility to take a virtual tour. To make the tour more realistic and to give virtual visitors a greater sense of participation, they can choose from one of the distillery tour guides available on the site. At the end of the tour they can sign their name in the virtual visitors' book, express an opinion about the tour and respond to company questions devised to pick up on consumer behaviour patterns and tastes. They are also asked to leave their address, a useful marketing strategy for expanding the company's mailing list and keeping in contact with future customers. For those who have been lucky enough to visit the Jack Daniel Distillery in person, they can download a photo of themselves with their tour group by clicking on 'Photo Pick Up' on the home page and typing in the date of their visit.

OTHER PRODUCTS, OTHER VISITS

Food and wine tourism is not just about visiting wineries, dairy farms, breweries, olive mills and distilleries. Virtually every single food or wine resource has the potential to stimulate the consumer's senses. Being able to view the whole process of production, from raw material to finished product, is bound to excite visitor curiosity particularly when they are able to feel the presence and taste the flavour of a region through its products. Any food and wine resource therefore has the power to become a resource for tourism. Other food production centres that have opened their doors to tourism include:

- The rice fields and farmhouses of Northern Italy, where visitors learn about rice cultivation in the past and in the present, the different varieties and their characteristics, how the end product is obtained and its different uses in cooking. Tours generally start with a visit to the rice field and end with sampling a traditional risotto, or for those fortunate enough, a tasting menu entirely based on rice, from the hors-d'oeuvres to the dessert (Piemonte, Lombardia, Veneto).
- Artisan bread makers, e.g. producers of Altamura bread in Puglia, *coppia* bread in Ferrara (Emilia Romagna) and Sardinian *carasau* bread.
- Cured meat factories. There are many renowned ham-producing companies in Spain and Italy who welcome visitors into their ageing cellars, explain the process of ageing and offer samples of the different cuts. There are also the smaller artisan producers operating in distinct regions in Italy, such as the Tuscan farmers who produce salami and prosciutto from the prized Cinta Senese pig, or the 'Culatello di Zibello tour' in the Po Valley where the meat is aged in traditional caves.
- Producers of traditional balsamic vinegar in Modena and Reggio Emilia.
- Producers of *foie gras*. Tours include being able to see where the ducks are bred in semi-liberty and a demonstration of *gavage* (force feeding); tours end with informal product tastings or even a sit-down meal. In France, producers often organize culinary tours, gastronomic weekends and cooking courses.
- Professional figures involved in the salmon supply chain: fishermen, salmon smoking factories, salmon retailers, etc. Tours are sometimes conducted by marine biologists. In Ireland, week-long gastronomy tours are organized during which guests follow the entire cycle of the fish's life. Lessons are practical as well as theoretical: participants learn about smoking techniques, the art of wine matching and enjoy tasting workshops.
- Pasta factories, where visitors can see pasta being made and enjoy a meal of hot pasta at the end of the tour.
- Snail farms, where the whole life cycle of a snail can be followed (Belgium).
- Salt works. In Marsala, Sicily, visitors are taken on a tour of the salt route and learn about industrial heritage and the windmills that were used in the early processes of salt making.
- Fruit production centres, where apples are delivered directly by the farmers to be selected, washed, packaged and stored. A tour of this type could begin in the apple orchards, follow parts of the automated production line and end with tasting the various types of product produced at the centre, e.g. fresh, dried or puréed apples.
- Artisan chocolate makers, where chocolate is still made according to age-old recipes. In Modica, Sicily, the tradition of making chocolate with *peperoncino* (chilli pepper) may have come from the Spanish who learned the art of chocolate making from the Aztecs; in the same area, chocolate is used as an ingredient for sweets filled with meat.

- Cocoa plantations, where tour visitors are taught the necessary skills to be able to appreciate the sensory characteristics of a *grand cru* chocolate, are taken through the different stages of transforming cocoa into chocolate, learn about and look at the traditional ways and methods used by the local people to prepare chocolate, and sample the products in a final tasting session; sometimes this can be complemented by chocolate-based beauty treatments (Mexico).
- Tea plantations, where tourists can learn how to pick the leaves during the harvesting season, see how the raw leaves are fashioned into tea and, while enjoying the beverage at the end of the tour, learn the ancient art of making tea (China).

There are also many other activities and initiatives that fall under the umbrella of food and wine tourism:

- Fishing tourism. Offering tourists something more than just a seaside holiday, it gives visitors the chance to experience a destination's underlying culture and to learn about responsible fishing practices as opposed to the unsustainable methods of the mass fishing industry. A tour could include going out in a fishing boat with local fishermen, learning how to catch fish with them and how to prepare the fish ready to eat either on board or back on land. Some fishing tours also offer the possibility of overnight accommodation with a fisherman's family.
- Farmers' markets. Visitors can have guided tours and meetings with the food producers.
- Farm days and stays. Joining in everyday farm activities such as fruit picking, helping with the grape harvest, milking the cows, etc., working guests usually get the chance to sample farm products, which more often than not they purchase to take home with them (e.g. bottles of wine, extra-virgin olive oil, jam).
- Model farms. These give young visitors the chance to learn all about work on a farm. Particularly important for inner-city children who have no experience of rural life, model farms generally cater for school groups. Even the youngest visitors can join in with different activities such as sowing and harvesting, and learn how raw materials are transformed before they arrive in supermarkets or appear on their table at home. Having direct contact with the farm workers and the farm animals and seeing how crops are grown and picked awakens city children's senses and helps to raise awareness about the importance of farming and the rural economy and the need to safeguard natural environments.
- Cookery schools and courses. Working alongside a chef, participants learn about regional products or those of a particular producer, develop their prowess in the kitchen and sit down at the end of the course to enjoy the meal that they have prepared during the lesson. They go home armed with new recipes and new skills.
- Sustainable and responsible tourism projects. With the aim of stimulating production and local economies in developing countries also through tourism, an example of this type of project is a tour of a coffee plantation, where visitors learn all about the cycle of coffee production from plant to bean selection to cup. They can also learn about the local coffee culture by participating in a traditional coffee ceremony in local people's houses. Coffee is also offered in specially designed visitor centres (Ethiopia).
- Monasteries. Apart from enjoying a historical or cultural visit, tourists can buy produce/ products such as honey, fresh fruit or liqueurs, cultivated or made by the monks.
- Environmental awareness programmes. These include initiatives to safeguard rural and mountain environments and their traditional activities, e.g. supporting alpine dairy farming. It is possible for a city dweller to adopt an animal and contribute to the expenses involved in breeding and looking after them. In exchange, they receive the dairy products

made from their 'own' herd. The cooperative ASCA in Anversa degli Abruzzi (Italy) has come up with a campaign called 'Adopt a Sheep, Defend Nature'. The people who adhere to this initiative can have lamb, milk, cheese, wool and fertilizer, and are welcome to stay on the farms that are members of the cooperative. In this way, they can participate directly in the working life of the farm and appreciate from close quarters what sheep breeding actually involves (grazing, birth, feeding, shearing, transhumance).

chapter 7

Supply Operators in the Food and Wine Tourism Industry

It is not just food and wine producers who are involved in the organization and management of gastronomic tourism. As well as tour operators and travel agents, there are many operators in the tourism sector who find they can increase business and professional satisfaction by stretching their core business to include services for food and wine tourists. As always, the best business results and the highest degree of customer satisfaction are obtained if services are linked to an area as a whole, rather than to just regional products.

There are also other actors in the field of gastronomic tourism such as information centres, tourism bureaus and institutes of education who take their role in food and wine tourism very seriously. In many cases, they have made it their mission to communicate the importance of food and wine tourism through a number of interesting educational initiatives.

ACCOMMODATION AND HOSPITALITY

The hospitality sector in the food and wine tourism industry does not always offer an adequate standard of accommodation to visiting tourists. Sometimes the buildings themselves are not suitable and do not offer comfortable guest accommodation, the standard of services at times is poor and staff do not always have the professional skills to respond appropriately to clients' needs. The lack of a professional approach can also create difficulties in business relationships with suppliers. Set out below are a number of suggestions that may help to address some of these issues.

It is advisable that hoteliers and accommodation managers in gastronomic tourism:

- Are familiar with the area and have first-hand experience of the region's resources and attractions, in order to be able to advise guests on where to go and what to do during their stay.

- Offer accommodation and hospitality, whenever possible, in buildings surrounded by the authentic local landscape (Fig. 7.1) and constructed with local materials and in the architectural style of the area. Examples of attractive and characteristic accommodation facilities include a splendidly restored half-timbered house in Burgundy, a 19th-century Milan town house with typical ornamental iron railings, an ex tuna-canning factory (*tonnara*) in Sicily, traditional stone cottages in the Cotswolds, an oast house in Kent, or a traditional Andalusian house with patio.

- Establish good relationships with local suppliers by using local produce whenever possible. Although it may be cheaper to order in bulk and buy alimentary goods from mass distributors, high-quality locally sourced supplies reflect the spirit, identity and flavour of a region.

- Foster good relationships with the host community.

- Oversee regular repair, upkeep and overall general maintenance of accommodation facilities.

- Ensure that the quality of facilities and services corresponds correctly to the category of accommodation; all too often, hotels in the same area and belonging to the same category (e.g. three-star) sometimes have totally different characteristics and standards.

- Maintain a professional approach in their dealings with clients and the supply side. Many smaller hotels and guesthouses do not offer discounts or special rates to travel agents or tour operators even when clients come through them. Moreover, when selecting operators and business partners on the supply side, choice should always be based on quality and business links in the area rather than trying to scrimp and save money. Suppliers' bills should also be paid promptly.

- Ensure that room rates (often far too high) correspond to the quality of the facilities and services on offer.

Fig. 7.1. Relaxing in a banana plantation (Gran Canaria, Spain).

- Consider breakfast time to be a special occasion for guests to enjoy regional produce (perhaps by proposing a gourmet breakfast menu); this is particularly important if clients have their other meals elsewhere.
- Make sure that they have plenty of informative literature to distribute to guests about the area and its resources, its produce/products and production.
- Stay in regular contact with local producers in order to book tours or visits for their guests.

Box 7.1. Case Studies: Accommodation and Hospitality.

- The tiny Chanric Inn in Calistoga, California (between Napa Valley and Sonoma Valley), offers a culinary destination with a focus on couples who want to be pampered unobtrusively. One of its strengths is the attention it gives to the food it serves its guests, which is all sourced locally. The breakfast, in particular, is a focal point: it is a gourmet, chef-prepared brunch that is tailored to specific dietary requests and it focuses on the seasons and locality of ingredients, utilizing fruit and produce from the organic garden of the property. The chef's cooking style is shaped by the Marine West Coast–Mediterranean climate of northern California wine country. They prefer to call the morning meal 'brunch' rather than 'breakfast' because the style is like a creative lunch. The food philosophy of providing fresh, locally sourced ingredients carries over into their selection of wineries in Napa and Sonoma. When guiding the guests to their personal favourites, they ask what the guest wants to experience. Many wineries have unique offerings, such as fine art, century-old wine caves, bocce ball courts and private tours and tastings. Knowing the guests' level of wine knowledge, their preference in wine styles and what attracted them to Napa Valley in the first place ensures a personalized experience. The same goes for being able to give informed advice about restaurants in the area. Northern California wine country has become almost as famous for its restaurants as it has for its wineries. Chanric Inn's proprietors visit those restaurants regularly to know 'who's hot and who's not' for their guests. But they also recommend the unexpected: not only top-end restaurants, but also, for example, Mexican food at the local Mexican grocery store, where you grab a burrito or taco to-go. In addition, local restaurant menus are freely available for the Inn's guests to consult. In this way, guests can make independent choices about where they would like to dine, but facilitated by the proprietors who make the restaurant reservations for them.
- The Royal Orchid Hotel in Bangkok, Thailand (part of the Sheraton chain of hotels), targets Western business and leisure clients. It has developed numerous examples of good hospitality practice, essentially to help Western tourists, overcome by culture shock and jet lag, on arrival in the colourful but chaotic capital city. One of their most interesting initiatives was to welcome guests by putting a basket of exotic fruit (of the type that can be found in local markets) in their rooms. Perhaps in itself not so original, but at the Royal Orchid guests also received a leaflet with a description of each of the fruits and instructions on how to peel and eat them. The organoleptic characteristics of each fruit were described in detail and, whenever possible, any similarities with the sensory qualities of 'Western' fruit were pointed out. In this way, hotel clients were introduced to the exciting tastes, colours and perfumes of an exotic new destination while being reminded of the sensory qualities of more familiar fruits at home. The fruit basket served as an incentive to hotel guests to venture out with confidence and explore the markets of Bangkok.

EATING ESTABLISHMENTS

The points made above with regard to accommodation facilities are also true for the food and beverage sector. As an integral part of the gastronomic tourism product, restaurants and other eating establishments have the opportunity to emphasize their links to their surrounding areas in a number of ways.

Recurring problems in the sector however include the over-dependence of some restaurants on being 'typical' or 'characteristic', and a certain resistance to reviewing product quality. In fact, many restaurant managers or owners unfortunately know very little about local produce and its culinary possibilities, and make little effort to find out about new products and market trends.

The ambience, atmosphere, type of cuisine and level of service offered by a restaurant provide excellent ways of communicating the personality and spirit of a region to a visitor.

Some useful suggestions:

- Over and above anything else, the actual building must blend in harmoniously with its surroundings and be pleasing to the eye (the exterior's architectural style and the interior's décor and furnishings). Perhaps we are stating the obvious here, but the context in which the gastronomic experience takes place strongly influences how much pleasure diners derive from the experience.

- Restaurant management and personnel must possess the necessary skills to prepare and present dishes, guarantee a satisfactory level of service and offer tasting menus and food and wine pairing advice to clients. In addition, an essential part of the service should be the ability to share their knowledge about the surrounding area and its attractions and resources.

- Whenever possible and if in keeping with the cuisine and style of restaurant, local produce should always be used (this is true for innovative and creative cuisine as well as traditional dishes). Even if only a small part of the menu is based around local produce, it will still serve to emphasize to clients the important role that the land plays in giving an area its spirit and identity. When guests enjoying a farmhouse holiday can sit down to a meal made from the farm's products, it not only heightens their sense of belonging to the farm, it also connects them with the wider region.

- Again, whenever possible, local suppliers and producers should be supported, particularly those who embrace sustainable practices and who may be experiencing difficulties in distributing their products to a wider market. Being constantly monitored by local restaurateurs and their clients can only have a positive impact on the quality of local production. It also gives a boost to the local economy and creates efficient and loyal supply-chain relationships. A restaurant working with local producers in a supportive and cooperative business environment will be able to offer clients top-quality cuisine and a fine dining experience. For those clients who show particular interest in local food and wine production, restaurant managers should also be able to advise them about which of their suppliers are open to visitors.

- Inviting local producers in to speak about their products and giving restaurant clients the opportunity to try and taste their products (e.g. through tasting sessions or cookery courses) is another excellent way to support local suppliers and inform visitors about regional produce at the same time.

- Including seasonal dishes on the menu is one of the best ways to introduce clients to the true quality and natural flavours of local products. Organizing 'themed' menus with dishes based on specific ingredients available only at certain times of year will also help to focus attention on the land, its producers and its resources.

The menu and wine list, along with the professional skills of the staff and of course the dishes themselves, communicate quite clearly the restaurateur's approach to offering clients quality products and an authentic and pleasurable dining experience.

Many smaller, simpler establishments do not always have a menu, although it is always advisable. Being able to take one's time to read a menu, without feeling rushed to make a choice, helps to put guests (especially foreign visitors) at ease. The menu and prices should always be clearly visible, perhaps written up on a strategically placed board, so that patrons can look forward to enjoying their meal knowing exactly how much they will be spending. This avoids any unpleasant surprises at the end when it comes to paying the bill.

Given the importance then of offering clients a clear and carefully put together menu, particular attention should be paid to making sure that:

- the menu is aesthetically attractive and pleasing to the eye;
- it reflects the ambience, cuisine and business philosophy behind the restaurant;
- the type of material used is appropriate and in good condition (the menu should be a pleasure to hold), and graphic layout and text organization are clear and attractive;
- descriptions and translations are clear, simple and efficient;
- it is not too long or too complicated (too many dishes can be confusing); and
- it is in keeping with the local surroundings.

The menu could also include some information about:

- the restaurant (when it was first established, some notes about the architecture of the building, etc.);
- the chef (business profile, philosophy and approach, etc.);
- the restaurant owners and their mission;
- the various dishes on the menu and their ingredients (giving special mention to the ingredients that go into making the most emblematic dishes);
- the tradition and significance of hospitality in the region;
- links with the surrounding area; and
- the essential spirit of those dishes that best represent the regional cuisine or that of the restaurant.

Restaurant staff obviously need to be knowledgeable about what is on the menu so that they can make suggestions or give further information about dishes when presenting them to clients.

Themed tasting menus give clients an excellent opportunity to sample the natural flavours of local produce and a chef's creative ability in the kitchen; however, it is important to offer just a few select dishes so that choice is not overwhelming. In the end, a successful menu is one that invites diners to enjoy an experience involving all five senses.

The wine list should also be easy to read and understand. As with the menu, it should be aesthetically pleasing. Well-designed, attractive wine labels can be attached to the list as they serve to attract the customer's eye, as well as giving information about the wine's origin, etc. A top-end restaurant naturally needs to offer a wide selection of wine, while a more modest establishment can easily get away with having just a few, carefully selected wines on its list. Whatever the case, the list is there to facilitate the client in making a choice and should never, as unfortunately often happens, make the client feel inadequate to the task. There are various ways in which wine can be linked to local producers. One way is by having a dedicated section displaying the labels of local wines. Another way is to give clients an opportunity to try different local wines during a meal by pairing each course with a glass of wine that has been especially selected to accompany the food. Special evening events, when producers present their wine to restaurant clientele, also serve to raise awareness of the strong links between food and wine production, while at the same time adding to the pleasure of the dining experience.

Further ideas that could be put into practice include:

- Creating a themed menu that focuses entirely on one specific gastronomic product that is representative of a region particularly noted for its prestigious production.
- Dedicating an area where the restaurant's own produce and/or local produce is displayed and sold. In many cases these areas make an attractive addition to the general ambience of the restaurant, particularly when the décor is in keeping with the style of the restaurant (e.g. wooden barrels and wine cases, jute sacks and other containers or implements on display).
- Inviting clients to view the restaurant's wine cellars to see the bottles that are on the wine list; in the case of enterprises that are also involved in food production, taking clients on a guided tour of the premises, for example, to see meats being cured or visit the ageing cellar to see how cheese matures.
- Offering diners the possibility of complimentary corkage, particularly when the restaurant is located in an area noted for wine tourism.

Restaurants that offer the right type of atmosphere and a truly commendable dining experience can, at the end of a meal, invite their clients to write their address on a specially designed card. In this way, they can stay in contact with clients by sending them news about future gastronomic events, information about new products, recipes, etc. Diners can also be asked to give feedback about the food and service.

Some of the above suggestions will also find favour with food critics and restaurant reviewers. In fact, in many ways they correspond to some of the criteria used by writers of restaurant guides to assess restaurant performance and practice in:

- the choice and quality of fresh produce;
- the chef's ability to produce creative dishes from primary ingredients;
- the quality and variety of the food;
- the use of local produce/products;
- whether the food is a true expression of regional identity and flavour;
- the type of menu offered and its coherence with regard to the region and the type of dishes proposed;
- the selection of wine and type of wine list;
- the professional behaviour of the staff in the kitchen and dining rooms;
- the quality of table settings (e.g. having the correct wine glasses, the correct cutlery); and
- creating a pleasing atmosphere and ambience.

Box 7.2. Case Studies: Eating Establishments

- Alice Water's legendary restaurant Chez Panisse in Berkeley, California, and its more informal, inexpensive Café, have always offered clients a menu based on healthy, seasonal, organic produce. Food is sourced from more than over 60 producers, the majority of whom work locally using sustainable methods of cultivation and production. In all cases, the focus is on safeguarding the environment and offering high-quality produce that is natural and full of flavour. In 1996, a foundation was set up to promote various programmes aimed at raising awareness in young people about the importance of eating healthy food. The foundation works closely with local schools, helping those involved by offering cooking lessons, planting organic gardens and encouraging food studies to be part of the normal school curriculum.

- Amerigo 1934 in Savigno (in the hills above Bologna) is really quite unique in Italy, in that it is highly praised by a number of restaurant guides, each one very different from the other and each applying a completely different set of assessment criteria. The *trattoria* offers traditional cuisine as well as more innovative regional dishes. Although creative, the dishes are usually simple and based on just two or three essential ingredients. Here the main focus is on seasonal availability and on the use of high-quality produce all of which is sourced locally, within a radius of 10–20 km (Fig. 7.2). The only exceptions are Piemonte beef, which in any case is supplied by a local butcher, and freshwater shrimps from Umbria. The restaurant's philosophy is clear and simple: 'to respect the original flavours and tastes of local produce and to rediscover old recipes or create new recipes from old'. Their approach to seasonality is illustrated by the fact that truffles or mushrooms are never on the menu all year round. The restaurant never uses frozen mushrooms or pre-prepared truffle sauces. In contrast, the ones that find themselves on the menu at Amerigo 1934 are the different types of mushrooms that can be found growing locally from month to month. For example, restaurant diners are able to enjoy morel mushrooms from March to June, plum agaric mushrooms from April to June, porcini mushrooms from May to November, girolles from June to November, chanterelles and trombetti from August to January. Business relationships with the small, local producers who supply the restaurant with fresh produce are based on mutual esteem and trust. A nearby water mill that has been operating since the beginning of the 17th century provides the restaurant with its flour. Potatoes come from the Cà Bortolani/Tolé plateau, chestnuts from Gavignano and organically grown fruit and vegetables are supplied by a farmers' cooperative in Valle Samoggia. Other local farmers provide the *trattoria* with hens, guinea fowl, ducks, geese, rabbits and other farmyard animals, while young goats come from the Savigno Plains, beef comes from the Modena White prize breed of cattle, prime pork from the Mora Romagnola pig bred in Montesevero and Montetortore, and freshwater salmon from Corno alle Scale. Altedo asparagus is supplied by a local consortium of producers and finally there is local game, cheeses and cured meats. As the area that supplies the restaurant is so small, sustainable practices are achievable and practical. The close business links between the restaurant and its suppliers bring tangible economic benefits to the local community, while the short distance that the produce travels from farm to table means the restaurant is an active supporter of the 'food miles' concept. By 'going local', energy consumption and air pollution are reduced and food freshness is guaranteed (with the advantage that chemical preservatives do not need to be added as is the case when products have to be stored for long periods

(Continued)

Box 7.2. Continued.

or transported long distances). This philosophy naturally extends to the choice of wine. Wines from the Colli Bolognesi feature prominently with approximately one hundred labels, all of which are listed in the *Carta Atlante dei vini e dei luoghi* (a map showing the location of vineyards and wineries) and are available by the glass at a reasonable price. Regional wines from Emilia Romagna are also well represented (subdivided into three smaller areas: Parma and the Colli Piacentini, Lambruschi Reggiani and Modenesi, and Romagna). Complimentary corkage is also offered. In Italian this has been translated into PTV ('Porta il Tuo Vino'), literally 'bring your own wine'. And this is not all. Apart from organizing special events and meals, usually based around a particular seasonal product, the restaurant also has its own shop, La Dispensa di Amerigo (Amerigo's Pantry). Many products available on the menu can also be bought in the shop, and are prepared and packaged by a firm owned by the restaurant. Clients who would like to complete their gastronomic experience in a relaxed way and stay overnight can choose to stay at the Amerigo 1934 Inn. The restaurant owners have created this small B&B, offering five beautifully restored rooms in one of the old houses in the centre of Savigno. Lastly, to

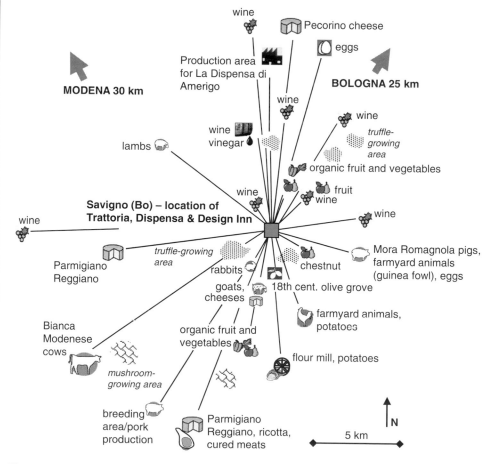

Fig. 7.2. Amerigo 1934's network of gastronomic produce and suppliers.

(Continued)

Box 7.2. Continued.

complete this extremely rich and varied offer, the restaurant has organized, on request by interested clients, guided visits to their suppliers or even a gastronomic tour of the entire region in cooperation with another leading restaurant in the area.

- The chef of La Bastiglia di Spello (Umbria, Italy) introduces his menu with a section entitled 'Alcune cose da dire' ('Some things to say'), with the aim of communicating to diners his commitment to high-quality, seasonal, local products:

> We only buy meat from farmers whom we know personally and whose products really stand out in the market; if at all possible we prefer to buy the whole animal, rather than individual cuts of meat.
>
> Our beans and pulses come from the areas around Spello, Colfiorito, Lago Trasimeno and the Martani mountains.
>
> The fish comes exclusively from the Mediterranean and is not farmed.
>
> All our vegetables are grown locally and we choose organic produce before anything else.
>
> The oil comes from the olive trees growing on the hills around us.
>
> We pick our own herbs according to the season.
>
> We make our own bread either here in the kitchen or in the ovens in Foligno.
>
> Our wines deserve a special mention elsewhere
>
> Whenever we can, we buy regional products, but we always have an eye out for the very best gastronomic produce on the Italian market.
>
> If advised beforehand, we are happy to create special menus for people with food allergies or intolerance.

- From Le Charlemagne at Pernand-Vergelesses in Burgundy, the view over the *grand cru* vineyards is so stunning that it is almost on a par with the exquisite cuisine of the area in giving food and wine tourists a truly memorable gastronomic experience. At the Bras restaurant in Laguiole, considered by many to be one of the most interesting gastronomic addresses in France, Chef Michel Bras brings the surrounding landscape into the restaurant by the creative use of special essences in his recipes, for instance, essence of fennel. Indeed, the restaurant has chosen as its elegant logo a silhouette of feathery Alpine fennel leaves (*Meum athamanticum*). The choice is not casual, as the fragile, wild plant grows on the high plateau of Aubrac far away from pesticide use and pollution. Michel Bras was born in Aubrac and the area continues to be a constant source of inspiration for his recipes. One of his signature dishes is in fact, 'sea bass with buttermilk and Alpine fennel, malabar spinach and bread and sage dumplings' (Floch, 1995).

- Some operators have begun offering people the chance to find out more about the use of wild herbs in the kitchen. Meetings and workshops, organized with the help of interested restaurateurs and botanists, begin by teaching participants about the properties of edible herbs and how to identify them. In follow-up sessions, the group first goes out into the countryside to pick the herbs and then they learn how to prepare dishes under the guidance of an experienced chef. A tasting session then follows and participants are taught the correct methods and vocabulary for carrying out an organoleptic analysis, and learn which other dishes or wine would be perfect accompaniments.

- The Goods Shed in Canterbury (UK) offers a very unusual but complete gastronomic experience (Fig. 7.3). As the name suggests, the building by Canterbury railway station was once used to store goods. Nowadays, food and wine lovers can find, housed

(Continued)

Box 7.2. Continued.

Fig. 7.3. Daily farmers' market, food hall and restaurant in Canterbury (Kent, UK).

under the same roof, a farmers' market, food hall and restaurant. All products sold in the market tend to come from local producers, farmers and fishermen working in Kent or the South London area. Apart from being able to buy meat, fruit and vegetables, fish, bread and cakes and speciality food products, visitors can enjoy the same products displayed on the stalls in the restaurant overlooking the market. The day's menu is written up on a blackboard, and, as well as enjoying watching the goings-on in the market from the terrace, diners can also watch the chef and his assistants at work in the open-plan kitchen. All those involved in The Goods Shed actively support sustainable practices and fair trade and their promotion of British cottage industries has put pressure on supermarkets to stock more British products. The informal atmosphere in the restaurant, the healthy, natural food and the simple but creative dishes with just the right touch of Mediterranean flair make this one of the best tables in the Kent area.

- Cases also exist of producers coming together to promote the region within which they work. In Vallagrina, Isera, Trentino (Italy), the local council has given an association of local producers and farmers the use of a 17th-century palace to house the *Casa del vino* (the 'House of Wine'), which the association describes as being a kind of 'embassy of local tastes'. There are 24 active members and they include both large established wineries and small, independent producers. All are involved in the production of Val Lagarina wine and are responsible for over 90% of wine production in the valley. The producers' undersigned intent is to cooperate in promoting the region and its

(Continued)

Box 7.2. Continued

products, to raise visibility in the market and to create and share economic benefits. Visitors to the *Casa del vino* can enjoy a meal and a glass of wine in the restaurant-bar, which showcases local wines and products such as wines, extra-virgin olive oil and cheese from the Trentino region. The chef uses fresh produce bought from small, local producers and the menu changes daily, offering just one dish accompanied by one of the wines of the *Casa del vino*. Themed evening events and tasting sessions, often in cooperation with local partners, such as MART (The Museum of Modern and Contemporary Art of Rovereto and Trento), offer excellent opportunities to promote art and boost the economy of the region.

TOURIST INFORMATION CENTRES AND BUREAUS

A tourist information centre is an absolute must for any locality wishing to attract and receive visitors. Having said that, unfortunately not all tourist destinations have one, and those that do in many cases often have centres that are poorly run and inefficient.

The minimum requisites for a tourist information centre or bureau serving a production region or *terroir* are that:

- It is easy to pinpoint and easily accessible.
- It is housed in welcoming surroundings, preferably within a building representative of the spirit and culture of the place (e.g. built with local materials and in the local architectural style); it is furnished with taste; and it is functional and technologically well equipped.
- Opening and closing times are clearly displayed and respected; ideally, office hours should be longer when demand is higher, at weekends and on public holidays, or during periods when the production cycle of a local product reaches its most interesting point and is most likely to draw greater visitor numbers.
- It is run by friendly, professional staff, able to respond efficiently to all enquiries, whether they come from tourists, tour operators or travel agents. They must be knowledgeable about the area and have first-hand experience of the area's resources: sites to visit where regional production takes place, restaurants, hotels and accommodation facilities, and cultural and other attractions. They should also be able to communicate in at least one foreign language. The organizational structure should be clear with each person taking responsibility for a specific task.
- It has a well-designed web site and enough good-quality leaflets and other materials to satisfy tourist demand. Information materials should be varied and meet visitor needs; e.g. tourists should be able to pick up charts, themed maps, leaflets, brochures or business cards showing the whereabouts of local producers, hotels and other accommodation options, shops, natural and cultural attractions. Books and guides about the area, or about local products and gastronomy, e.g. recipe books, should also be on sale.

Wine routes or indeed any route that has been specifically designed for visitors to explore the flavours and tastes of a particular production area deserve a special mention. Food and wine routes are governed by local and/or national legislation (e.g. in Italy, they come under a law passed on 27 July 1999, under the section entitled 'Wine Routes', and published in the *Gazzetta Ufficiale* no. 185 on 9 August 1999; since then further regional laws have been passed).

When wine routes are really open and operating (and not just present on a map, as so often happens), the main problems seem to be:

- an overall lack of coherence or structure, with individual producers often seeming not to have grasped what role they should play within the system;
- over-dependence on promoting a tourist product that, in truth, if tourists try to explore and go beyond the road signs, is underdeveloped and does not correspond to regional reality;
- a lack of information and services with regard to booking accommodation and visits to wineries, farms and other regional production centres;
- an inadequate knowledge of minor regional resources that might be interesting for visitors, particularly off-the-beaten-track paths or lesser-known monuments; and
- an inability to propose itineraries linking different tourism experiences around a common theme that would give visitors a complete taste of what the region has to offer during their stay.

Box 7.3. Case Studies: Tourist Information Centres and Wine Routes.

- The city of Beaune (France) is one of Burgundy's main tourist attractions. The tourist information centre (www.ot-beaune.fr) is situated right in the heart of the city opposite its most famous building, the Hotel Dieu. The centre is run efficiently and effectively and provides an excellent model of best practice. The organization behind a successful tourism information centre is extremely complex and requires a detailed organogram in order to respond satisfactorily to all the diverse needs of visiting tourists. In this particular case, the Beaune bureau is divided into three main sections that are responsible for dealing with the general public, with operators in the tourism sector, with local producers and the press:
  - Service Accueil et Bureau des guides interprêtes régionaux (Accueil et information du public/Boutique Atheneum de la Vigne et du vin. The boutique is well-stocked with books and guides, wine, design objects and gadgets, maps and other materials related to tourism in the area/Services et prestations liées à l'organisation des voyages et des séjours: billetterie – excursions, visites guidées, dégustations, sites et monuments, activités de loisirs et de pleine nature, spectacles; réservations – hôtels, chambres d'hôtes, campings, meublés de tourisme/Dîner de Gala de la Vente des Vins des Hospices de Beaune/Assistance et conseils/Services de guides-interprêtes régionaux/Observatoire Local du Tourisme).
  - Service Marketing et Communication (Relations avec les professionnels organisateurs de voyages, assistance et conseils, éductours, réceptions/Relations avec la presse, assistance et conseils, accueils de presse/Relations avec les opérateurs touristiques régionaux, assistance et conseils/Gestion de l'information touristique: base de données touristiques, photothèque/Editions des dépliants et brochures, site internet/Foires, salons, workshops et opérations extérieures/Relations avec la presse, assistance et conseils, accueils de presse/Publicité/Plan de promotion commerciale/Vente et commerce).
  - Direction générale, administrative et financière (Aménagements touristiques/Affaires générales et ressources informatiques/Comptabilité et gestion/Coordination touristique/Démarche qualité/Direction et représentation/Partenariat, clubs, affiliations et labels/Personnel et formation/Vie statutaire).

(Continued)

Box 7.3. Continued.

- The Sagrantino wine route in Umbria is one of the most popular and best organized routes in Italy. It is an excellent example of product diversification and integration. Five municipalities are involved: Montefalco, Bevagna, Gualdo Cattaneo, Giano dell'Umbria and Castel Ritardi. The area, which has enjoyed DOCG status, has a strong gastronomic tradition and is famous for its wines; in particular, Sagrantino di Montefalco, made from a local red grape variety. The area is also known for its extra-virgin olive oil production and its hearty country cooking. The gastronomic resources of the area are integrated well with its environmental and cultural heritage of medieval hill-top villages and precious works of art. The wine route was created by the five municipalities who joined together and set up an association to promote and manage the route. It has been fully operative since 2003. There is an information point inside the association's legal head-quarters in Montefalco and another information stand inside the city council building in Bevagna. The association now counts over 130 members, almost 35% of whom are wine producers. The majority of members (almost 50%) are involved in the hospitality sector or in catering, although their annual fees contribute to less than 25%. Other members include public bodies and banking institutions, providers of tourism services such as transport companies and travel agents, olive mill owners, farmers and local craftsmen who are not necessarily connected to the alimentary sector.

  The association offers a variety of services to its members, including: advertising and promotion at tourism fairs and exhibitions both at home and abroad; providing information and promotional material about individual members' business activities and distributing this information to visitors to the area; organizing courses and workshops for professional development; coordinating and assisting in applying for regional and European funding; and organizing road signs to guide tourists to wineries, farms, hotels, restaurants, etc. A designated department deals with the organization of local, national and international events including familiarization trips for journalists and operators in the sector and maintaining contacts with the press. There is also a Sagrantino Wine Bar in Berlin.

  For the tourist, the association offers: information and assistance, accommodation reservations, sightseeing tours and guided visits to the wineries, themed tours and packages and bicycle hire. There are also plans to open a wine bar and shop to promote all the Wine Route products.

  The association's communication strategies are managed by an efficient public relations team who make sure that the area, its producers and produce/products are constantly in the public eye. The Wine Route's web site (also translated into English and partly into German; www.stradadelsagrantino.it) is full of information about the area and association members. Web site content is updated weekly. In 2009, the web site was nominated as the best wine route Internet site in Italy. The association's network also deals with scientific research and publications. It finances projects for integrated tourism development in the area. Apart from the professional courses for business leaders and their employees, it has also set up courses for the unemployed. Food and wine appreciation courses have also been organized for residents to give them a sense of participation and to raise awareness about the importance of the area's rich gastronomic heritage. An upcoming project is the realization of a new system of footpaths. Since the Sagrantino Wine Route was set up, the number of bed places has doubled and tourist arrivals have increased by 150% with a 72% increase in overnight stays.

THE TOUR OPERATOR

The typical tasks of a tour operator, such as organizing package travel, drawing up itineraries and putting together holiday brochures, will be discussed in greater detail in Chapter 8; however, it is worth underlining here that tour operating, in some countries, is often not as efficient or as effective as it should be, especially in the food and wine tourism sector. In fact, tour operators need to address a number of issues if they are to attract and satisfy a target that tends to shy away from organized travel, preferring to make their own travel arrangements.

Tour operators and retail travel agents who intend to include gastronomic destinations in their holiday packages may like to consider some of the suggestions below. In order to enter the food and wine tourism market successfully and satisfy demand, they should:

- Acquire a thorough knowledge of gastronomy and the food and wine sector.
- Send internal staff who already have some specialist knowledge of the sector on fact-finding trips to gastronomic regions; if this is not practicable or possible, external consultants, experienced in gastronomic tourism, need to be employed to carry out critical field research. A useful point to remember is that an 'outsider' may very well discover strengths in a destination that people who have lived there for years may never have noticed.
- Adopt a multidisciplinary approach and create culturally valid itineraries for different targets (e.g. integrating sports activities with cultural visits and gourmet tasting sessions); this 'customized' approach should attract independent travellers as well as groups.
- Be in a position to offer a personalized service if required, able to draw up custom-made itineraries on request.
- Avoid at all costs making trite or false claims about the area to be visited; holiday brochures should be truthful and precise, depicting the destination and its cultural identity as it really is. Itineraries and programmes of activities should be well-constructed beforehand and match the descriptions as set out in the brochures.
- Avoid labelling and selling holidays as 'gastronomic stays' when in reality what is offered is just accommodation (and nothing more) in a region known for its gastronomic produce; even worse if the accommodation is located in an area that has no links at all with food or wine production in the region.
- Always respect the carrying capacity of a destination, whether it is a small farm or a large internationally renowned winery; designing tours for small, manageable groups should always take precedence over constructing commercialized packages for large groups. A tour operator can only guarantee a satisfactory experience and encourage exchange between the host community and tourists if visitor numbers are limited.
- Choose their suppliers according to the quality of their offer (and not only according to cost); they should always reflect regional best, having implemented environmentally friendly policies and carrying out their business activities in a professional manner. Tour operators should also make sure that clients are well informed about their suppliers and their business practices.
- Refrain from demanding huge discounts or free offers, especially from visitor accommodation facilities, as quality of service may suffer as a result.[1]
- Always honour any business agreements made with suppliers (restaurants, production enterprises, accommodation facilities, etc.) and distributors.
- Check a new holiday product down to the very last detail before launching it on to the market.
- Select distributors (including travel agents and other points of sale) who have a serious and professional approach, who are informed about the product and demonstrate a commitment

to it; this can be facilitated by proposing the occasional incentive or educational visit to give the 'seller' first-hand experience of a product before it is proposed to clients.

- Make sure that there is a wide selection of informative material available for clients on all aspects of the destination, including geography, history, gastronomy, art, science and culture. The tour operator should also be prepared to give advice to clients should they require further information, e.g. suggestions with regard to helpful web sites to visit or books or guides to read.
- Invite clients to pre-trip meetings to explain the holiday programme in detail and make sure they all have the correct information; it is also a chance for everyone in the travel group to get to know each other.
- Give a percentage of their profits to support sustainable projects in the destination area (e.g. conservation projects).
- Employ professional personnel to accompany groups (e.g. guides, drivers), who are knowledgeable about the destination and can transmit this knowledge to visitors; they should also be familiar with the gastronomic aspects of the holiday.
- Foster good relations between clients and their travel guides or escorts; for instance, some tour operators who organize adventure or activity holidays, where it is vital that a relationship of trust exists between the tour leader and the group, include photos and profiles of the instructors in their brochures, so that clients already have a good idea about the person who will be assisting them during their stay. This idea could easily be extended to include not only biographies of guides and escorts, but also of other people that visitors will meet while on the trip, e.g. food and wine producers.
- Avoid being overly ambitious when it comes to programming activities; clients should never feel that they are having to participate in a *tour de force*, so journey times, number of stopovers, visits, tasting sessions and so on should be scheduled realistically with their comfort in mind. Clients also need some time on their own to be able to pursue their own interests, to be free to make their own discoveries or just simply wind down at the end of a day and reflect on the day's events.
- Monitor client satisfaction both during and after the holiday and modify itineraries if improvements are deemed necessary; clients should be given feedback questionnaires at the end of a trip and any eventual criticisms should be dealt with promptly and considered in a positive light, as an opportunity to improve the quality of the holiday product even further.
- Stay in contact with clients by organizing after-trip meetings or keeping in touch through e-mails and electronic newsletters, etc.

THE TOUR GUIDE

The tour guide, responsible for individual visitors or groups in a gastronomic destination, must be able to give detailed information about every aspect, including natural attractions, works of art, museums, archaeological sites, etc. They also have the task of leading visitors to a better understanding and fuller appreciation of the food and wine resources in the area. This means visiting and explaining the rural landscape, describing the cultural aspects, giving some information about the history of food and wine production in the region and illustrating the various phases of sensory analysis. Giving specific information about individual products should be left to the producers themselves or to staff in charge of visitor reception at the farms or wineries included in the itinerary. It should also be remembered that gastronomic tourism attracts a number of targets, ranging from 'novices' to 'multi-interest visitors' to 'experts', as we have seen in Chapter 3.

The set of general suggestions below will help to make a guided visit more professional and pleasurable for visitors:

- The route the visit takes should be based around a coherent theme (for more information on this point and other aspects of itinerary construction, see Chapter 8). Once the theme has been established, the route needs to be worked out, taking into consideration the distance to be covered and means of transport (e.g. minibus, bicycle or on foot), how long it will take to cover the entire route and where and when to include stops along the way. When there are a number of different ways to reach a destination, the more interesting/ attractive route should always be chosen over more direct but busier roads.

- When planning a guided visit, it is important to take into account the geomorphological features of a site or, in the case of a city centre, its urban layout. For instance, visitors to a medieval hill-top town should begin at the bottom and then gradually wind their way to the top, discovering along the way the history and architecture of the town; or if the site happens to go back to Roman times, it is important to point out how the city was built according to a system of perpendicular roads. A guide needs to make a place come alive for visitors; by exploring urban development over the centuries, visitors will come away with a much greater understanding of how the city's changing fortunes are reflected in its buildings (e.g. by beginning a tour in the Renaissance heart of a city, then taking visitors further afield to admire the city's Liberty buildings before ending the tour inside an exciting contemporary space built to host trade fairs and exhibitions).

- A guided visit should always be an occasion for visitors to learn more about the importance of the region's natural resources, its art and its gastronomy. However, it should also be an occasion for visitors to meet the local residents. Taking a small group to have an aperitif in a local bar, well off the main tourist track, is an excellent way to come into contact with residents and share in a normal, everyday activity.

- A guided tour needs to be carefully planned and studied. All the places that will be included in the itinerary must be visited and checked beforehand. Furthermore, a multi-disciplinary approach will make it much more interesting and stimulating for the group. Visitors will appreciate a guide who arrives punctually, who is able to interest and involve all the members of the group, who can give explanations without being too long-winded and who can pass with ease from one subject to another. Story-telling skills are invaluable; knowing when to pause and how to modulate tone of voice so that everyone can hear are extremely helpful skills to engage the group and keep everyone's attention. The subject, the level and complexity of discourse all have to be studied and moulded to the interests, age and number of people on the tour. Finally, the guide must always adhere to the tour programme and make sure that the group stays together.

- By the end of a guided tour, the tourist should have a good idea of all the different aspects of the destination: culturally, socially, gastronomically, etc. Some specific aspects should also have been gone into in more depth (e.g. through a tasting session, visiting a winery or strolling across a local farmer's fields).

GASTRONOMIC CULTURE CENTRES

A great number of gastronomic culture centres exist both in Italy and abroad whose mission is to inform and educate the public about the world of gastronomy and high-quality food and wine products. Through various initiatives, they educate people to appreciate the importance of being able to savour the flavour of a region through its dishes and products. We have selected some of the best examples in Box 7.4.

Box 7.4. Case Studies.

A centre for tourists and residents

COPIA, the American Center for Wine, Food & the Arts, a multifunctional centre that was explicitly created to educate both tourists and residents about food and wine culture, unfortunately closed down in 2008. In spite of its closure, COPIA is still worth looking at as a model for a gastronomic cultural centre. Located in the wine-growing region of Napa Valley, home to hundreds of wineries, COPIA's aim was to attract tourists to the centre to learn about viticulture in the valley, before visiting the area and its wineries. Initiatives to involve and educate visitors included:

- Wine. Exhibitions, tasting sessions, courses and other special events organized for different targets, from beginners to connoisseurs, with wine as the central theme. Participants could learn the art of wine selection and develop their skills in wine tasting. Included in the programme of COPIA's daily activities was: 'Daily Wine Class, Wine Tasting 101'. This class gave interested visitors the basic notions of wine tasting that could then be put into practice once they set off to tour the Napa wineries. More experienced visitors could opt for 'Wine Tasting 102: Taste, Quality & Price or Introduction to Wine and Food Pairing'. 'Winery of the Week, The Wine Spectator Tasting Table' introduced tourists to a particular Napa winery, giving them the chance to taste and try wines from their cellars. Other special programmes included guided monthly wine-tasting sessions, food and wine pairing workshops and general meetings. Visitors could also pick up wine information leaflets, articles and recipes.
- Food. Numerous events were also organized to educate visitors in the art of food tasting. Cooking lessons were held in the 'Food Theater' with participants being able to taste the different dishes prepared during the lesson. A varied programme of activities included a daily food class, special meals, and conferences and meetings with renowned food experts, chefs and producers. Visitors to the centre could also enjoy a meal at Julia's Kitchen. The restaurant's French-American cuisine was based around fresh, organically grown products from COPIA's own gardens. Diners could watch their meals being prepared in the open kitchen and participate in a range of special evening events organized around different themes, such as food and music or food and cinema. In the less formal American Market Café, visitors could have a quick seasonal sandwich or choose from a selection of gourmet cheeses.
- The arts. A permanent exhibition entitled 'Forks in the Road: Food, Wine and the American Table' treated visitors to an interactive explanation and analysis of contemporary American thought with regard to the production and consumption of food. In addition, the centre organized temporary exhibitions that looked at food and wine through the mediums of modern art, photography and crafts. Concerts, films and conferences all on the food/wine theme completed the rich calendar of events.
- The Edible Gardens. Covering an area of approximately 3.5 acres along the banks of the Napa River, the 'Edible Gardens Tour' completed the COPIA experience. Modelled on the 16th-century Jardins du Villandry in France, visitors could stroll through the gardens and admire the native fruits, plants, herbs and flowers of Napa Valley. Cultivated

(Continued)

Box 7.4. Continued.

according to organic and biodynamic methods, the garden's produce was used in Julia's Kitchen and the cooking lessons in the 'Food Theater'.

- The Copia Store. Visitors could buy a selection of wines, books, products and gadgets.

The web site also contained articles, recipes and food and wine suggestions.

Higher education training

The Pollenzo Agency houses the University of Gastronomic Sciences, an elegant restaurant, a four-star hotel and The Bank of Wine. It is located in Pollenzo, an ancient hamlet of Bra (Piemonte, Italy, where the International Slow Food Association also has its headquarters). The modernized space that the complex now occupies was once the model farm of King Carlo Alberto of Savoy and is the perfect place to showcase the philosophy of Slow Food and its relationship between mind and taste.

- The University of Gastronomic Sciences was opened in 2004 under the auspices of the Slow Food Association, together with the Regions of Piemonte and Emilia Romagna. It is the first university entirely dedicated to the culture of food. It was set up with the aim of creating an international research and training centre. It promotes sustainable farming methods, supports the preservation and protection of biodiversity and favours an organic relationship between gastronomy and agrarian sciences. The university offers a 3-year first-level degree course followed by a 2-year second-level degree. The programme adopts a multidisciplinary approach to the study of gastronomy, plus studies in the humanities, sciences and economics. At the end of their university training, students are awarded the title of 'Professional Gastronome'. The programme of studies (accounting for approximately one-third of the entire course) also includes several internships in regions of Italy and in production regions abroad. Food production laboratories and work and learning spaces have been specifically created for the students. The University's mission is to create highly professional figures, to promote manual crafts and conserve traditional methods of food production. The University also offers a Master in Italian Gastronomy and Tourism and a Master in Food Culture and Communications, both taught entirely in English.
- The Bank of Wine was established with the idea of creating archives for the best examples of regional wine production and to promote the culture of wine in Italy. The most renowned and best-loved Italian wines are all stored here in the original 18th-century wine cellars. Taking a tour of the cellars, open for both independent and guided visits, is like taking a stroll through the vineyards of Italy. Wine lovers can also reserve and buy their favourite wines on condition that they leave the bottles in the Bank for a fixed period of time. The Agency organizes tasting courses for journalists and Bank members, vertical wine tastings, dinners, training courses, and weekends dedicated to viticulture and oenology led by the Bank's wine producers.
- The neo-gothic building, which is now a luxury four-star hotel, also dates back to the time of King Carlo Alberto of Savoy. In keeping with its location inside the Agency complex, each of its 47 bedrooms is named after the 'grand crus' of Barolo, Barbaresco or Roero.
- Guido's Restaurant is named after a living legend of Piemonte cuisine, Guido da Costigliole, who became famous for his reinvention of traditional Piemontese meat dishes. Although the restaurant is not actually part of the Agency complex, it shares

(Continued)

Box 7.4. Continued.

exactly the same values and objectives, and is an expression of the Agency's aim to be a frame of reference for gastronomic culture.

The opening of the University has made the area (already on the tourist track thanks to the fame of Slow Food) even more attractive to visitors: the town now offers a wide choice of hotel accommodation, B&Bs, restaurants, wine bars and specialized shops.

Further training for professionals and experts in the field

- ONAOO (National Organization of Olive Oil Tasters; www.oliveoil.org) was set up in 1983. The Association has its headquarters in Imperia (Liguria, Italy), a maritime port, whose industrial and productive activities have traditionally been connected to the agro-alimentary sector (e.g. pasta and extra-virgin olive oil: there are hundreds of olive farms in the valleys further inland).

  The Association, an offshoot of the Italian Chamber of Commerce, has since its outset been able to count on the strong support of a group of renowned Italian olive oil tasters. ONAOO's mission is to promote and protect the art of olive oil tasting.

  The concept that quality control of extra-virgin olive oil can be limited to monitoring chemical, microbiological and physical characteristics has long since been abandoned. Today's professional tasters judge the quality of extra-virgin olive oil by conducting a thorough sensory analysis, paying particular attention to the oil's aroma and flavour. These panels of experts therefore guarantee that prime extra-virgin olive oils reach consumers, who do not normally have the specialist knowledge or the techniques to be able to distinguish between a good-quality olive oil and a defective one.

  ONAOO was the first olive oil tasting school in the world. Because of its location in Liguria, it is excellently placed to transmit the traditional techniques and cultural heritage of this world-famous olive-growing region and of Italian olive oil production, in the Mediterranean basin. The school provides a lively platform for debates and information exchange about the culture of olive oil.

  People come from all over the world to attend its courses. The aim of the school is to give students a complete panorama of olive oil production, from the study of agronomy to transformation techniques, and from sensory analysis to marketing strategies. The full-immersion courses, which run for 2 to 5 days, also give course attendants a complete geographical perspective of the world's olive-growing regions beginning with the Mediterranean, the cradle of olive oil production.

  The courses are organized to satisfy different needs and levels. Higher level, in-depth training courses are available for those who already have some expertise in olive oil tasting, while people without professional experience but a passion for olive oil are introduced to the techniques of sensory analysis in order to distinguish a good quality extra-virgin olive oil from a defective one. The lessons are theoretical as well as being practical. The main courses offered are: Technical Courses for Aspiring Olive Oil Tasters; Practical Course in the Techniques and Culture of Olive Growing to increase production, to contain costs and to improve the quality of olive oil; Oil Pressing Techniques and Training Course for Olive Growers; Professional Diploma Courses and Further Training Courses.

  The Association maintains relationships with higher education institutes and scientific research organizations and has many international members. It also organizes

(Continued)

Box 7.4. Continued.

annual trips to Spain, Greece, Morocco, Portugal and other olive oil-producing countries all over the world.

- Trieste is the principal port for coffee imports in Italy and the whole of the supply chain can be found here, from the city's coffee importers to its historic cafés, where coffee is still drunk today in the authentic atmosphere of *belle époque*. It was here in 1933 that Francesco Illy founded his company and developed a pressurized packing system for preserving coffee. Illy is also responsible for establishing a University of Coffee to promote the culture of coffee. The University organizes courses and workshops at different levels for producers and professionals. The courses vary in content and include bar management and marketing, coffee tasting, coffee aroma analysis, practical sessions on how to make the perfect moka, espresso or cappuccino, and coffee- or chocolate-themed dinners.

  The courses for professional bar staff explore the world of coffee from every angle. Beginning with the raw material and ending with how to treat clients to a stylish, perfectly made cup of coffee, every aspect is covered: from the plant, the bud, the bean and the production process to the different methods used to make espresso, cappuccino and other types of coffee drinks.

  Coffee lovers are also catered for. The University offers courses to further people's knowledge about coffee and to teach them the art of appreciating and distinguishing coffees from different growing regions, similarities and differences in roast, and the varying notes and aromas. They also learn the correct techniques to prepare coffee and how to conduct a tasting analysis. The majority of courses are held at the Illy University in Trieste, but Illy has also opened a number of branches outside Italy. In addition, the University also takes its courses on tour to high-profile gastronomic destinations. The courses either follow a general programme, taking place over 1 or 2 days, or they can be specially organized on request. Course participants receive a certificate of attendance at the end of the course.

NOTE

[1] Contracts between tour operators and their suppliers tend to be one of the following types. (i) 'Buy out', by which a tour operator (usually a large company with ample financial resources) purchases in advance and at a much lower cost than the published rack rate a large number of bed places, assuming the risk if the bed places remain unsold. (ii) 'Allotment', by which a tour operator is allocated a certain number of bed places and other services at a discounted price compared with the rack rate (but less advantageous than 'buy out') up until a fixed date; the tour operator then has the option of confirming the allotment by this deadline. If the option is not confirmed, the available bed places and/or services are taken over again by the supplier. (iii) 'By commission' or 'confidential tariffs', which represent the least risk for a tour operator, although economically less advantageous than the other two types of contract, as the tour operator only receives a commission on sales.

chapter 8

Designing a Life Experience: Itinerary Planning and Organization

Tourism differs quite substantially from other types of leisure activities. As an activity, tourism lasts longer but other leisure pursuits are 'used' with more frequency. Consumer choice is strongly influenced by market trends and many people choose a particular destination or type of holiday because they see it as being fashionable and a confirmation of their social status. Tourism entails going on a journey and putting physical distance between the consumer's place of residence and their final holiday destination and also implies a return home. It generally requires more financial investment than other activities and the suitability or quality of the product cannot be tested out beforehand. Buying a holiday product therefore presents a number of risks for the consumer. A holiday experience for most people is, in effect, a part of their life story, albeit a small part played out in 'some other place'. As in everyday life, there are surprises, unexpected meetings and unforeseen events. Everyday needs must be met but in a different context to the daily routine, while dreams and expectations have to be fulfilled, to avoid disappointment with the choice of product.

Holiday planners must therefore be in tune with their clients, able to share their ideas, identify their likes and dislikes and understand their dreams and anxieties. In essence, they must be able to successfully plan and manage a part of their clients' lives. The task of the tour planner is even more delicate when people buy a holiday package, because they are in fact delegating responsibility for their choice to the person in charge of creating the itinerary.

The ability to construct a life experience in the way that tour operators (or travel agents and tour guides) are required to do is a skill that is extremely useful for many actors in the tourism industry, particularly in the food and wine sector. Being in a position to give helpful advice to guests and suggest well-planned itineraries that respond to their needs and interests can make all the difference in market placement. Hospitality enterprises such as hotels, B&Bs, farmhouses, wineries and restaurants that enter into interactive communication with their clients are placed in a much higher position in a competitive market. In gastronomic tourism it is also important that visitors receive detailed information about the surrounding area and suggestions for exploring the region. The best way to do this is for the person responsible for guest relations (and indeed for communicators and planners) to visit the surrounding area in person, draw up a series of recommendations based on personal experience, and then use this as a basis to design various itineraries according to the different targets.

PACKAGE TRAVEL

The European Council Directive 90/314/EEC on package travel, package holidays and package tours (European Union, 1990) is a useful document to refer to in order to get a clear understanding of what is meant by the term 'package travel'. In spite of the fact that it dates back a number of years (1990), it still gives us a valid description and definition. According to the directive, 'package' means the pre-arranged combination of not fewer than two of the following – transport, accommodation, tourist services not ancillary to transport or accommodation – when sold or offered for sale at an inclusive price. Tourist services in the package include itineraries, visits, excursions and the support of a tour guide or representative for the duration of the holiday. At the moment of booking the consumer accepts and enters into an agreement with the organizer or retail party on the specific arrangements for the holiday package. Organizers or retailers are in actual fact bound by the directive to offer or sell packages at an all-inclusive price and must not charge for individual services included in the package. The specific costs of the single components of the holiday are not made known to the client. Tour operators can play on the 'all-inclusive' nature of a package and offer attractive conditions to their customers. For example, they can offer standard services at discounted prices by making direct agreements with the supply side. However, they can also offer high-quality services or a rich programme of activities, tailoring their offer to suit individual needs, which requires specialized knowledge on the part of the operator and time-consuming research. In this case the price of the holiday will necessarily be higher. When creating a customized tour, it is essential that the tour operator gives the client the necessary information and possibilities of choice, so that the final itinerary absolutely matches the interests and expectations of the client.

The directive also states that the service offered in a holiday package should cover a period of more than 24 hours or include overnight accommodation.

The law clearly sets out the minimum requisites needed to construct a general holiday package for the mass tourism market, but at the same time, it leaves tour operators with enough freedom to be able to create customized packages to satisfy the needs and expectations of individual clients. Consequently, operators in the food and wine sector are in an excellent position to create appealing packages based around themes and activities that will interest and attract different targets with divergent needs.

Tour operators responsible for holiday planning and organization must keep in mind, however, that demand in the food and wine sector, more than in other tourism sectors, has a strong tendency towards independent, autonomous travel. In fact it is not an easy task to convince a gastronomic tourist, used to making their own travel arrangements, to buy a ready-made holiday package.

Nevertheless, it is also true that in many cases the ability to organize an independent holiday experience is not always supported by ample enough knowledge about what the chosen destination has to offer. It is virtually impossible for a first-time visitor to be informed about all the resources in a region, particularly in such a specialized area as local produce and production. An overwhelming number of natural and cultural attractions, accommodation facilities, restaurants and leisure or sports activities can also be confusing. Without inside knowledge, it is difficult for the prospective traveller to make the right choice. In spite of the plethora of information that a tourist can pick up about a gastronomic destination in books, guides, magazines, brochures and other published material, there is still plenty of space for manoeuvre. A cultural tour operator with a creative professional approach can offer tourists a valid alternative to independent travel. Even when tourists are well-informed about a destination before setting off, they may not be prepared for the emotional impact that the beauty of the natural environment will have on them, or for the intensity of their physical reaction as they become immersed in a totally new sensory experience. An operator intending to offer gastronomic tours should therefore take into account and take advantage of people's inexperience and lack of knowledge about their chosen destination. Last but not least, tour operators can also save their clients a great deal of time and money by organizing all the details of a trip (including insurance) and managing any eventual problems or complaints.

As demand in the food and wine sector is so strongly independent, organized packages must be particularly enticing and appealing, much more so than in any other sector of tourism. Tour operators need to have a professional approach and offer a variety of carefully planned itineraries, based around coherent themes that are flexible enough to be tailored to individual tastes and interests.

With demand being so fragmented, operators can find themselves dealing with a wide target with very different expectations. The way they respond to these diverse needs can take them in a number of directions. As we have already seen, the target in gastronomic tourism displays wildly varying characteristics: aware consumers and Sunday excursionists, experts and novices, sports lovers and culture vultures, to name just a few. Operators therefore have many options open to them. Tour packages can be either flexible or tightly structured but must always offer an original and interesting holiday experience. They can specialize in offering a highly personalized service, working alongside the client who actively participates in planning and organizing the trip. They can offer a myriad of extra services and activities, including short visits that can still guarantee a fulfilling experience for the client. The aim at all times is to provide clients with the opportunity to learn more about the destination, to promote cultural exchange, to encourage visitor participation and to create moments of relaxation and enjoyment that stimulate both physical and emotional well-being.

As operators begin to create tour itineraries for their clients, there are a number of important factors to keep in mind. The region or area that is chosen as a holiday destination must communicate its identity clearly to the visitor. The interplay of elements that together form the region's character or personality should gradually be unveiled and revealed, beginning with the distinguishing features of its landscape. The supply side must create conditions that permit visitors to establish a rapport with the host destination. Tour planners must always be aware of the importance of the quality of the visitor experience and be sensitive to the sensations and emotions evoked by a gastronomic product.

PREPARING AND DESIGNING THE BROCHURE

The principal way to reach the general public and publicize a package holiday or tour is through the distribution of catalogues or brochures, whether in the more traditional printed format or as electronic versions. The European Council Directive 90/314/EEC comes in useful here as well, to help us define the essential characteristics of what is meant by the term 'brochure'. It states that a brochure:

> shall indicate in a legible, comprehensible and accurate manner both the price and adequate information concerning: the destination; the means, characteristics and categories of transport used; the type

of accommodation, its location, category or degree of comfort and its main features, its approval and tourist classification under the rules of the host Member State concerned; the meal plan; the itinerary; general information on passport and visa requirements for nationals of the Member State or States concerned and health formalities required for the journey and the stay; either the monetary amount or the percentage of the price which is to be paid on account, and the timetable for payment of the balance; whether a minimum number of persons is required for the package to take place and, if so, the deadline for informing the consumer in the event of cancellation.

How does an operator go about conceiving and designing a holiday brochure? The first all-important point to remember is that it is an extremely complex task to plan and produce a brochure. It has to be successful in communicating the image that the tour operator wishes to convey to the target market, the philosophy and business approach of the operator, as well as holiday proposals and offers. All this requires professional knowledge, an adequate budget, the monitoring of resources and time-management skills. Planning a brochure from scratch to launch a new activity entails a considerable length of time. Even adding new offers to an established programme is not a quick process. In fact, it can take as long as 2 years, from the research phase to the final realization of the project, for a new destination to appear in a catalogue. Significant time is also needed just to update offers and prices for the following season.

The type of holiday offered, the number of activities included, the duration of the holiday and the particular sector that is being dealt with (e.g. food and wine tourism), together with the tour operator's market image and position, all put a distinctive stamp on the brochure.

A brochure is not just a promotional tool; in a sense it also functions as a business card. It is therefore extremely important to take the appropriate steps to plan and produce a brochure. The stages in Fig. 8.1 have been analysed by necessity into a logical sequence, although in reality they are normally implemented simultaneously.

Analysis sheets: support tools for consultation, data revision and planning

Being able to refer to an analysis sheet when carrying out research and collecting data can be very helpful both during the investigation phase and later when analysing results. Notes can be added with regard to possible future business contacts and suppliers, as well as comments about regional services, resources and attractions.

The analysis sheets are also useful for making notes about the most important features of a gastronomic destination and for jotting down general impressions during the visit. When it comes to writing up observations after the visit, the notes taken during field research will be especially invaluable to compile an informative and accurate report. The inclusion of photos, promotional literature and any other relevant material will give the report even more weight.

The analysis sheets presented in Figs 8.2 to 8.5 can all be modified to reflect the different research objectives of individual tour operators.

CULTURE AND GASTRONOMY TOURS

Organizing the tourist experience, whether to do with food and wine tourism or not, revolves around the very substance of package travel: the itinerary. This is especially true when a package involves a tour rather than a stay in one place.

Learning to create and construct packages for food and wine tourism requires professional skills and knowledge that can keep abreast with the latest trends. A successful itinerary clearly needs to be well researched beforehand, and certain fundamental elements need to be taken into account during the planning, programming and management phases. These have been listed below.

Actions to take: reading up on the subject, statistical research (using both primary and secondary data), case analysis, field research and analysis

PROJECT PLAN	initial analysis

Analysis of opportunities offered by the area and the market in question
Planning for strategic product development
• area analysis (attractions, destinations, natural resources and landscape appeal, socio-economic aspects, administrative aspects; permits, opportunity and potential, safety and security, potential partners, policies for development and future projects, cultural identity and awareness of host community, external image, SWOT analysis)
• market analysis: demand, supply, competition, financial analysis and forecasts relating to socio-economic factors that could influence tourist product development
• assessment of development opportunities for the product (environmental and socio-economic impact and sustainability, quality)
• policy development (requisites, necessary resources, time management, budget, market segmentation, identification of target, market positioning, product, communication tools and promotion, prices, distribution and sales)
• formulation of theme-based products (development, consolidation, quality control, modification and improvement)
• assessment of alternative possibilities

METHODOLOGY – STRATEGIES FOR PRODUCT FORMATION	production

Research analysis
• prepare analysis sheets
• verify area opportunities and project coherence (appeal/theme, professionalism, environment, degree of tourist development, socio-economic factors)
• contact operators and make control visits to check services and infrastructure (accommodation/eating places/production centres/viability and accessibility/walking and cycling paths/transport/tourist services, cultural, leisure, sport, etc./usability)
• verify and analyse field research comparing results with data collected from bibliographical research
Product planning according to the following criteria:
• quality/category, coherence in terms of regional identity, functionality/position, professionalism, client/target needs
• itineraries/activities
• choice of partners and suppliers
• stipulation of supply contracts
• compiling and editing the text/graphic design and images
• pricing
• brochure production (design layout, information, texts, photos)
Strategies for promotion and commercial distribution
• advertising, fam trips, events; choice of direct or indirect distribution channels (agents, electronic marketing, mailing; public and private organizations, associations, important clients, end users)

CONTROL – VALIDATION/MODIFICATION	market

• Test (test visits) and market launch
• Monitoring (financial performance, client feedback, internal human resources, external partners, customer relations and complaints management)
• Assessing alternatives after having analysed business performance results
• Professional know-how (continuous training and professional development opportunities through courses, conferences, seminars, workshops and meetings)
• Adjustments and improvements to the product (new themes, activities, partners, events)

Fig. 8.1. Guidelines for brochure planning.

The ability to construct itineraries is one of the most important factors for the creation of services in cultural tourism: it can determine the success or failure of a tourist product, whether it concerns a destination or a company operating in the tourism sector.

AGROFOOD PRODUCTION CENTRES
Individual business name/Company name Address   Tel.   Fax   E-mail   Web site
Type of production/market   –   Reference markets
Name of person in charge (owner/visit organizer/person responsible for customer relations)
Notes on company history and business characteristics
VISITOR RECEPTION   VISITS   PROGRAMMES Open to the public   yes/no/pre-booked visits only   days and times Booking advised   Closed on …   Closed during … When to visit (best period and why)   When not to visit (why) Individual visitors welcome   Groups welcome: min./max. no. of visitors accepted Languages spoken: English/French/German/Spanish/Italian/other Visitor guide (quality, tour features, ability to communicate and adapt to target)
TYPE OF TOUR – DESCRIPTION   independent   guided Complete/partial tour   (what is included/what is missing) Outside (vineyards, olive groves, pastures, animal enclosures …) Inside (production areas …)
TASTING yes/no   Designated area yes/no   (description of type of ambience) No. of places Tasting guide/expert (quality, main features of tasting session …) Type of service (at the bar/seated, technical/informal, equipment/different combinations …)
SALES POINT   Designated area   yes/no   (description of the type of ambience) Products on sale   Prices
VISIT LENGTH and PRICES Average length of visit – Price per person (with/without tasting session) Other notes on visit and tasting
OTHER organized SERVICES/ACTIVITIES CATERING SERVICES on site/off site   outsourced (see Food & Beverage Sector) ACCOMMODATION on site/off site   outsourced (see Hospitality Sector) OTHER cultural activities, excursions, sports activities; courses and workshops, internships; working partnerships with external business enterprises and other organizations …
NOTES ON AMBIENCE AND WELCOME Ambience/Environment/Location/Professionalism/Courtesy/Quality/Sustainability/ Atmosphere/Surrounding area

Fig. 8.2. Analysis sheet: food production enterprises.

Having a system of structured itineraries in place offers significant advantages:

- It gives clients the opportunity to discover an area and learn to appreciate a hitherto unknown environment in a privileged way, as the tour will have been tested by someone who already knows the region well.
- It stimulates visitor curiosity, as 'themed' tours offer something fresh, new and original compared with the usual more conventional holiday propositions.

FOOD & BEVERAGE SECTOR
Individual business name/Company name
Type of restaurant   notes
Address   Tel.   Fax   E-mail   Web site
Name of person in charge (owner/person responsible for customer relations…)
Name of chef   notes
Notes on company history and business characteristics
Closed on …   Closed during …   Languages spoken: English/French/German/Spanish/Italian/other
CATERING SERVICES   No. of people catered for   Garden/Terrace Services   Smoking area   Cuisine (regional/national/international/pizzeria/other)   (fish/meat/other)   Wine list   Olive oil (origin)   Menu description (types of dishes, tasting menus, special menus for groups …)   Average price for complete menu (individuals and groups, freebies)   Notes on: ambience, service, food
ANCILLARY SERVICES   ACCOMMODATION   on site/off site   outsourced   (see Hospitality Sector)
OTHER SERVICES   car park, coach park …   Organized activities for guests: visits to wineries, farms and other gastronomic destinations…   Partnerships and agreements with external services (visits to other production centres and gastronomic destinations, other organized visits, excursions, sports, cultural activities …)
NOTES ON AMBIENCE AND WELCOME   Ambience/Environment/Location/Professionalism/Courtesy/Quality/Sustainability/ Atmosphere/Surrounding area

Fig. 8.3. Analysis sheet: food and beverage services.

- It encourages visitors to prolong their stay in a destination, making the visitor experience more proactive and therefore more satisfying.
- It increases a sense of belonging to the chosen destination, even if it lasts just for the duration of the holiday.
- It fosters cultural exchange between visitors and the host community, even for residents who are not directly involved in tourism services.
- It is a precious resource for the host community, offering numerous occasions to discover, learn more about and lay claim to their place of residence, all factors that reinforce respect for the immediate environment and strengthen a sense of community and common identity.
- It boosts more active participation in civic matters, as the host population becomes more aware of the need to safeguard regional identity and protect the environment through the development and implementation of sustainable practices.

To sum up, having a structured approach to itinerary planning raises visibility in the market, adds value to the tourist offer, and gives a destination and its operators a distinctive edge over competitors, while at the same time improving the quality of life for both tourists and residents.

HOSPITALITY SECTOR		
Individual business name	Company name	Type of accommodation
Category Address Tel. Fax E-mail Web site		
Name of person in charge (owner/person responsible for customer relations) Notes		
Notes on company history and business characteristics		
Closed on … Closed during … Languages spoken: English/French/German/Spanish/Italian/other		
ROOMS/BEDS Number and type Rooms/facilities/services for disabled guests Pets accepted yes/no Groups welcome (max. no. of persons) …		
CATERING SERVICES internal/ external outsourced (see Food & Beverage Sector)		
ANCILLARY SERVICES car park, coach park Organized visits (production centres, gastronomic destinations, cultural visits …) Spa centre Sports facilities Fitness trails, cycling and footpaths Sports equipment for hire Other services – activities for guests Partnerships and agreements with external services (visits to other production centres and gastronomic destinations, excursions, sports, cultural activities …)		
RATES (for the current and following year) BB/HB/FB Seasonality – rack rates and lowest rates Special offers (children, seniors) Agreements with Tour Operators and Agents Commissions/prices for individuals Commissions/prices for groups (min. no. of people, free offers) Contractual agreements (confidential tariffs, allotment, buy out)		
NOTES ON AMBIENCE AND WELCOME Company/Location/Main office/Professionalism/Courtesy/Ambience/Services/ Quality/Surrounding area/Sustainability/Atmosphere Best and worst times to stay		

Fig. 8.4. Analysis sheet: hospitality services.

To construct a 'themed' itinerary that can satisfy the diverse needs of different types of targets, but is planned with total respect for the environment and the socio-economic characteristics of a region, is a considerable and delicate task. An itinerary that has a specific medium/ long-term programme, is constructed according to the principles of sustainability and includes the very best a region can offer, will without doubt have a positive ripple effect. In terms of marketing and promotion, the region can only benefit, but the impact on regional organization and companies operating in the area is also positive. For example, there is greater stimulus to be innovative, to create efficient organization systems and networks and put management strategies in place that are both balanced and forward-looking.

Itinerary planning is therefore an activity that concerns most, if not all, tourist operators. It is certainly an essential *modus operandi* for tour operators, travel agents, tourism bureaus, travel consultants and associations, indeed any professional figure involved in tourism services. It is

LOCALITY Cultural heritage sites/Monuments/Museums or similar cultural resources/ Sightseeing walks or similar cultural activities
Address and contact details   Directions   Notes (history, art, geography)   Name of the person in charge   (director, owner, person responsible for PR)   Organization and management   Accessibility   parking   ticketing   Cost of visit   Possibility of guided tours   Conditions and ease of visit   State of repair   Safety and security   Further studies: resources, publications, links to similar themes, etc.
Closed on …   Closed during …   Languages spoken: English/French/German/Spanish/Italian/other   Groups welcome (max. no. of persons)   High season/low season   Best/worst periods to visit
NOTES ON AMBIENCE AND WELCOME   Atmosphere/Location/Professionalism/Courtesy/Services/Quality of experience/ Sustainability/Regional integration/Network–agreements–visitor cards with other regional organizations or facilities
LOCALITY – Tourist organization and/or services   Company name and contact details   Activity (type – guided visits, excursions, sports, health and well-being, leisure)   Services (description, type, length of time, areas of competence, external partnerships)   Human resources (no. of workers, business profiles and professionalism, flexibility, courtesy, helpfulness)   Languages spoken: English/French/German/Spanish/Italian/other   Rates and free services   Descriptive notes (impressions, simulated visits and services)

Fig. 8.5. Analysis sheet: regional attractions and tourist services.

equally important for anyone involved in welcoming visitors to their place of business, whether it is a rural B&B, a centre for regional production or a gastronomic destination such as a winery or local restaurant.

Themed itineraries (including those that offer courses in painting and drawing, pottery, photography, languages, music, yoga, cooking, etc.) provide the general tourist product (the destination) with a distinct identity and a more complete offer. This is also true for individual businesses because itineraries create a lasting link between those businesses and the region in which they operate. As a result, what they have to offer visitors are products that tend to be more exciting, more original and more attractive.

Technical strategies for itinerary planning

In order to give visibility to a region and make it an attractive and interesting destination, tourism operators need to follow a precise methodology to construct itineraries as the ultimate aim is to provide visitors with the opportunity to discover a region in an enjoyable way. The need for a rigorous approach is especially true for areas that are famous for their food and wine production as regional characteristics are so complex.

Putting together an itinerary or tour is like assembling a number of small parts, each one closely linked to another. As there are so many variables to be taken into account, it is often better not to impose a strict time sequence or try to rank the variables into order of importance. To facilitate novices in itinerary planning, the variables that need to be considered are set out in order below. However, each variable needs to be analysed in conjunction with the others. As each variable is acted upon, it is important to predict what the outcome of that action will be on the other variables and manage the consequences.

Although each variable can take on a different significance for an itinerary to function effectively, it is important to keep in mind that incorrect or superficial analysis, even of apparently insignificant factors, can have negative consequences on how useful and how enjoyable the itinerary will eventually turn out to be.

The correct methodology to draw up an itinerary for a cultural and gastronomic tour must therefore be based on the principles of accurate research, professionalism, application, intuition, rationality and flexibility. A multidisciplinary approach and multiple analyses must then be applied to all the potential variables in force, each one linked to the other.

The whole process of itinerary construction is therefore based on careful analysis and research, both of which are indispensable for making sure that the operative phase that follows is planned logically. Adopting a protocol to set down strategies and actions, of the type used for creating a marketing plan, can be extremely helpful when organizing all the work necessary to draw up an itinerary.

Know the region

An itinerary is basically a discovery trail that takes place over a fairly large area. Choosing an area by tracing over a few lines or curves on a map is not sufficient. In order to obtain a satisfactory result it is necessary to look carefully at all the various components of the chosen region. These include: geographical features, natural resources, culture and society, economy and production, local legislation and entrepreneurship (Figs 8.6 and 8.7).

It is vital that the identity and image of a particular region as perceived by the outside world corresponds to the cultural identity as lived and manifested by the host population. The degree to which a region can be analysed is strictly related to how much detailed planning goes into creating the itinerary.

A regional analysis should present evidence of elements that can be incorporated into an itinerary and guarantee its success. In other words, the suitability of an area or region needs to be verified. This can be done by:

- confirming that the region meets the expectations of the itinerary planner with regard to fundamental prerequisites, assessing whether more possibilities emerge once further knowledge has been gained by visiting the area, and taking note of any opportunities to link a series of 'themed' activities together to give a complete visitor experience; and
- checking that the objectives of the itinerary match the needs and characteristics of the target and that they correspond to the type of programme that has been devised, e.g. means of transport chosen, degree of difficulty, period and duration; choice and type of services and facilities, safety and security measures.

The procedure adopted to analyse a region and evaluate its strengths and risks as a visitor destination can be divided into distinct phases:

- Bibliographical research and desk analysis. Preliminary studies aimed to collect information before carrying out field research in the destination and to estimate time needed for the visit.

Fig. 8.6. Olive grove near the medieval abbey (Abruzzo, Italy).

These initial studies will also be useful in subsequent stages whenever there is a need to verify any aspects.

- Field research. The structure of an itinerary can vary according to how detailed or complex the proposed programme of activities is. This obviously depends on the nature of the tour and its intended target. Each and every element of the programme needs to be tested personally by the itinerary organizer and, whenever possible, at different periods of the year and in different climatic conditions. It is important not to underestimate any risks that could impact negatively on the real visitor experience. The need to study, create and properly test itineraries before allowing them to become public and enter the market requires a great deal of time investment. To be able to produce a complete and thoroughly tested itinerary therefore needs accurate time planning and management.

- Critical feedback, control and adjustment. It is absolutely essential that analyses (e.g. SWOT analysis or customer feedback surveys) are carried out at regular intervals; without this information it would be impossible to improve and update the product and meet evolving consumer needs and expectations. The distribution of regional resources and tourism infrastructure needs to be mapped out, together with available services, suppliers and possible business partners. This helps to establish not only the principal places of interest to be visited but also any breaks or stops en route. Feedback on all these aspects allows

Fig. 8.7. The terraced slopes of Cinque Terre (Liguria, Italy).

the itinerary organizer to constantly review the end product and helps in the selection of facilities and services that are coherent with the leitmotiv and quality of the offer.

Basic instruments that are useful for getting to know an area first-hand are:

- derived maps, topographic and thematic maps, including those showing the geological features of an area or the flora and fauna, nautical and weather maps, etc., GPS and other satellite tracking systems, GIS (Geographic Information System);
- journals and other publications on tourism and related topics, e.g. nature, art, history, traditions, cooking, local crafts;
- electronic instruments for recording and storing images, e.g. a digital camera, video camera, scanner; and
- orientation instruments, e.g. a compass, altimeter, curvimeter, binoculars.

Aims and objectives

The way in which a cultural and gastronomic tour is set up and organized depends very much on who is behind the project. A national or local tourism board will have a completely different approach to itinerary planning compared with a tour operator or a private operator. With quality and sustainability being the core characteristics of any itinerary, the aims and objectives of a public organization will be tied to their role as a public institution and will focus on highlighting regional resources, while a tour operator or a private enterprise will be more concerned with marketing strategies and profit margins. In the case of a private operator, the aims and objectives behind constructing the itinerary will very much reflect their relationship with the area and their competitors. Benchmarking, selecting possible business partners and suppliers, and identifying the target are all important actions to be taken in order to realize the ultimate aim of the itinerary: visitor satisfaction.

Market analysis and decision making

This phase involves:

- market segmentation and choice of target(s);
- knowing about and analysing tourism products already on offer in the market, being informed about case studies and being aware of real and potential competitors operating in the same sector; and
- deciding where to position the product.

Continuous action research and up-to-date analysis of what is happening outside the region are useful for making comparisons and can facilitate decision making in itinerary planning. For example, reading specialist publications and trade journals, attending conferences on tourism or fairs and exhibitions, even visiting other areas, all provide up-to-the-minute information on which to base decisions concerning itinerary construction and management. Sometimes changes to the original programme may need to be made or the level of quality measured; knowing about successful external business practices can be enormously helpful in making the necessary adjustments. However, external business models may not always be appropriate and should be thoroughly tested before being applied in a totally different context. Every region and every enterprise has its own set of characteristics that condition market decisions.

Analysing project success potential and project management requirements

Once research and analysis have been carried out and a region assessed with regard to having the necessary requisites for a potentially successful tour, it is then possible to begin to actively programme the tour. This stage of planning requires having a clear and accurate idea of what resources are available in order to meet the aims and objectives of the project. To be able to draw up an itinerary in the secure knowledge that it will meet intended goals means having the support of human resources in terms of professional skills, and having sufficient financial and technological resources.

As has already been mentioned, the structure of an itinerary is based on the organization of a number of variables and interdependent elements (Fig. 8.8). Combining those elements together, to create an offer that is efficacious and corresponds to clients' needs and expectations, is not an easy task. It requires ability and skill. In fact, one of the principal factors in determining the success of a tour lies in the ability to tie all the disparate elements together to create a rational and logical trail with a clear theme that will appeal to and satisfy the target.

CHOOSING THE THEME

The choice of theme is fundamental as it gives an itinerary a distinct identity and makes it unique. A recognizable theme also marks it out from other more generic tourist products on the market. It means offering something to the visitor that is original and enticing, a product that reflects the region's productive resources and cultural heritage. The theme must obviously be appropriate for the intended target and lie within the competencies, in terms of knowledge and skills, of the people responsible for the planning and eventual management of the itinerary.

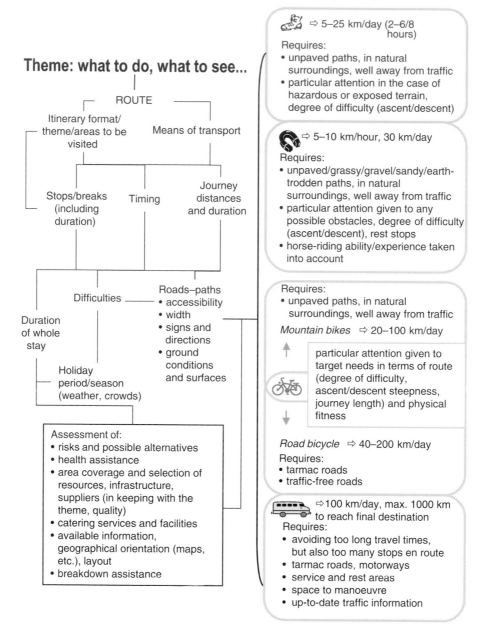

Theme: what to do, what to see...

ROUTE

Itinerary format/theme/areas to be visited

Means of transport

Stops/breaks (including duration)

Timing

Journey distances and duration

Difficulties

Roads–paths
- accessibility
- width
- signs and directions
- ground conditions and surfaces

Duration of whole stay

Holiday period/season (weather, crowds)

Assessment of:
- risks and possible alternatives
- health assistance
- area coverage and selection of resources, infrastructure, suppliers (in keeping with the theme, quality)
- catering services and facilities
- available information, geographical orientation (maps, etc.), layout
- breakdown assistance

⇨ 5–25 km/day (2–6/8 hours)
Requires:
- unpaved paths, in natural surroundings, well away from traffic
- particular attention in the case of hazardous or exposed terrain, degree of difficulty (ascent/descent)

⇨ 5–10 km/hour, 30 km/day
Requires:
- unpaved/grassy/gravel/sandy/earth-trodden paths, in natural surroundings, well away from traffic
- particular attention given to any possible obstacles, degree of difficulty (ascent/descent), rest stops
- horse-riding ability/experience taken into account

Requires:
- unpaved paths, in natural surroundings, well away from traffic

Mountain bikes ⇨ 20–100 km/day

particular attention given to target needs in terms of route (degree of difficulty, ascent/descent steepness, journey length) and physical fitness

Road bicycle ⇨ 40–200 km/day
Requires:
- tarmac roads
- traffic-free roads

⇨ 100 km/day, max. 1000 km to reach final destination
Requires:
- avoiding too long travel times, but also too many stops en route
- tarmac roads, motorways
- service and rest areas
- space to manoeuvre
- up-to-date traffic information

Fig. 8.8. Structuring an itinerary: principal factors.

A food and wine itinerary naturally focuses on one or more products in a given area. There are manifold ways of presenting an itinerary but the general theme must obviously appeal to the intended target. We can, for example, find specialized tours that are directed at an exclusive market. There are educational tours with hands-on activities for all the family. Some tours are simply focused on entertainment while others are more serious and scientific. However, there is always a risk of a tour turning out to be unexciting or unoriginal or, at the other extreme, to be so full of technical details that it completely overwhelms the participants. The chosen theme therefore must reconcile a number of diverse approaches. It needs to be original and well researched, with just the right amount of detail to satisfy visitor curiosity. It should present the area and its products in a simple, direct way, yet be rich in content and capable of arousing interest. It must have a multidisciplinary approach, drawing together all the different resources of a region and offering a wide range of activities. The overriding factor is always to build a strong link between visitor experience and the region.

Set out below are some examples of exciting or original experiences that tourists can enjoy in different regions and in different situations. In each case, the visitor's sensory perception of a gastronomic product is heightened by combining it with one or more resources in the region (e.g. art, history, geography, geology, literature, flora and fauna, architecture, anthropology, religion, economy).

In a wine region, a tour could be dedicated to visiting wine estates where the same type of grape is grown (e.g. discovering the different nuances of Nebbiolo wine in Piemonte, Italy). But imagine the impact on visitors during a wine-tasting session when a connection is made between the intense colour of the wine and the vivid brush strokes of a famous painting. Again, to heighten visual and sensory perception, the round, soft, supple taste of the wine could be compared with the undulating forms of the hills where the grapes are grown. It is even possible to link the structure of a wine with that of its cellars, whether they are traditional wine vaults or high-tech, state-of-the-art wine storage spaces.

In alpine regions, a tour could concentrate on comparing the different types of cheese produced. Or, even more exciting from an organoleptic point of view, titillate visitors' sense of smell by revealing to them the link between the microclimate of the region, the abundant growth of aromatic plants in the meadows and the particular aroma of the cheese that comes from the milking herd that grazes there.

In olive-growing regions, visitors can be given the opportunity to discover the similarities and differences in taste of the same type of olive oil, produced according to the same methods, but cultivated on different olive farms.

On a cultural tour of a historic centre that includes a visit to a famous ghetto, visitors will remember far more about the place, its history and its inhabitants if, after having learned about Hebrew traditions, they sit down and enjoy a kosher meal together at the end of the tour.

Other ideas for making connections to create unusual but stimulating tours include:

- linking a particular region with its immediate neighbours and exploring their linguistic, cultural or culinary ties;
- combining food and literature by giving visitors the chance to enjoy a literary feast in the same place as the setting of a great novel;
- illustrating the culinary traditions of an area by seeking out the food, wine, farm animals, etc. depicted in great works of art (e.g. the *cinta* pig in Lorenzetti's fresco *Il Buon Governo* in the Palazzo Pubblico in Siena);
- while visiting places where food or wine is produced, the personal histories are retold of the people who, with inspiration and vision, adopted innovative production methods to create rare, gastronomic delicacies; and
- discovering the organoleptic and cultural similarities in products that, although coming from two very distinct and distant areas, are inextricably linked because of emigration or seasonal migration.

The linking together of a region's resources, its history and its people through a 'themed' itinerary has a very strong impact on visitors. Sensations and emotions evoked during the holiday stay with them long after the tour is over, and are relived every time they tell friends or family about the pleasure or excitement derived from their culinary, cultural and sensory experiences… exactly like Proust's madeleine!

LENGTH OF TOUR AND STOPS EN ROUTE

How long a tour lasts and the distance it covers depend on the season, the type of area chosen, the number of visits and activities that will be included, and of course, the means of transport that will be used.

TRANSPORT

Itinerary planners have an ample choice of transport means: from trains, coaches, minibuses, cars, jeeps, mountain bikes, ships and boats to horses. The final decision depends on the intended target and the type of tour that has been organized. There are, of course, also walking holidays, where no other form of transport is necessary, once tourists have arrived at the start destination. Organizing a tour that requires the use of more than one form of transport obviously needs careful planning and timing to make connections smooth and efficient. Overall distance and length of tour obviously need to be considered. Other factors like the distance between destinations en route, stop-offs and refreshment breaks also need to be taken into account, as well as the time of year, road or route conditions and the choice of navigation instruments.

Planning suitable distances between destinations, particularly for hiking or trekking trails, requires not only deciding on the maximum number of kilometres to be covered each day, it also needs to predict the minimum distance that a tour participant can walk to be able to fully enjoy the hike and the surroundings without it becoming boring or unsatisfactory (see Fig. 8.8).

ROUTE CONDITIONS

Road conditions obviously affect journey times. The itinerary planner therefore has to be aware in advance of any possible problems (e.g. road works) and whether there are any alternative routes in case of hold-ups. The planner also needs to look into whether the route chosen is well signposted, whether there are rest or service areas along the way, and once in the destination if there is adequate room for manoeuvre and parking.

Narrow roads, badly maintained road surfaces, winding mountainous roads, etc. will all have an influence on the duration of a tour. In the case of a walking tour, the time it takes a hiker to cover a certain distance depends on the kind of terrain (smooth and sandy, grassy, rocky), whether it is on the flat or if there are any steep gradients. Figure 8.8 illustrates the correlation between length and type of tour and means of transport.

STOPS EN ROUTE

For the tour experience to be enjoyable and pleasurable, it is absolutely essential that there are frequent breaks en route. Decisions need to be made about the whereabouts (e.g. is it just a break for refreshments or is it a cultural or gastronomic visit to tie in with the general theme of the tour?). When, how often and how much time is dedicated to a stop also need to be carefully calculated. Apart from making sure that there are rest stops or moments of relaxation to give tour participants a break from travelling, planners need to give clients the opportunity to have some free time, particularly when they are on an organized, guided tour.

If breaks are not accurately timed and do not fit in well with the programme of activities, the tour may turn out to be less than satisfactory. Also, when people are on a guided tour they expect the tour schedule to be respected. If the itinerary has to be changed or journey time extended because breaks or visits have taken longer than predicted, clients are not going to be very happy. Generally speaking, a visit to a wine or food production centre usually lasts on average about 60–90 minutes. The length of time spent on a visit depends on how much importance is given to that particular visit within the complete itinerary.

HOW LONG AND WHEN

The time of year and the duration of the tour depend on a set of variables that have already been described above: theme, area and distance, means of transport, the number of visits and, of course, the intended target. The type of infrastructure and the services and facilities available in the area to visitors are other variables. These are often conditioned by seasonality. It is also impossible to define an ideal time to visit a region without taking into account seasonal changes in weather and temperature. Apart from meteorological conditions, the tour organizer also need to be informed about peak holiday periods and the possibility of finding places uncomfortably crowded. The best time to visit a winery, farm or oil mill is to go when visitors can see for themselves the fruit of the producer's labours. Joining in the grape harvest or being able to see the olives being pressed obviously make for exciting moments. However, enquiries should be made to find out exactly if, how and when visitors and groups are catered for. Available services and prices in the area need to be checked, as well as visitor numbers, again to avoid peak times and crowds. In actual fact, if general conditions are favourable and if opportunities for themes present themselves, a tour created out of season can be a very attractive proposition indeed. Not only is it easier to create itineraries for specific targets, tour participants will enjoy a more relaxed and personalized welcome from producers and their staff, and prices are generally considerably lower. The organization of a special event or exhibition can be the catalyst for an off-peak visit. And, while it may not be the season for visitors to assist in the main production activities, they can still enjoy and learn a lot by seeing a different stage of the production process.

SELECTING THE SUPPLY AND RESOURCES

As we have already mentioned, the itinerary organizer needs to check that the resources and attractions in the area are appropriate in terms of visitor interest, that they are easily accessible and that they are in keeping with the main theme of the tour. This means personally visiting farms, wineries and other food and wine production centres in the area as well as local places of cultural interest. Possible business partners, local tourism operators and suppliers of tourist services will also need to be selected. The right type of accommodation must be chosen, along with suitable catering facilities. Opportunities for relaxation and entertainment also need to be explored, e.g. spas, sports and leisure centres. The tour planner needs to think about pleasant places to stop and break the journey, as well as the main cultural or gastronomic destinations. Selection in all cases must be based on the quality and professionalism of the supply, as visitor expectations must be met at all times.

Planning the route format: linking area resources and themes

The geographical aspects of a region and the thematic aspects of the holiday are the two main factors influencing the shape a tour takes in a given destination. In fact, designing a tour route implies identifying and integrating a basic set of variables, such as:

- the main themes of the holiday;
- the geomorphological and cultural features of the area;
- the richness, value expressed and location of resources;
- the presence and distribution of tourist facilities and services (accommodation, restaurants, etc.); and

- technical aspects (length of stay, means of transport, type of rest stops, length of journey times between stopovers, etc.).

When a *terroir* and its productive region lie within a clearly marked and distinct geographical context (e.g. a plateau, a hilly region or an easily recognizable plain), the most complete and exhaustive way of revealing its spirit and identity to visitors is by designing a circuit or daisy route (Fig. 8.9).

The daisy route is particularly suitable for areas where the tourist pull factor is based on a particular resource or attraction that epitomizes the region's dominant culture: the tour route can therefore be designed around this core resource/attraction, making it the starting point from which excursions can then be organized to visit other resources or local places of interest (Fig. 8.9). These further excursions should complement the main theme of the holiday and give visitors a better and fuller understanding of the region and its resources.

Opting to design a tour using the daisy route format can also be conditioned by what the region has to offer in terms of accommodation facilities and other tourist services. In fact, choosing the same hotel or accommodation facility as a base for the entire stay can often work out to be more economical, as hotel owners are more likely to offer lower rates for groups who stay for a few days or more. From a logistical point of view, a one-base stay also makes baggage handling easier, as loading and unloading suitcases is kept to a minimum, as well as facilitating business relationships with external personnel (e.g. tour guides), who are

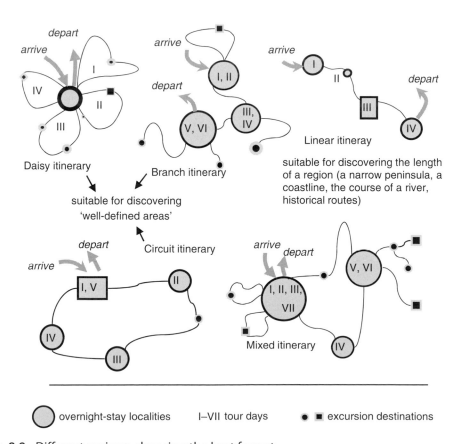

Fig. 8.9. Different regions: choosing the best format.

more likely to be based in the region's main centre. A good example of a 'daisy route' itinerary is a gastronomic tour of the heel of Italy, based in Lecce. From here, visitors can be taken to discover the wines of the Salice Salentino and Manduria areas, the ancient underground olive mills of Squinzano, Scorrano, Vernole and Casarano, the delicious almond sweets and artisan durum wheat pasta of Maglie, and fish from the Ionian Sea (in Gallipoli) and the Adriatic Sea (in Otranto).

A circular or circuit route on the other hand is perfect for visiting areas that have a number of special resources or attractions, particularly if there is some kind of theme that links them together and if there are sufficient tourist services and facilities to accommodate visitors comfortably as they travel from one place to the next (Fig. 8.9). With this type of itinerary, the tour starts and finishes in the same place. Choosing where to begin and end a tour depends on a number of factors, e.g. its proximity to an airport or other transport hubs, or it could simply be the best place to introduce a region, before setting off to explore all its other attractions. Some examples of circuit routes are gastronomic and cultural tours of historic centres in the Pianura Padana or Sicily (Italy), Andalusia in Spain, the coastal localities of Bretagne (France) or Cornwall in the UK. Also in the UK, people with a passion for 'real' beer can enjoy visiting historic taverns and pubs and take ale and bitter brewery strollings in Kent, Yorkshire, the Cotswolds or even London. In Belgium, a circular tour of Brussels and a circular tour in the area between Flanders and Vallonia both present a great opportunity for circuit routes based on enjoying influences of the different cultures in the region and above all beers (e.g. Lambic, Trappist, Saison, Oud Bruin or Flanders' red beers). As we have seen with London and Brussels, city centres lend themselves easily to this type of circular itinerary. In Cognac (Poitou-Charentes, France), a circular tour taking in its most famous distilleries is another good example of a city centre circuit.

When the aim of an itinerary is to tour the length of a peninsula, a stretch of coastline, the course of a river or even an ancient trade or pilgrimage route, a linear route is ideal (Fig. 8.9). This type of route also lends itself to connecting key destinations on a Grand Tour when there are long distances to be covered. For instance, a linear route is the only way to take tourists on a satisfactory journey down the Adriatic coast, enabling them to discover the subtle differences in taste and the varieties of fish soup that can be had according to the local catch. At each different stop, visitors will appreciate and enjoy a different composition of spices, aromas and flavours. The same format can also be used for a bicycle tour along the banks of the Po River, the longest river in Italy (approximately 660 km). The tour will lead visitors on a trail of gastronomic pleasure, as they discover alpine cheeses and cured meats in the valleys of Piemonte, truffles in the Langhe region, and rice and gorgonzola cheese in the Lombardia plains. As the tour continues down the course of the river to Emilia Romagna, visitors will come across the delights of Parmesan cheese, Parma ham and balsamic vinegar. And, as they approach the Po Delta, they will enjoy sweet melons and watermelons before a final feast on Po Delta clams. In the Mosel Valley in Germany, a linear route will take visitors along the wine road. As their journey progresses, tourists will be able to appreciate how the geography, soil and microclimate of the *terroir* induced the Romans to begin cultivating grapes there 2000 years ago. In a similar way, a linear itinerary (or branch route, depending on how far inland the winery tour goes) is the best format for visiting the Niagara Peninsula Viticultural Area and the wineries dotted along the south-west shores of Lake Ontario in Canada.

Finally, an itinerary that is constructed around a branch route format (which can easily be applied to the geographical regions cited above) is the best way to visit an area that has several principal attractions thanks to their tourist pull factors or that make sense from a logistical point of view. In essence, a branch route enables tourists to stay in a number of different destinations linked together, each one in itself worthy of visitor attention, but also geographically close to other resources or attractions (Fig. 8.9). Visitors can then be taken on further local excursions from each of the main destinations. This format is, for example, an ideal way to visit distilleries in the Armagnac area in the South of France. In this particular case, the tour needs to be based in at least two towns, Eauze and Condom. From here, tourists can be taken into the rolling countryside to explore the numerous Armagnac distilleries in the region, from small, family-owned businesses to large, industrialized production centres.

A branch route is also the perfect formula for visiting river or mountain valleys and exploring some of the lesser known tributaries or minor valleys along the way. A good example is a tour along the Adige Valley (Italy), beginning in Verona and travelling north to the Austrian border. Good branching-off points include gastronomic stops to discover the extra-virgin olive oil of Lake Garda, apples and associated products in the Val di Non, wines along the wine route just outside Bolzano and speck in Val Pusteria.

As always, it is the theme of the route that is of strategic importance. In fact, different routes can be organized within the same area according to different themes and the target that they wish to appeal to. For example, the city of Siena (Italy) and its surrounding area can be explored in a number of ways (Fig. 8.10):

- Daisy route. This format can be used when the aim of the tour is to explore the city's medieval past and its political, social and economic relations with its feudal neighbours: Chianti (to the north-east), the Crete Hills and Val d'Orcia (to the south-east), the Metallifere Hills (to the south-west) and the city of towers, San Gimignano.
- Circuit route. If instead the focus of the tour is on wine, a visit to the city of Siena is not even necessary, as the area around Siena can be divided into four main wine-producing regions: Chianti (to the north-east); the south-east where the most prestigious wines to be found are Brunello di Montalcino, Nobile di Montepulciano and Orcia Rosso; the area around Massa Marittima and its Monteregio wine route; and San Gimignano (to the

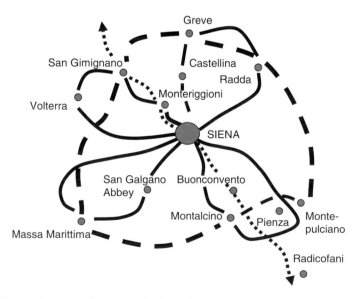

Fig. 8.10. Different themes: choosing the best format.

north-west) and its famous white wine, Vernaccia. To give the tour's wine theme an even stronger focus, wineries that also offer visitor accommodation could be the perfect choice for overnight stays.

- Linear route. This tour would begin in France and follow the ancient Francigena road, the very same route that medieval pilgrims took, passing through the Siena region and stopping off in San Gimignano on their way to Rome.

For itineraries or discovery trails that do not use motorized means of transport, e.g. walking, cycling or horse-riding tours, it is absolutely essential that routes are marked by clear signs and that tourists are well-equipped with mapping instruments to orient themselves:

- Signs should be placed at sensible intervals along the entire length of the route. Signs marking the route can be made from a variety of materials from natural wood to varnished metal (Fig. 8.11). The key elements are that they should be simple, clear and precise. Interpretive panels giving additional information about geographical features, the flora and fauna of the area or food and wine products of the region will make the route more interesting and informative.
- Maps also need to be clear and easy to read and handle. Themed maps can become useful tools of information for visitors and facilitate their stay in the area. GPS/satellite navigators in this sense can also be invaluable instruments for today's travellers.

Fig. 8.11. Signs along a *winefoothpath* (Alsace, France).

THEME, INTERDISCIPLINARY APPROACH AND TARGET IN THE GASTRONOMIC TOUR

Organizing and planning for tourism, as we have seen, signifies programming and managing the visitor's life for the whole duration of the holiday. Putting together an itinerary therefore means creating a plot or scenario with points of reference that are important for making the experience a success. If we look at it from this point of view, the itinerary is rather like a story woven around the client who takes on the role of main character.

Apart from having a professional attitude and adequate technical knowledge, a good operator in cultural and food and wine tourism who wishes to create successful itineraries must be able to identify coherent and easily recognizable themes that will become the leitmotiv for the trip. In addition, as the itinerary unfolds, the tour planner must be able to narrate each chapter in detail, and enchant and involve the participants. This can only be done with an interdisciplinary approach.

If food and wine tours concentrate exclusively on the gastronomic aspect, they run the risk of becoming boring and repetitive. Requests for tours to be organized purely around a gastronomic theme (e.g. only visiting food or wine enterprises and participating in tasting sessions) usually only come from experts in the sector (e.g. visiting delegations of wine tasters, restaurant owners, food and wine importers). But even when this is the case, including a visit to a nearby cultural attraction or extending an invitation to an art exhibition or musical event can be a pleasant surprise for all the participants. Being creative in this way assumes an even greater relevance when trying to appeal to prospective clients who do not have a professional interest in the sector and whose motives for travel are leisure, culture and/or sport as well as an interest in food and wine.

A captivating theme linked to the region's resources and a multidisciplinary approach are the keys to creating a winning food and wine tour.

Boxes 8.1 and 8.2 outline some examples of successful food and wine itineraries.

Box 8.1. Case Study: Using Symbols and Images in Art to Construct a Food and Wine Itinerary.

Let us begin by imagining that we have to create a gastronomic tour in one of the greatest wine regions in the world: Champagne. The target is a small group of people with a passion for food and wine. They are all professionals, aged between 45 and 60, with medium-high cultural backgrounds, and a propensity to spend money on the things they enjoy.

Further information is as follows.

- Length of tour: a long weekend.
- Period: spring.
- Accommodation: three/four-star hotel.
- Transport: minibus.
- Assistance: driver-tour leader, guide for city/town tours, wine experts and oenologists for winery tours and tastings.

A preliminary survey of this region in the north-east of France reveals some principal characteristics:

- It has always been considered to be the northernmost point for top-quality wine production.
- It is characterized by its chalky subsoil, which goes down to a depth of about 200 metres.

(Continued)

Box 8.1. Continued.

- Heaters are often placed in the vineyards to protect grape buds and shoots from the continental climate and icy nights.
- It is divided into five sub-regions: Montagne de Reims, Vallée de la Marne, Côte des Blancs, Côte de Sezanne and Côte des Bar (see Fig. 8.12).
- Three grape varieties are grown in the area: Pinot Noir, Pinot Meunier and Chardonnay.
- The vineyards extend over an area of approximately 34,000 hectares.
- There are about 15,000 winegrowers.
- The average size of a wine estate is about 1.5 hectares.
- Countless bottles of champagne are stored in 260 km of tunnels, carved out of the chalk soil, under the city of Reims.
- It was the first region to be given the AOC seal (Appellation d'Origine Contrôlée).
- Six official itineraries of the Champagne region already exist; the local wine route was inaugurated in 1950.

The results of this preliminary analysis illustrate how difficult it is to have a complete and comprehensive understanding of wine production in the Champagne region. In addition, the high number of individual small producers in the area together with the presence of large prestigious champagne houses makes it doubly difficult for an

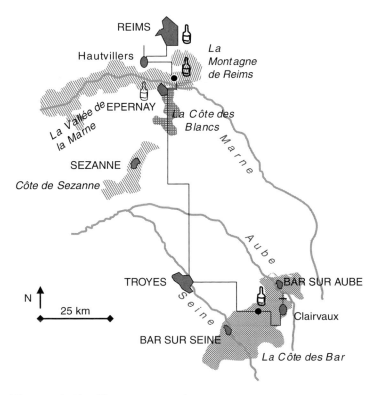

Fig. 8.12. Itinerary in the Champagne region.

(Continued)

Box 8.1. Continued.

itinerary organizer to decide on the best and most appropriate wineries to include on a tour.

The planner needs to ask two questions:

- What to choose as a starting point? The tour must introduce visitors to more than one aspect of the region. Visits to wine production centres need to be integrated so that they form part of a complete 'themed' experience.
- What form should the itinerary take? It must be kept in mind that the aim of the tour is to give visitors a complete picture of the region, in spite of its complexity.

One way is through art. The city of Reims, together with Epernay, is known the whole world over as the capital of champagne. It is also famous for its splendid Gothic cathedral; with its 2303 beautifully sculpted statues, it is an eloquent expression of the medieval world. The cathedral is also a symbol of the rebirth of the city after the devastation of the First World War. It was added to the list of UNESCO World Heritage Sites in 1991. Numerous possibilities exist to link this wondrous work of art to the area and champagne production. Twenty-four kings, including Clovis, the first king of France, were crowned and consecrated here and champagne just happens to be the wine of kings. We can find vine leaves and oak leaves sculpted out of stone (wine barrels are made from oak trees). One of the stained glass windows, completed in 1954 and presented to the cathedral by local wine producers, beautifully illustrates step by step how champagne is made. Dom Perignon, the monk who is credited with inventing champagne, is also depicted in the same window. Exactly in this spot, in the right-hand nave of the cathedral, we have a possible starting point for explaining the methods of champagne production – a more unusual location for visitors to be introduced to champagne than in the wine cellars, as normally happens. A 2- to 3-hour stroll will then enable visitors to get a glimpse of some of the other city monuments before ending up at the Maison Mumm. The *maison* is instantly recognizable by its late 19th-century mosaic façade. With wine again as the focus, we have art and gastronomy combined together. It can be interesting and stimulating for visitors to come across artistic styles from different periods and see how they were used in the world of food and wine production.

From here visitors can then be taken to the wineries and vineyards chosen according to clients' needs. A champagne-tasting session in one of the main champagne houses is obviously a must. An interesting detour could also be made to see the deep quarries dating back to Roman times that were used to extract the stone with which the city was built. They are actually used today as *caves de champagne*. A visit to the Abbey of Hautvillers (burial place of Dom Perignon) would also make for a fascinating stop. The gastronomic aspect of the tour could then be explored more fully by taking a trip out to the vineyards of a small, independent producer to learn more about the characteristics of the soil and the climate and their influence on grape cultivation. Having the occasion to meet the producer or an oenologist who can explain traditional wine press methods and give visitors a chance to try a more traditional champagne will generate great excitement and emotion for the tour participants.

Once in Epernay, a visit to CIVC (Comité Interprofessionnel du Vin de Champagne) would be just the right occasion for the tourists to enjoy a brief lesson on the techniques of champagne tasting, specifically designed for their technical skills.

(Continued)

Box 8.1. Continued.

Then, leaving behind Reims and Epernay, the tour could continue south to the beautiful city of Troyes. With its medieval centre, 15th-century half-timbered houses and yet another gorgeous Gothic cathedral, it is a perfect place to explore, before setting out to visit the vineyards further south, where the Pinot Noir reigns supreme.

One of the first things to point out to visitors in Troyes, map in hand, is that, if observed from above, the layout of the historic centre closely resembles the shape of a champagne cork (Fig. 8.13). In the magnificent cathedral, the surface area covered by stained glass windows is the largest in Europe. One of the windows, the renowned *Mystic Wine-Press*, emphasizes the religious significance and symbolism of the grapevine. It was here at the Council of Troyes in 1128 that Saint Bernard of Clairvaux first outlined the Rules of the Knights Templar. And it was Saint Bernard who first brought the Pinot Noir grape from Burgundy to produce a still wine. Also in the centre of Troyes is the church of Saint Urbain, one of the finest Gothic buildings in Champagne. Here visitors can admire the *Vierge au Raisin* (*Virgin of the Grapes*), a masterpiece of Renaissance sculpture. Finally, when all the sightseeing is over and cultural curiosity has been satisfied, the gourmets among the group will enjoy sitting down to a meal of *andouillette*, the famous tripe sausage of Troyes.

The tour planner could also add a further dimension to the trip by including a shopping stop. In fact, Troyes is also famous for its exquisitely woven cloth that has been attracting buyers since medieval times. Today, its outlet malls attract shoppers with its designer stores and brand labels.

An outing along the valley of the Aube and a visit to the ruins of Clairvaux Abbey could complete the tour. Here in the Aube countryside, the group can enjoy a visit to a famous champagne house. The Cistercian wine cellars built during the time of Bernard can be found within the grounds, providing a tangible presence of the past and the influence of

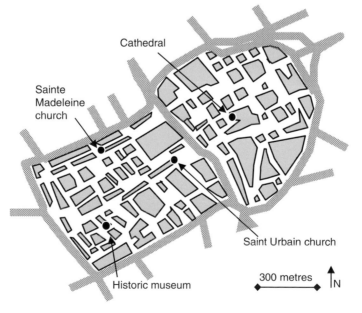

Fig. 8.13. Troyes: layout of the historic centre in the form of a Champagne cork.

(Continued)

Box 8.1. Continued.

Cistercian monks on wine production in the area. This is also an occasion for the group to get a deeper understanding of champagne vinification, for example the nature and function of *liqueur d'expedition* and *zero dosage*.

The Champagne tour, as we have outlined above, therefore takes visitors on a trail of discovery beginning with art, architecture and history that blends beautifully with the sparkling wine and gastronomic delights of the region. The monuments and works of art, from different epochs and in a variety of different styles, provide the leitmotiv of the tour and give participants the chance to deepen their artistic knowledge as well as gaining more gastronomic expertise.

Having decided on the structure of the itinerary, the final programme could look something like this (accommodation is on a B&B basis: three-star hotel in the centre of Reims, four-star hotel in the vine-growing hills of Epernay and a four-star hotel in the centre of Troyes).

Day 1:

- Guided visit of Reims cathedral and the historic centre.
- Free time for lunch.
- Tour and tasting session in a champagne house in the historic centre.
- Evening meal in a characteristic bistro. Overnight in Reims.

Day 2:

- Tour and tasting session in a champagne house in Reims.
- Lunch in Hautvilliers – visit to the Abbey of Hautvilliers.
- Afternoon outing to the vineyards of a small, independent *vigneron* and wine tasting.
- Transfer to the hills of Epernay. Spa and beauty treatment, evening meal and overnight stay.

Day 3:

- Guided visit to CIVC.
- Free time for lunch in Epernay.
- Transfer to Troyes.
- Free time.
- Evening meal and overnight stay in hotel (one of the typical half-timbered buildings of Troyes, dating back to the Renaissance).

Day 4:

- Morning guided visit to Troyes cathedral and historic centre.
- Lunch in the centre of Troyes (characteristic local restaurant serving *andouillete*).
- Afternoon visit to centuries-old family business in the Aube countryside (brief stop to see the ruins of Clairvaux Abbey).
- Free time for evening meal. Overnight stay in Troyes.

Day 5:

- Free time for shopping, visiting museums, etc.
- Lunch in hotel.
- Departure.

(Continued)

Box 8.1. Continued.

This is just an outline of a possible programme. It would naturally have to be more descriptive and informative if it were to be presented to the general public.

The title given to the tour depends very much on the target. The name obviously has to generate curiosity and give a promise that reflects clients' expectations and interests. 'Bubbles and Glass' could be a good solution to attract first-time visitors to the Champagne region or those who have had little or no experience of wine tasting. 'Glorious Gothic Cathedrals and the Wine of Kings', a title that has more didactic connotations, could easily be inserted into a brochure proposing more traditional cultural tours. However, if we want to give a more technical slant and appeal to our small group of food and wine connoisseurs, 'Glass, Chalk and Perlage' is the perfect title. In three words, it sums up the magnificent stained glass windows of the cathedrals, the delicate glass of champagne flutes, the chalky soil of the Champagne *terroir* and the cave and, finally, the fine perlage of the wine, all of which our tourists will experience first-hand during the tour.

Box 8.2. Case Study: the Importance of the Target when Constructing a Themed Itinerary.

As we have already seen, the way an itinerary is planned and developed depends very much on the intended target. The region where the tour will take place must possess resources and features that correspond to the characteristics displayed by the potential target, their expectations and interests. Once these have been identified, it is then the itinerary planner's task to come up with a theme which will bring visitor and region together in a satisfying way. Because visitor needs and interests are so varied, it is possible to organize different itineraries to the same area.

This time the task is to create a tour to the countryside south of Siena. This particular area of Tuscany, with its harmonious landscape and food and wine production of the highest order, is one of the most sought-after gastronomic destinations in Italy, if not Europe. The region's produce rightly enjoys an international reputation for excellence. We just have to think of its great wines such as Brunello di Montalcino and Nobile di Montepulciano or perhaps the lesser-known Rosso Orcia Doc. The area is also famous for Pecorino cheese from Pienza and Cinta Senese ham.

We have two very different targets who would like to tour the same area, a group of mature people attending classes at a university for senior citizens and a group of younger, multi-interest visitors (food and sport). The itineraries will have to be planned in such a way as to reflect the main interests of each group and different choices will therefore have to be made with regard to destinations, visits and activities. With the first group, the main emphasis will be on culture, while with the second, gastronomy will be the main focus.

Cultural tour

In the first case, the group from the university for senior citizens is a non-specialized target. They are from Puglia in the south-east of Italy and have asked the tour organizers to draw up an itinerary that will take them on a cultural tour of Tuscany. No particular requests have

(Continued)

Box 8.2. Continued.

been made with regard to destinations or topics other than the desire to explore different facets of the region over a time span of 4 days.

The principal points to be considered during the planning phase are as follows:

- To give visitors an experience of the region where the quality of the experience really stands out in terms of facilities and services.
- To offer them cultural occasions which go beyond visiting churches and monuments.
- To come up with a theme or topic that will not only give them the *raison d'être* for visiting the main destination, but will accompany them along the route. The journey from Puglia to Tuscany is quite long and visitors will need a break along the way. A lunch stop in Abruzzo would be a perfect solution. After thoroughly studying various possibilities, a theme emerges centred around the powerful Piccolomini family. One member in particular, Enea Silvio Piccolomini, who later became Pope Pius II, exercised enormous influence in Tuscany, but not only there. In Celano, in Abruzzo (a perfect spot for a break), the Piccolomini presence is marked by an imposing and formidable castle that today also hosts an interesting museum.
- To add a gastronomic aspect to the tour so that group members are introduced to some of the excellent food and wine produce of the regions that they pass through on their journey. They can be taken to visit farms and wineries and enjoy specially devised tasting menus on their way through Abruzzo and once they reach their main destination south of Siena. On each visit, the group will need to be received by personnel capable of involving them and leading them on their first tasting session. In this particular case, the gastronomic experience is not the focal point of the trip, but it is an exciting addition to the main theme that is focused on giving them a cultural experience.

The outline of the programme would look something like this.

- Target: a group from the university for senior citizens, Puglia.
- Transport: minibus.
- Duration: 4 days/3 nights.
- Requested destination: Tuscany.
- Tour: 'In the footsteps of Enea Silvio Piccolomini (Pope Pius II)'.
- Accommodation: three-star hotel in Montepulciano.
- Sites visited: Celano (Castello Piccolomini and museum), Pienza (Palazzo Piccolomini, cathedral, focus on the urban layout), Siena (focus on the frescoes of Pinturicchio in the Biblioteca Piccolomini), the Duomo of Montepulciano and guided walk to see the principal monuments of the city; guided tours of Siena and Pienza.
- Other visits: ancient wine vaults in Montepulciano (including wine tasting), dairy farm (cheese tasting: Pecorino – sheep's cheese – from Pienza).
- Meals: one evening meal and lunch in the hotel, other meals focused on the local cuisine of Abruzzo and Tuscany in traditional, local restaurants.

Food and wine tour

In the second example, the itinerary must be constructed around a group of sports and food lovers from the Trentino area of north-east Italy. The group is composed of both singles and couples, with an average age of 45. As experienced gourmets, they have specifically requested a wine tour of the Crete Senesi area.

(Continued)

Box 8.2. Continued.

This target therefore requires a different set of priorities focusing on the following:

- Identify a period of the year when countryside life is at its most appealing. As wine production must necessarily be at an interesting stage to satisfy the group's curiosity, they would probably find the grape harvest to be the most captivating moment of the entire cycle of production. This is a rather delicate phase for producers to welcome visitors to their cellars, as it is the busiest time of the year with all the machines and workforce involved in the harvest; but as this is a small group of wine connoisseurs travelling in a small minibus, they may very well grant them the privilege. The group will appreciate the visit even more once they realize that a special concession has been made for them. If the visit has to be made at another time of year, they can still experience a sense of being privileged guests by being given a special tasting session or being involved in other activities on the estate.

- As wine is partly the main focus and with tour participants already having some experience of oenology, the tour can concentrate on the more technical aspects of wine (from which the title of the tour originates). The group will appreciate having the opportunity to find out about the production of Rosso Orcia Doc, which is not as well known as other wines in the area, and to be given the chance to discover its organoleptic characteristics. The visitors therefore would need to visit a winery that can organize not just a tour of the vineyards but a meeting with an oenologist as well. Interest in food and gastronomy can be satisfied by visiting farms and other small local businesses involved in food production.

- Include in the tour an occasion for the group to be together out in the open air. Being fit and active, they will enjoy a long hike across country, particularly if the objective is to reach a place where they can discover and taste local food and wine.

- The tour must give group members a sense of the distinctive 'personality' of the area. It is therefore essential that the choice of accommodation is not a hotel with standardized services and facilities that could be found anywhere; it must reflect the special characteristics of the region. As the area is also a renowned destination for thermal baths and spa tourism, this could be another component to include. Keeping the theme of wine as the tour's leitmotiv, the group could enjoy a vinotherapy session at a local spa.

- Finally, the programme needs to include a cultural component. The group should be introduced to the region's artistic and historic heritage by visiting Pienza and Trequanda. The visits should not be too technical or didactic however, as art in this case is not the core focus of the tour but a pleasurable addition.

The basic outline of the programme is as follows.

- Target: food, wine and sports lovers from Trentino, singles and couples, average age 45.
- Transport: minibus or small coach (16 places).
- Duration: 4 days/3 nights (in the autumn).
- Requested destination: Tuscany–Crete Senesi.
- Tour: 'The Red Wines of the Crete Senesi'.
- Accommodation: characteristic three-star accommodation.

(Continued)

Box 8.2. Continued.

- Sites visited: Montalcino (wine tasting in two wine cellars, one of which belongs to a large-scale producer, followed by a stroll in the historic centre), Montepulciano (wine tasting in traditional wine vaults led by an oenologist).
- Guided visits: Pienza (traditional dairy farm, cathedral, focusing on the urban layout), Trequanda (a walk in the hills of the Crete Senesi followed by a visit to a pig farm famous for its production of Sienese ham, food tasting paired with the red wine Rosso Orcia Doc).
- Other activities: spa and beauty treatments (vinotherapy).
- Meals: special menu-tasting lunches and dinners (local production: sheep's cheese, truffle, oil, *ribollita* – thick Tuscan bread and vegetable soup, *pan co' santi* – sweet loaf).

Bibliography

Angelini, R. (ed.) (2007) *La vite e il vino*. Bayer Crop Science, Milan, Italy.

Antonioli Corigliano, A. and Viganò, G. (2004) *Turisti per gusto: Enogastronomia, territorio, sostenibilità*. De Agostini Editore, Novara, Italy.

Associazione Italiana Sommeliers (2005) *Il mondo del Sommelier*. Associazione Italiana Sommeliers Editore, Milan, Italy.

Associazione Italiana Turismo Responsabile (1998) Carta d'identità per viaggi sostenibili. http://www. ebnt.it/gestione_file/Documenti/12_2006_5_26_Carta AITR turista sostenibile.pdf (accessed 31 March 2010).

Augé, M. (1997) *L'Impossible voyage. Le tourisme et ses images*. Édition Payot & Rivages, Paris.

Beeton, S. (2005) *Film-induced Tourism*. Channel View Publications, Clevedon, UK.

Bencardino, F. and Prezioso, M. (2007) *Geografia del turismo*. McGraw-Hill, Milan, Italy.

Berardi, S. (2007) *Principi economici ed ecologici per la pianificazione dello sviluppo turistico sostenibile*. FrancoAngeli, Milan, Italy.

Billi, S. (2005) L'ottica del beneficio. Territorio e prodotto turistico nell'economia dell'esperienza. In: Dall'Ara, G. and Morandi, F. (eds) *I sistemi turistici locali*. Halley Editrice, Camerino, Italy, pp. 121–153.

Brodo, V., Mojoli, G. and Surrusca, A. (2001) *Salumi d'Italia. Guida alla scoperta e alla conoscenza*. Slow Food Editore, Bra, Italy.

Bruner, E.M. (2004) *Culture on Tour: Ethnographies of Travel*. University of Chicago Press, Chicago, Illinois.

Budd, J. (2002) *Great Wine Tours of the World*. New Holland Publishers, London.

Buhalis, D. and Laws, E. (2001) *Tourism Distribution Channels: Practices, Issues and Transformations*. Continuum, London.

Bureau International du Tourisme Social (1996) Montreal Declaration. http://www.bits-int.org/ files/1177334236_doc_Montreal Declaration.pdf (accessed 31 March 2010).

Butler, R. (2006) *The Tourism Area Life Cycle: Conceptual and Theoretical Issues*. Channel View Publications, Clevedon, UK.

Butler, R.W. (1980) The concept of a tourist area cycle of evolution: implication for management of resources. *Canadian Geographer* 24, 5–12.

Calvino, I. (1988) *Under the Jaguar Sun*. Harcourt Inc., Orlando, Florida.

Cane, E. (2010) I bambini, i viaggi e i loro gusti. Un modello di accoglienza in azienda enogastronomica a misura dei piccoli visitatori. Graduation thesis, University of Gastronomic Sciences, Pollenzo (Bra), Italy.

Capatti, A. (2003) Il Buon Paese. In: *Introduzione alla Guida Gastronomica d'Italia 1931.* Touring Editore, Milan, Italy, pp. 6–31.

Caroli, M.G. (2006) *Il marketing territoriale. Strategie per la competitività sostenibile del territorio.* FrancoAngeli, Milan, Italy.

Casarin, F. (1996, 2007) *Il marketing dei prodotti turistici. Specificità e varietà.* G. Giappichelli Editore, Turin, Italy.

Castoldi, G. (2000) *Manuale di tecnica turistica e amministrativa.* Hoepli, Milan, Italy.

Chiorino, F. (2007) *Architettura e vino.* Electa, Milan, Italy.

Christaller, W. (1964) Some considerations of tourism location in Europe. *Papers in Regional Science* 12, 95–105.

Cinelli Colombini, D. (2007) *Il marketing del turismo del vino. I segreti del business e del turismo in cantina.* Agra Editrice, Rome.

Coccossis, H. and Mexa, A. (2004) *The Challenge of Tourism Carrying Capacity Assessment: Theory and Practice.* Ashgate, Aldershot, UK.

Cogno, E. and Dall'Ara, G. (1999) *Comunicazione e tecnica pubblicitaria nel turismo.* FrancoAngeli, Milan, Italy.

Costa, P. and Manente, M. (2000) *Economia del turismo.* Touring Editore, Milan, Italy.

Croce, E. (2008) Prodotto turistico ed enogastronomia: punti critici e forme di integrazione. In: Romano, M.F. (ed.) *Nuovi turismi. Strumenti e metodi di rilevazione, modelli interpretativi.* Edizioni ETS, Pisa, Italy, pp. 171–190.

Croce, E. and Perri, G. (2002) L'offerta di 'turismo culturale' in Italia da parte dell'intermediazione: una rassegna delle proposte dei Tour Operator. In: Manente, M. and Furlan, M.C. (eds) *Per un osservatorio sul turismo culturale: Motivazioni e comportamenti nella domanda.* CISET University of Venice, Venice, Italy, pp. 57–71.

Croce, E. and Perri, G. (2007) *Carta dei prodotti agroalimentari del Po.* Meridies (for UNISG), Chieti, Italy.

Croce, E. and Perri, G. (2008) *Il turismo enogastronomico. Progettare, gestire, vivere l'integrazione tra cibo, viaggio, territorio.* FrancoAngeli, Milan, Italy.

Croce, E. and Perri, G. (2009a) Comunicazione, immagine, identità: impresa alberghiera e territorio. *OA – Ospitalità Alberghiera* (Federalberghi Veneto, Venice) 67, 34–37.

Croce, E. and Perri, G. (2009b) Il paesaggio, sfondo scenografico o realtà geografica da gustare nel turismo enogastronomico. *Quaderni della Ri- Vista. Ricerche per la progettazione del paesaggio* (University of Florence) 11; available at http://www.unifi.it/ri-vista/11ri/11r.html (accessed 3 April 2010).

Croce, E. and Perri, G. (2010) *Carta delle produzioni agroalimentari di Cisternino in Valle d'Itria.* Meridies, Chieti, Italy.

Cunningham, W.P., Cunningham, M.A. and Woodworth Saigo, B. (1997) *Environmental Science: A Global Concern.* McGraw-Hill, New York.

Dallari, F. and Grandi, S. (2005) *Economia e geografia del turismo. L'occasione dei Geographical Information Systems.* Patron, Bologna, Italy.

Del Corno, L. (2007) *A tavola con Omero.* BUR, Milan, Italy.

Ejarque, E. (2003) *La destinazione turistica di successo.* Hoepli, Milan, Italy.

European Commission (1999) Sustainable tourism and Natura 2000: guidelines, initiatives and good practices in Europe. Final publication based on the Lisbon seminar. http://ec.europa.eu/environment/nature/info/pubs/docs/nat2000/sust_tourism.pdf (accessed 6 December 2009).

European Union (1990) European Council Directive 90/314/EEC on package travel, package holidays and package tours. http://eur-lex.europa.eu/LexUriServ/LexUriServ.do?uri=CELEX:31990L0314:EN:NOT (accessed 2 April 2010).

Fennel, D. and Malloy, D.C. (2007) *Codes and Ethics in Tourism: Practice, Theory, Synthesis.* Channel View Publications, Clevedon, UK.

Floch, J.M. (1995) *Identités visuelles.* Presses Universitaires de France, Paris.

Gambera, A. and Surra, E. (2003) *Le forme del latte. Manuale per conoscere il formaggio.* Slow Food Editore, Bra, Italy.

Gambero Rosso (2005–2007) *Viaggiarbene*. Gambero Rosso Ed., Rome.

Giaoutzi, M. and Nijkamp, P. (2006) *Tourism and Regional Development: New Pathways* Ashgate, Aldershot, UK.

Giordana, F. (2006) *La comunicazione del turismo tra immagine, immaginario e immaginazione*. FrancoAngeli, Milan, Italy.

Goldstone, P. (2001) *Making the World Safe for Tourism*. Yale University Press, New Haven, Connecticut.

Grasso, M. (2009) *Tour operator e agenzie dettaglianti. Strategie e marketing delle imprese di viaggio*. FrancoAngeli, Milan, Italy.

Hall, C.H., Sharples, L., Mitchell, R., Macionis, N. and Cambourne, B. (eds) (2003) *Food Tourism around the World: Development, Management and Markets*. Elsevier Butterworth-Heinemann, Oxford, UK.

Hall, C.M. and Page, S.J. (2006) *The Geography of Tourism and Recreation. Environment, Place and Space*, 3rd edn. Routledge, London.

Hall, D., Kirkpatrick, I. and Morgan, M. (eds) (2005) *Rural Tourism and Sustainable Business*. Channel View Publications, Clevedon, UK.

Hausmann, C. (2005) *Marketing & Strade del vino. In viaggio tra saperi e sapori*. Agra, Rome.

Holloway, J.C. (2004) *Marketing for Tourism*. Prentice Hall/Financial Times, Harlow, UK.

Illy Università del Caffè (2008) Piccolo galateo organolettico dedicato agli amanti del caffé. Paper. Illy Università del Caffè, Trieste, Italy.

Innocenti, P. (2007) *Geografia del turismo*. Carocci, Rome.

International Council for Local Environmental Initiatives (1994) *Local Agenda 21 Model Communities Programme* International Council for Local Environmental Initiatives, Toronto, Canada.

International Union for Conservation of Nature and Natural Resources, United Nations Environment Programme and World Wide Fund for Nature (1991) Caring for the Earth: A Strategy for Sustainable Living. http://coombs.anu.edu.au/~vern/caring/caring.html (accessed 23 February 2010).

ISTAT (2009) Capacità degli esercizi ricettivi. http://www.istat.it/dati/dataset/20091214_00/ (accessed 3 April 2010).

Jamieson, W. (2006) *Community Destination Management in Developing Economies*. The Haworth Hospitality Press, Binghamton, New York.

Kotler, P., Bowen, J.T. and Makens, J.C. (2009) *Marketing for Hospitality and Tourism*, 5th int. edn. Pearson, Upper Saddle River, New Jersey.

Leed, E.J. (1991) *The Mind of the Traveler. From Gilgamesh to Global Tourism*. Basic Books, New York.

Lozato-Giotart, J.P. (1993) *Géographie du tourisme: de l'espace regardé à l'espace consommé*, 4th edn. Masson, Paris.

Lozato-Giotart, J.P. (2008) *Géographie du tourisme, de l'espace consommé à l'espace maîtrisé*, 2nd edn. Pearson France, Paris.

Lozato-Giotart, J.P. and Balfet, M. (2007) *Management du Tourisme: les acteurs, les produits, les marchés et les stratégies*, 2nd edn. Pearson France, Paris.

Lundgren, J.O. (1984) Geographic concepts and development of tourism research in Canada. *Geojournal* 8, 17–25.

McKercher, B. and Du Cros, H. (2002) *Cultural Tourism: The Partnership between Tourism and Cultural Heritage Management*. The Haworth Hospitality Press, Binghamton, New York.

Manente, M. and Furlan, M.C. (2002) *Per un osservatorio sul turismo culturale: motivazioni e comportamenti nella domanda*. Ciset, Venice, Italy.

Marconi, M., Fajner, D., Benevelli, G. and Nicoli, G. (2007) *Dentro al gusto. Arte, scienza e piacere nella degustazione*. Edagricole, Bologna, Italy.

Michael, C.M. (ed.) (2003) *Wine, Food, and Tourism Marketing*. The Haworth Hospitality Press, Binghamton, New York.

Michelin (2005–2007) *Italia. Alberghi & Ristoranti*. Michelin et Cie Propriétaires-Éditeurs, Clermont-Ferrand, France.

Minca, C. (1996) *Spazi effimeri*. Cedam, Padova, Italy.

Ministero delle Politiche Agricole Alimentari e Forestali (2010) Prodotti di qualità. http://www. politicheagricole.it/ProdottiQualita/default (accessed 2 April 2010).

Ministero per i Beni e le Attività Culturali (2009) Culture in Italy basic figures. http://www.beniculturali. it/mibac/multimedia/MiBAC/documents/1258713763980_MINICIFRE2009ingleseSTAMPA. pdf (accessed 2 April 2010).

Miossec, J.M. (1977) Un model de l'espace touristique. *L'Espace Geographique* 6, 41–48.

Montanari, M. (2002) *Il mondo in cucina. Storia, identità, scambi.* Gius. Laterza & Figli, Rome-Bari, Italy.

Montanari, M. (2004) *Il cibo come cultura.* Gius. Laterza & Figli, Rome-Bari, Italy.

Motion Picture Association of America (2006) The Economic Impact of the Motion Picture & Television Industry on the United States. http://www.mpaa.org/press_releases/mpa us economic impact report_final.pdf (accessed 1 April 2010).

Motion Picture Association of America (2009) The Economic Impact of the Motion Picture & Television Industry on the United States. http://www.mpaa.org/EconReportLo.pdf (accessed 1 April 2010).

Negri Arnoldi, F. and Tagliolini, B. (2003) *La guida al turismo culturale. Dalla formazione all'attività professionale.* Carocci, Rome.

Normann, R. (2001) *Service Management: Strategy and Leadership in Service Business*, 3rd edn. John Wiley and Sons, Chichester, UK.

Normann, R. and Ramirez, R. (1994) *Designing Interactive Strategy. From Value Chain to Value Constellation.* John Wiley and Sons, Chichester, UK.

Normann, R. and Wikström, S. (1994) *Knowledge and Value: A New Perspective on Corporate Transformation.* Routledge, London/New York.

Paolini, D. (2000) *I luoghi del gusto. Cibo e territorio come risorsa di marketing.* Badini & Castoldi, Milan, Italy.

Pastore, R. (2002) *Il marketing del vino e del territorio: istruzioni per l'uso.* FrancoAngeli, Milan, Italy.

Pavese, C. (1950) *La luna e i falò.* Einaudi, Turin, Italy.

Pechlaner, H. and Weiermair, K. (2000) *Destination management. Fondamenti di marketing e gestione delle destinazioni turistiche.* Touring Editore, Milan, Italy.

Perri, G. (2004) Modalità per la strutturazione di itinerari turistici. In: Cisternino, C. (ed.) *Manuale delle procedure per operatrici dell'ospitalità e dell'accoglienza turistica in Bed and Breakfast.* Schena Editore, Fasano (BR), Italy, pp. 89–91.

Perri, G. (2008) Cartographic reflections: from method to prospects. *Gastronomic Sciences* (University of Gastronomic Sciences, Pollenzo (Bra), Italy) 3, 36–41.

Perri, G. and Croce, E. (2007) *Carta dei prodotti agroalimentari del Po.* University of Gastronomic Sciences, Pollenzo (Bra), Italy.

Perullo, N. (2005) Turismo enogastronomico: una ricetta superata? *La Rivista del Turismo* (Milan, Italy), 4/2005, 31–34.

Peter, M. (2008) *Tourism Impacts, Planning and Management.* Elsevier, Amsterdam.

Petrini, C. (2005) *Buono, pulito e giusto. Principi di nuova gastronomia.* Einaudi, Turin, Italy.

Petrini, C. and Padovani, G. (2005) *Slow Food Revolution. Da Arcigola a Terra Madre: una nuova cultura del cibo e della vita.* Rizzoli, Milan, Italy.

Plog, S.C. (1974) Why destination areas rise and fall in popularity. *The Cornell HRA Quarterly* 14, 55–58.

Rispoli, M. and Tamma, M. (1995) *Risposte strategiche alla complessità: le forme di offerta dei prodotti alberghieri.* G. Giappichelli Editore, Turin, Italy.

Robert Mondavi Winery (2010) Winery Tours & Tastings. http://www.robertmondavi.com/rmw/at_ the_winery/tours http://www.robertmondaviwinery (accessed 10 February 2010).

Rocco, A. (2005) Un viaggio tra schermo e bicchiere. *Cinema&Video International* Jan/Feb 2005; available at http://www.cinemaevideo.it (accessed 7 November 2007).

Savelli, A. (2003) *Sociologia del turismo.* FrancoAngeli, Milan, Italy.

Sereni, M. (2006) *Storia del paesaggio agrario italiano.* Laterza, Rome-Bari, Italy.

Slow Food (1989) Il Manifesto Slow Food. http://associazione.slowfood.it/associazione_ita/ita/manifesto. lasso (accessed 21 February 2010).

Slow Food (2005–2007) *Guida agli Extravergini.* Slow Food Editore, Bra, Italy.

Slow Food (2010) Presidia in Italy. http://www.presidislowfood.it/pdf/italian_slowfood_presidia.pdf (accessed 10 February 2010).

Soldati, M. (1971) *Vino al vino.* Mondadori, Milan, Italy.

Sommers, B.J. (2008) *The Geography of Wine. How Landscapes, Cultures,* Terroir, *and the Weather make a Good Drop*. Plume Press/Penguin, New York.

Taiti, F. (2003–2010) Osservatorio sul turismo del vino. http://www.cittadelvino.it/node/50 (accessed 2 April 2010).

TCI (2004–2009) *L'Annuario del Turismo (e della Cultura)*. Touring Editore, Milano, Italy.

Touring Club Italiano (1931) *Guida gastronomica d'Italia*. Touring Club Italiano, Milan, Italy.

Tourism Australia (2006) Wine Tourism Snapshot. http://www.tourism.australia.com/content/Niche/niche_snapshot_wine.pdf (accessed 1 September 2009).

Tourism New South Wales (2000) Wine Tourism Development Information. Understanding your tourism market. http://corporate.tourism.nsw.gov.au/Sites/SiteID6/objLib13/understanding_your_market.pdf (accessed 30 March 2010).

Turri, E. (1979) *Semiologia del paesaggio italiano*. Longanesi & C., Milan, Italy.

UNESCO (2004) Val d'Orcia. http://whc.unesco.org/en/list/1026 (accessed 4 February 2010).

UNESCO (2010) World Heritage List. http://whc.unesco.org/en/list (accessed 27 March 2010).

Urry, J. and Sheller, M. (2004) *Tourism Mobilities: Places to Play, Places in Play*. Routledge, London.

Valery (1841) *L'Italie confortable, manuel du touriste*. Renouard, Paris.

Van Der Borg, J. and Costa, C. (1993) *The Management of Tourism in Cities of Art. TRC Meeting in Ostersund, Sweden, April 1993*. Libreria Editrice Cafoscarina, Venice, Italy.

Vaudour, E. (2003) *Les terroirs viticoles*. Dunod, Paris.

White, R.E. (2003) *Soils for Fine Wines*. Oxford University Press, New York.

Williams, S. (1998) *Tourism Geography*. Routledge, London.

Wilson, J.E. (1999) Terroir. *The Role of Geology, Climate, and Culture in the Making of French Wines*. University of California Press/The Wine Appreciation Guild, Berkley, California.

World Commission on Environment and Development (Brundtland Commission) (1987) *Our Common Future*. Oxford University Press, Oxford, UK.

World Conference on Sustainable Tourism (1995) Tourism Charter for Sustainable Tourism. http://www.gdrc.org/uem/eco-tour/charter.html (accessed 31 March 2010).

WTO (1985) Tourism Bill of Rights and Tourist Code General Assembly of the World Tourism Organization, Sophia, Romania. http://www.world-tourism.org/sustainable/doc/1985%20TOURISM%20BILL%20OF%20RIGHTS.pdf (accessed 31 March 2010).

WTO (1997) Manila Declaration on the Social Impact of Tourism. http://www.univeur.org/CMS/UserFiles/70%20Manila.PDF (accessed 31 March 2010).

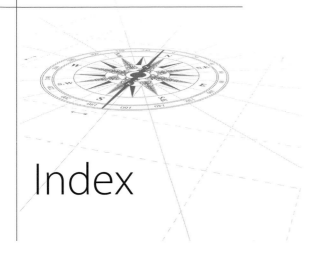

Index

Page numbers in **bold** refer to figures and boxes.

access 90
accessories ordering 91
accommodation 27, 48, 104, 137–139
activities 114–115, 151
actors
    contribution 14
    external 77
    internal 78
    supply-side 5, 18–19, 46, 47, 87–115, 150
    tourists 45–59
    see also operators; tourists
'Adopt a Sheep, Defend Nature' 136
ageing rooms **71, 121**
agrofood **162**
aims 168–169
American Centre for Wine, Food & the Arts
    (COPIA) **153–154**
Amerigo 1934, Savigno, Italy **143, 144**
analysis
    desk 166
    frequency 167–168
    geographic 20, **21**
    market 50, **51**, 169
    positioning **72–73**
    projects 169
    self-evaluation 106–107
    sensory 99–103, 112–113, 125, 129, 130
    sheets 112, **113**, 160, **162–165**
    SWOT 88
    see also evaluation

appeal factors 71–72
    see also attractors
approaches 40–44, 46, 150
archaeology, industrial 92, 121, 132
architecture
    experience enhancement 91–92
    geomorphology reflection **93**
    identity factor 44
    styles 128–129, 133, 138, **181**
    'temple to wine and art' project 118–119
    underground 132
    see also buildings
arrival 118
    see also welcome
art
    culinary traditions illustration 171
    exhibitions **153**
    itinerary construction **178–183**
    landscape observer impact 21
    link with food and wine tourism
        92, 118–119
    pleasurable addition **185**
    users 55
associations 4–5, 56–57, 126,
    146–147, **149**
atmosphere 113, 142
attitude changes 3, **4**
attractors 26, 27, **28–29**, 30, **165**
    see also appeal factors
Aube Valley, Champagne, France **181–182**

augmentation **67**
   see also expansion
authenticity 10, 138
awareness, consumer 56

banana plantation **138**
Bank of Wine **154**
Barbaresco, Piemonte, Italy 120
Beaune, Burgundy, France **148**
bee-keeping enterprise **114**
beer 101, 128–129
behaviour
   changes, eating 3
   descriptors 45
   effects 11
   experiential approach 46
   human, complexity 38
   impact 104
   model 23–24
   purchasing 46, 47, 48
   recommendations 58–59
   targeting factor 49–58
Benziger family winery, Glen Ellen, Sonoma, California 119–120
Biodynamic Vineyard Tram Tour 119–120
bonding 39
branding 75
   see also images; logo; symbols
Bras, Michel **145**
bread 69–70, **113**, 134
breweries 128–129
   see also beer
brochures 64, 159–160, **161**
buffalo 124, **125**–126
buildings 90, 92, 121, 140, **154**
   see also architecture
Butler's model 34–37

California 116–120
Cantillon brewery, Brussels, Belgium 128
Cantina Sociale Produttori del Barbaresco 120
car parks 90
carrying capacity 12–13, 17, 36, 150
   see also saturation
Cartella delle principali specialità gastronomiche delle regioni italiane 3
cartography 42, 44
   see also maps
'Casa del vino', Isera, Trentino, Italy **146**–**147**

case studies
   accommodation and hospitality **139**
   centre for tourists and residents **153**–**156**
   communication **78**–**80**
   eating establishments **143**–**147**
   information centres and wine routes **148**–**149**
   itinerary construction **178**–**183**
   themed food and wine familiarization trip **85**–**86**
   young visitor wine tasting programme **114**
Cathars, France **77**
certification 5, 17, 20
   see also quality; standards
Chalk Hill Estate, Sonoma, California 122
Champagne **178**–**183**
Chanric Inn, Calistoga, California **139**
cheese
   comparison tours 171
   core product or ancillary component **70**–**71**
   cultural landscape, inherent part 2
   farms 60, 123–128
   promotion 75
   tasting 100–101, 126
   see also farms
Chez Panisse, Berkley, California **143**
children 108–115
chocolate 102, 134
choice 38, **139**, 159
Cinque Terre, Italy **168**
Cisternino, Itria Valley, Italy **79**
City of Taste, Rome 5
City of Wine (Ciudad del Vino), Elciego, Spain 105
CIVC (Comiteé Interprofessional du Vin de Champagne) **180**, **182**
Clairvaux Abbey **181**–**182**
Clos Pegase winery, Calistoga, California 118
Cooperative of Milk and Fontina Cheese Producers, Valle d'Aosta, Italy 126
cocoa plantation tours 135
codes of practice 58
coffee 101, **156**
Comiteé Interprofessional du Vin de Champagne (CIVC) **180**
communication
   channels 81–82
   client/supplier 157–158
   destination identity 73–**86**
   distribution policy role 81
   guidelines 75

methods **78**, 84, 140, **145**
planning 74–75
policy 89, 95
pre-trip meetings 151
problems 73
strategies 73–75, 89, **149**
techniques 64
tools **79**
see also brochures; information;
    targeting
communicators, professional 57
companies 55
concepts 5, 15, 16, **19**–22, 121
consumption practices 47, 48
contact methods 142, 151
contamination, methanol 4–5
contracts 150, **156**
cookery 122, 135, 171
see also gastronomy
COPIA (American Centre for Wine,
    Food & the Arts), Napa Valley,
    California **153**–**154**
Coppia Ferrarese 69–70
corkage 106, 142
costs 25, 137, 138, 141
cru 19, 20, 121
Culatello di Zibello 69, **70, 71**
Culinary Tour 122
culture
    component **185**
    food and wine link 49–50
    gastronomy link 2–3, 152–156
    integrated tourism 6–9
    tours 160–177, **183**–**184**
    see also architecture; art

dairies 123–128
decision making 96–97, 169
decline 35
demand 10, 18, 159
destination
    comparison 69–70
    construction 63
    development 11–14, 35, 60–68
    fleeting acquaintance 10
    identity communication 73–**86**
    knowledge 18–19
    multiple experiences **41**
    successful, key points 2
    types, macro-categories 26–27
    see also experience; product

displays 104, 142
distilleries 132–133
distribution 25–26, 27, 37, 80–82
diversification **149**

eating establishments 140–**147**
    see also restaurants
ecosystems 12
    see also environment; sustainability
education 49, 126, **153, 156**
    see also learning
efficiency, economic 12
environment
    awareness programmes 135–136
    elements **21**
    evaluation tools 18–44
    good practices awareness
        promotion **14**
    omnipresence 15
    protection, cardinal principles 13
    quality **16**
    tourism impacts **9**–11,
        36–37, 39
    see also sustainability
Epernay, Champagne, France **180**
equipment ordering 91
etiquette 58–59
    see also behaviour
European Council Directive 90/314/EEC
    158, 159–160
evaluation 18–44, 99, 101, 106–108,
    166–167
    see also analysis
events 4–5, 105, 142
evolution **4**, 31–40
exhibitions 82, **153**
expansion 65, 88, 104–106
    see also augmentation; extension
experience
    authenticity 10
    construction ability 157–158
    consumption 18
    creation 17, **41**
    designing 157–186
    enhancement 91–92
    human factor importance 17
    Jameson 132–133
    myths 47
    negative, effect 65
    total **103**
    see also destination

extension 68, 88
    see also augmentation; expansion

fairs 82
fam (familiarization) trips 82–**86**
farmers **14**, 135, **146**
farms
    days and stays 135
    illustrated map **111**
    visitors 54, 135
    visits 60, 123–128, 134
    young tourists **109**, 135
    see also cheese
feedback 167–168
films **78**
fishing tourism 135
flavour, geographical **19**
flows 23–31
foie gras production tours 134
food and beverage sectors **163**
food halls **146**
food production enterprises **162**
food visitor, *defined* 47–48
France 1–2
Fromagerie Gaugry, Gevrey-Chambertin,
    Burgundy, France 126–128
fruit 134, **139**
Fuksas, Massimiliano 133

Galantino Olive Mill, Bisceglie, Puglia,
    Italy 131
Gambero Rosso 4, 5
gardens 120, 122, **153–154**
Gastronomic Guide to Italy 2
gastronomy 2–3, **28–29**, **39**–40, **43**,
    152–156
geography
    analysis 20, **21**
    flavour **19**
    mental 19, 76–77
    sense development 40
    taste 1
    theories 22–40
geomorphology 92, **93**
good business practice 116
Goods Shed, Canterbury, UK **145–146**
grapes 117–118, 120
    see also vineyards; wineries
Graves, Michael 118
greenways 7–9

groups 47–58, 90, 118
    see also packages
growth 35, 37
    see also expansion; extension
Guida gastronomica d'Italia 2
guide
    attributes 151–152
    behaviour impact 104
    knowledge 120, 131
    oenology 123
    restaurant, performance and practice
        criteria 142
    visit success contribution 94–95, 97–98
guidelines
    brochure planning **161**
    business practices 89–90
    communication 75
    olive oil evaluation 101
    organization 90–91, 96–103
    presentation 90–91
    sustainable codes of practice adoption 58
    tasting sessions 98–103
    tourist product creation 88–108
    welcome 89–90, 108–115
guides 2–3, 4
    see also literature; maps
Guido Pastor **114**
Guido's Restaurant, Pollenzo, Piemonte,
    Italy **154–155**
Guinness Storehouse, Dublin, Ireland
    128–129

Hazard Analysis and Critical Control Points
    (HACCP) 106–107
herbs **145**
Herederos de Marqués de Riscal, Spain 105
heritage, Italy 60
hierarchies 24, 31, 33
hiking **8**
history 1–6, 41–42, 132, 171
    see also education
hospitality 137–139, 157–158, **164**
host community 11, 62, 78
House of Wine **146–147**
Hugel & Fils, Riquewihr, France 123
hygiene 6

identity 2, 44, 73–86
Illy, Trieste, Italy **156**
image 33–34, 75, 77

images 75, **103**, **178–183**
impacts **9–11**, 21, 36 37, 39
information
    aids 118
    asymmetric, problems 81
    availability 25
    centres and bureaus 147, **148–149**
    distribution 80–82
    materials 151
    provision 93–94, 139
    web site 89
    see also brochures; communication;
        events; media; signs
inhabitancy, affective 21–22
instruments 168
    see also tools
integration
    complexity 82
    elements 67 68
    product **66**, **149**
    services and facilities 105
    tourism types 6–9
interactions 68
    see also involvement; participation; tasting
involvement 35, 102–103, 106, **107**, 123, 142
    see also tasting
Italian Touring Club 2
Italy 2–3, 5, 48, 60, **61**
itinerary
    construction 161, **178–186**
    form **180**
    mental geographical 19
    multi-product 170–171
    package tour 160–165
    planner's questions **180**
    planning 164–177, **184**
    priorities, focusing **185–186**
    structured 162–163, **170**, **182**
    successful **178–186**
    themes 164, 165, 170–172, 178, **183–184**

Jack Daniel's Distillery, Lynchburgh,
        Tenessee 133
Jameson Experience 132–133
journals 168, 169

Kendall Jackson Winery, Lynchburg,
        Tennessee 122
knowledge 18–19, 120, 131, 141, 166–168
Kotler model 66–**67**

La Bastiglia, Spello, Umbria, Italy **145**
La Dispensa di Amerigo, Savigno, Italy **144**
La scienza in cucina e l'arte di mangiar bene 3
labelling 5
    see also certification; quality
land use **4**
landscape
    authentic 138
    interpretation **41**
    olive-growing areas 130
    –region relationship concept 19, 20–22
    as regional identity 2, **77**
    terraced slopes **168**
    use **145**
layout importance 113
Le Charlemagne, Burgundy, France **145**
'Le tour de Bourgogne á vélo' 8
learning 6, 23, **54**, 152
    see also education
legislation 5, 147, 158
    see also regulations
leitmotiv 178
    see also images; logo; symbols
lighting 90
links
    art 92, 118–119
    concepts 19, 121
    culture 2–3, 49–50
    quality 15, 17
    resources/theme 171–172, 173–177, 178
    sustainability 17, **39–40**
list, wine 141–142
L'Italie confortable, manuel du touriste 2
literature 3, 44, 93–94, 139, 166
    see also guides
logo **145**
    see also symbols
Lozato-Giotart's theory 25–31
Lundgren model 23–24

Maiatica olive plant 132
Maison Champy, Beaune, Burgundy,
        France **114**, 121
maison de champagne 95, **96**
Maison d'Olivier Leflaive, Burgundy,
        France 122–123
'Make Your Own Blend Tour' 120–121
management 140, 169
manuals 2–3
*Map of Agro-alimentary Produce in Cisternino, Itria
        Valley* **79**

maps
    area knowledge aid 168
    artistic 3
    dairy farm **124**
    down on the farm **111**
    gastronomic production, Po Valley,
        Italy **43**
    provision 177
    thematic 42–44, **79**–80
    tourism positioning **72**
    vineyards and wineries **144**
market analysis 50, **51**, 169
markets, farmer **14**, 135, **146**
matching 122
    see also pairing
meat 69, **70, 71**, 101, 134
Mecenate 1
media 4–5, **78–79**, 84–85
menus 115, 140–141, 142, **145**
Midleton Single Distillery, County Cork,
    Ireland 132
milieu, *defined* 20
milk 125, 126
    see also cheese; dairies
mills, olive 129–132
Miossec's model 31–34, 37
model, behaviour 23–24
models
    area evolution 31–34, 37
    augmented tourist product
        66–**67**
    core product/ancillary components
        69–73
    destination life cycle **34**–37
    geographic 22–31, 40
    psychographic travel **37**
    spatial 23
    tourist product as variable services 65
monasteries 135, **181–182**
Mondavi Wine Club 122
Mondovino 4
Monteschiavo Olive Mill, Maiolati
    Spontini, Marche, Italy 131
moutard **107**
movement, tourist 23–25, 46
mozzarella, buffalo 123–126, **125**
multipolarization 30–31
museumification 33–34
museums 106, 125
mushrooms **143**
Mystic Wine-Press **181**
myths, experience 47

Napa Valley, California, USA 75, **76**
Nardini Distillery, Bassano del Grappa, Italy 133
National Organization of Olive Tasters
    (ONAOO), Imperia, Italy **155**
networks 25, 68, 139, **144**
Normann model 65

objectives 168–169
oenogastronomy 45, 48, **105**
oenology 123
olive 8, **72**, 129–132, **155**, 171
olive oil 101, 129–130, **167**
'The Olive Oil Greenway' 8
ONAOO (National Organization of Olive
    Tasters), Imperia, Italy **155**
Open Cellars (*Cantine Aperte*) 5
opening hours adherence 89
operators 40, 65, 81–82, 137–156
    see also actors
organization
    familiarization trips 82–**86**
    guidelines 90–91, 96–103
    production areas tour **127**
    visits 117–118, 124, **127**
organoleptic similarities 171
orientation, instruments 168
origins 1–6
    see also history
Osterie d'Italia 4
outside 119
    see also landscape; panoramas

packages 158–159
    see also groups
pairing **100**, 122, 123
panoramas 64, 66, **111**, 120, 129
    see also landscape
participation 67–68
    see also involvement
partners 80–81, 82, 138, 150–151
pasta factories, tours 134
Pasteur, Louis (1822–1895) 121
Peju Province Winery, Napa Valley, California 122
Penfolds Winery, Australia 120–121
perceptions 64–65, 77, 113
personnel 90, 95, 140, 151, **153–154**
    see also guide; staff
Pienza, Tuscany, Italy **176**, 183–184, 185–186
Pietrantonj winery, Abruzzo, Italy 121
place *see* destination; region; *terroir*

planners 157
planning
    concepts **19**
    decisions, before guided visit 96–97
    elements, tourist product 65
    guided tours 152
    production area tours **127**
    route format 173–177
    sustainability practices 13
    see also itinerary
Plog's psychographic travel model **37**
polarization 30–31, 33
policies 13, 31, 33, 89, 95
positioning analysis **72**–73
presentation, guidelines 90–91
press releases 84–85
prices 25, 137, 138, 141
problems, eating establishments 140
product
    agro-alimentary 88
    areas 120
    breakdown 66–**67**
    components 17, **63**–64
    core 65, 69–70, 88
    core or ancillary **70**
    creation 88–108
    integration **66**
    life cycle **34**–35, 36
    private/public aspects comparison 65
    sensory profile 99
    transformation 60–68, 69
    viewpoints 64–65
    see also destination
professionalism 57, 94–95, 151, **153–154**
programming 151, **184**, **185–186**
projects 118–119, 135, 151, 169
promotion 5, 75, 82, 89, **146–147**
    see also brochures; communication;
        information; media
prototypes 48
publications 2–3, 99, 168
Puglia 132
purchasing 46, 47, 48, 103–104
    see also shops

quality
    accommodation category matching 138
    certification 5, 17, 20
    concepts 15, **16**
    control **155**
    defined 14
    emotional 17
    product characteristics 14–17
    self-evaluation 106–108
    standardization 17
    –sustainability link 17
    –*terroir* link 15
questionnaires 107–108

rates 138
    see also prices
recommendations 58
region
    identity 2, **77**
    knowledge 166–168
    –landscape relationship concept 19, 20–22
    multipolarized 30–31
    personality distinctiveness **185**
    transformation to tourist product 60–68
    see also terroir
regulations 6, 91, 99
    see also legislation
Reims, Champagne, France **179–182**
rejuvenation 36
research 47, 48, 166, 167
resources
    abundance 60
    breakdown **61**
    core 65, 69–73, 88
    selection 173
    theme linking 171–172, 173–177, 178
responsibility 135
restaurants 140, 142, **145–146**, **154–155**
rice cultivation tours 134
risk assessment 106–107
Robert Mondavi Winery, Napa Valley,
        California 117–118
Romans 1
routes 5, 147–**149**, 152, 172–177, **174**
Royal Orchid Hotel, Bangkok **139**
rules 110–112
    see also guidelines

Sagrantino wine route, Umbria, Italy **149**
salmon supply chain tours 134
salt works 134
satisfaction 62, 107–108, 151
saturation 31, 33, 35
    see also carrying capacity
scenery 92
    see also landscape; panoramas

Science in the Kitchen and the Art of Eating Well 3
sensory analysis 99–103, 112–113, 125, 129, 130
shops
    COPIA **154**
    dairy produce sales 126
    exclusive brands 133
    itinerary inclusion **181**
    layout importance 123
    leather handicrafts 125
    restaurant menu items sales **144**
Sideways **78–79**
Siena, Tuscany **183**
'Signature tour and tasting' 117
signs 75, **76**, 90, **177**
    see also information
skills requirement 140, 157
    see also training
slogans 75
Slow Food 4–5
snail farm tours 134
social conditions, evolution **4**
social justice 12
sourcing, local produce 138, 140, 142, **143, 145**, 146
souvenirs 121, 122, 123, 133
space 23–31, 113
Spielman, Sylvie 121
sports lovers 55
staff 94–**96**, 141
    see also personnel
standards 14–17
    see also quality
Stevenson, Robert Louis 75
studies 47, 48
    see also case studies
supply
    actors 5, 18–19, 46, 47, 87–115, 150
    business partners, selection 138
    chain tours 134
    local sourcing 138, 140, 142, **143, 145**, 146
    operators 137–156
    selection 173
surveys 107–108
sustainability
    –gastronomic tourism link **39**–40
    guidelines 58
    practices 11–14
    projects 135, 151
    –quality link **16**, 17

SWOT analysis 88
symbols 3, 70, 75, **178–183**

'Table d'Olivier' 123
targeting 47–58, 159, **183–186**
taste, geography 1
tasters, involvement 102–103
tasting
    certificates 133
    education **153**
    guidelines 98–103
    interactive game 123
    product physical characteristics description 112
    room **52**, 91, 113
    score sheets 112, **113**
    teaching **145**
    themed menus 141, 142
    visitor involvement role 102–103
    young visitors programme **114**
tea plantation tours 135
technical aspects, itinerary inclusion **185**
techniques 99
Terra Madre 4–5
territory 19–20, **21**
terroir
    concept 5, 19–22
    defined 20
    discovery desire 3
    excellent lesson on meaning of 121
    –quality link 15
    suitability 74
    transformation to tourist destination 60–68
themes
    attractions linking 61
    cartography 42–44
    choosing 169–172, **176**
    familiarization trips **85–86**
    format choosing **176**
    itinerary 164, 165, 170–172, 178, **183–184**
    mapping **79–80**
    menus 140–141, 142
    resources linking 171–172, 173–177, 178
    stops 19
theories 22–40
    see also models
timings, visit 90–91, 119, **185**
title, tour **183**
tools **79**, **127**, 160
    see also analysis, sheets

tourism
  described 157
  positioning maps **72**
  positive effects expectation 11
  research 47, 48
  spatial configurations **28–29**
  –sustainability link **39**–40
  types integration 6–9
  typologies 25, 135
Tourism Research Australia, study 17, 18
tourists
  categories 45
  characteristics 51–57
  flows and space configuring 23–31
  movement 23–25, 46
  product, *defined* 62
  settlements distribution 25–26
  typologies 37–38, 45–58
  young 108–115, 135
tours
  conducting 97–98
  geographic sense development 40
  guided 87–88, 129
  itinerary planning 160–178
  length 172, 173
  operators 40, 150–151
  organizing 90–91
  self-guided 118
  shortening stratagems 113
  types 117–118
  when 173
training 95, **154–155**
transformation 60–68, 69
transport 119, 172
trattoria **143**
travellers 2–3, 38
  see also tourists; visitors
Trieste, Italy **156**
Troyes, Champagne, France **181, 182**
truffles 6
Tuscany, Italy **42**
typologies 25, 26–27, 37–38, 45–58, 135

University of Coffee (Illy), Trieste, Italy **156**
University of Gastronomic Sciences, Pollenzo,
  Piemonte, Italy 5, **154**

Valentini, Francesco Paolo 88
Valtellina Dairy Group (Latteria Sociale
  Valtellina), Delebio, Italy 126

Vannulo Dairy, Capaccio Scalo, Campania,
  Italy 123–126
Vias Verdes greenway 8
Vienna–Prague Greenway 8
Vierge au Raisin **181**
vinegar, balsamic 134
vineyards **8**, 119–120, **144**
  see also grapes; wineries
Vini d'Italia 4
Vino al vino 3
VIPs/exclusive guests 57
Virgin of the Grapes **181**
visitors, types 48–57, **114**, 118, 135
visits
  facilitating 120
  guided, suggestions 152
  organization 117–118, 124, **127**
  timing 90–91, 119, **185**
  types 134–136
  see also tours

web site, essential information 89
web tours 131, 133
welcome
  exotic fruit baskets,
    provision **139**
  guide role 95
  guidelines 89–90, 108–115
  methods 118
  proprietor 95
  quality, self-evaluation 106–108
  reasons 87–89
  slogans or images 75, **76**
  style 95–**96**
  total experience factor 102–**103**
whiskey **56**, 132–133
Wine Cities 5
Wine Routes 5, 147–**149**
Wine to Wine 3
Wine Tourist Movement 5
winefootpaths 9, **177**
wineries
  ageing room **121**
  architectural style 118–119
  design 92
  distinctive personality 92
  maps **144**
  tasting sessions 100, **114**, 122
  tour ideas 116–123
  visitors, *definition* 47
  see also vineyards